Women, Intimate Partner Violence, and the Law

Interpersonal Violence Series

Series Editors
Claire Renzetti, Ph.D.
Jeffrey L. Edleson, Ph.D.

Parenting by Men Who Batter: New Directions for Assessment and Intervention
Edited by Jeffrey L. Edleson and Oliver J. Williams

Coercive Control: How Men Entrap Women in Personal Life
Evan Stark

Childhood Victimization: Violence, Crime, and Abuse in the Lives of Young People
David Finkelhor

Restorative Justice and Violence Against Women
Edited by James Ptacek

Familicidal Hearts: The Emotional Styles of 211 Killers
Neil Websdale

Violence in Context: Current Evidence on Risk, Protection, and Prevention
Edited by Todd I. Herrenkohl, Eugene Aisenberg, James Herbert Williams, and Jeffrey M. Jenson

Poverty, Battered Women, and Work in U.S. Public Policy
Lisa D. Brush

Child Victims and Restorative Justice: A Needs-Rights Model
Tali Gal

Battered Women's Protective Strategies
Sherry Hamby

Men Who Batter
Nancy Nason-Clark and Barbara Fisher-Townsend

When Men Murder Women
R. Emerson Dobash and Russell P. Dobash

Comparative Perspectives on Gender Violence: Lessons From Efforts Worldwide
Edited by Rashmi Goel and Leigh Goodmark

Religion and Intimate Partner Violence: Understanding the Challenges and Proposing Solutions
Nancy Nason-Clark, Barbara Fisher-Townsend, Catherine Holtmann, and Stephen McMullin

Violence Against Women in the 21st Century: Transnational Perspectives of Empowerment and Subjugation
Edited by Kristen Zaleski, Annalisa Enrile, Eugenia Weiss, and Xiying Wang

State Sanctioned Violence: Advancing a Social Work Social Justice Agenda
Melvin Delgado

Collaborating for Change: Transforming Cultures to End Gender-Based Violence in Higher Education
Edited by Susan B. Marine and Ruth Lewis

Women, Intimate Partner Violence, and the Law
Heather Douglas

Women, Intimate Partner Violence, and the Law

HEATHER DOUGLAS

OXFORD
UNIVERSITY PRESS

OXFORD
UNIVERSITY PRESS

Oxford University Press is a department of the University of Oxford. It furthers the University's objective of excellence in research, scholarship, and education by publishing worldwide. Oxford is a registered trade mark of Oxford University Press in the UK and certain other countries.

Published in the United States of America by Oxford University Press
198 Madison Avenue, New York, NY 10016, United States of America.

Library of Congress Cataloging-in-Publication Data
Names: Douglas, Heather, author.
Title: Women, intimate partner violence, and the law / Heather Douglas.
Description: New York : Oxford University Press, 2021. |
Series: Interpersonal violence series |
Includes bibliographical references and index.
Identifiers: LCCN 2020027065 (print) | LCCN 2020027066 (ebook) |
ISBN 9780190071783 (hardback) | ISBN 9780190071806 (epub) |
ISBN 9780190071813 (oso)
Subjects: LCSH: Women—Violence against. | Abused women—Legal status, laws, etc. | Intimate partner violence—Prevention. |
Family violence—Law and legislation.
Classification: LCC K5191.W65 D68 2021 (print) | LCC K5191.W65 (ebook) |
DDC 344.7303/28292—dc23
LC record available at https://lccn.loc.gov/2020027065
LC ebook record available at https://lccn.loc.gov/2020027066

DOI: 10.1093/oso/9780190071783.001.0001

9 8 7 6 5 4 3 2 1

Printed by Integrated Books International, United States of America

I really felt hunted by him. Wherever I turn, you kind of get used to looking over your shoulder kind of at everything. . . . It was really like a hunting thing . . . like a manhunt.

—(Ingrid, interview 3)

CONTENTS

ACKNOWLEDGMENTS

This project started a long time ago. In 2013 I submitted an application for a grant to explore women's experiences of legal system responses in the context of intimate partner violence (IPV). The grant application was successful, and thanks to an Australian Research Council Future Fellowship grant (FT140100796) and the support of the University of Queensland Law School, I was able to take the time to embark on the 178 interviews and the many emails, telephone calls, and court attendances that underpin this book.

I started the interviews in December 2014 and finished them at the end of 2017. But there were many interruptions to this project. In 2015 I took up development and leadership of the National Domestic and Family Violence Bench Book, a resource for Australian judges to use when dealing with cases involving IPV. As a legal scholar interested in improving law's response to IPV, I considered this an important role, and given what women were telling me about the shortfalls in their interactions with the courts, it seemed perfectly timed. I wrote up the last parts of this book through the Australian Autumn of 2020, when much of the world was in lockdown during the COVID-19 pandemic. As I wrote, I heard about the many women who were isolated in violent homes, unable to call for help, and realized that improving legal responses to IPV was as urgent as ever.

These are all the practical reasons for why this book took so long to write. But I also confronted deeper challenges. I continue to be in contact with some of the women I met during these interviews. Sometimes they are flourishing, but other times things are not so good. As I published various articles drawing on the women's stories, more women have also called and emailed me to share their experiences. I have tried to respond to every call and email. Often I have referred women to a legal center, a helpline, or a support service, occasionally to the police. Sometimes women I have never met have contacted me just to share their story, and I listen. There is an emotional intensity in this kind of research that is very different from what one experiences while researching the law on the books. The lingering question for me is, have I represented the stories of the women I have interviewed with integrity? This has bothered me throughout, and I hope the answer is yes.

There are always many people to thank for help with a project like this. These interviews could not have happened without the support of a number of people and agencies. Thanks to all the IPV support service workers and lawyers who have contributed their knowledge and time over so many years and who helped me recruit women for this study. In particular a big thank you to Cecilia Barassi Rubio, Leona Berrie, Barb Crossing, Caroline Fitzpatrick, Maree Kaiser, Angela Lynch, Lulu Milne, Batasi Morris, Rachel Neil, Linda-Ann Northey, Mark Ryan, Julie Sarkozi, Rebecca Shearman, and Hayley Smith. Thanks also to the services that facilitated this research, allowing me to use their space, their interpreter services, and their tea and coffee facilities: Domestic Violence Action Centre, Domestic Violence Assistance Program, Galang Place, Immigrant Women's Support Service, Queensland Indigenous Family Violence Legal Service, Women's House, Women's Legal Service (Brisbane), Working Against Violence Support Service, and WWILD Sexual Violence Program. The value of your work is inestimable; you have saved the lives of many women.

Sincere thanks to my "research community." Francesca Bartlett, Ana Borges Jelenic, Kerry Carrington, Kate Chapple, Kathy Daly, Molly Dragiewiscz, Robin Fitzgerald, Bridget Harris, Robyn Holder, Heather Nancarrow, Zoe Rathus, Michele Robinson, Stella Tarrant, Kate Thomas, Julia Tolmie, Tamara Walsh, and Jane Wangmann. All read various chapters or versions of them and/or kept the conversations and encouragement going. Leigh Goodmark read most of the chapters and plied me with her words of wisdom when I thought I might give up. I thank the crew at the Monash Gender and Family Violence Prevention Centre—Kate FitzGibbon, JaneMaree Maher, Jude McCulloch, Sandra Walklate, and Jasmine McGowan—for involving me in other projects along the way. Thanks to Nicole Watson for letting me read early versions of her work; I hope one day to be such a good storyteller. Clare McGlynn and Nicole Westermarland at Durham University welcomed me for three months in 2016 when I was very fortunate to be supported as a fellow at the Institute of Advanced Studies. I appreciated the opportunity to present on IPV and legal systems abuse while there. I also appreciated spending time at Humboldt University, hosted by Professor Dr. Susanne Baer and Professor Dr. Tatjana Hörnle, during the Berlin Winter of 2018. While there I had time and space to write the proposal for this book. Thanks also to the research assistants who supported my work in all sorts of ways: Jennifer Bell, Naomi Smith, Jess Downing-Ide, Beck Markey-Towler, Emma Fell, and Rachna Nagesh.

Aspects of the women's stories, from a cross-sectional perspective, have been published in various journals, including *Criminology & Criminal Justice*; *Australian Journal of Family Law*; *Journal of Family Violence*; and *International Journal for Crime, Justice and Social Democracy*. I thank these journals for their important work.

A big thank you to my family who I love so much—Zac and Felix, and especially Paul and Isabella, who lived with me through this project and listened to my endless frustrations about how the law seemed to continually fail the women I spoke to; they read drafts and never stopped encouraging me all those millions of times I nearly gave up.

Most of all, I want to thank all the women who were prepared to be interviewed. There would be no book without you. I learned so much from you all and hopefully your knowledge can underpin greater understanding and future improvements to legal and other responses to IPV. I wish I had more space to tell all your stories.

1

Introduction

> That's what—everyone thinks "she was so loved"—but if they really stopped to ask the question, how bad would the physical, mental and emotional abuse have to be before you were content to walk away from all you owned, from your home, your possessions and all your money, facing hundreds of thousands of dollars in debt? How bad would it have to be for you to stare down three and a half years of legal proceedings, court dates, letters, police visits, difficulty in finding work, reconnecting with family and friends? How bad would it have to be? Nobody wants to ask that question. That's really what is behind every woman's flight. (Colleen, interview 2)

I met Colleen twice for interviews over the period of the study that underpins this book. At some point toward the end of our second interview, I suggested to her that things seemed a lot better than they were when we first talked. She had made some notes, included in the epigraph to this chapter, that she wanted to record to explain her move into emergency accommodations with her child to "his friends, family, the butchers that you go to, the accountants, and the [tradesmen] that regard you as a madwoman." Her comment encapsulates the experiences of many of the women I talked to who had fled intimate partner violence (IPV) and, in

Women, Intimate Partner Violence, and the Law. Heather Douglas, Oxford University Press (2021). © Oxford University Press.
DOI: 10.1093/oso/9780190071783.003.0001

leaving, had also gone to law. Their journeys were often harrowing, long, and expensive, and the women were regularly disbelieved or ignored.

How 65 abused women from diverse backgrounds interacted with the legal system and "legal system actors," including child protection workers, police, lawyers, and judges, in response to IPV is the subject of this book. Every year millions of women globally turn to law as an integral part of their strategy to live lives free and safe from violence. Sometimes they turn to the police for help and apply for civil protection orders, family court orders to help them manage their children's contact with a violent father, and orders to avoid deportation after separation from an abuser. Sometimes, because of the violence, child protection services (CPS) takes their children away. While separation from an abuser may seem like a solution, far from signaling an end to violence, it often drives legal engagement that in turn provides new opportunities for perpetrators to continue their abuse (DeKeseredy, Dragiewicz, & Schwartz, 2017; Dobash & Dobash, 2015; S. Miller, 2018, pp. 106–109). Countless abused women are enmeshed in a variety of overlapping, complex, and often inconsistent legal processes and have both fleeting and longer-term connections with legal system actors.

Despite researchers' urgings to decenter the law and to look for alternative approaches and strategies to mainstream legal responses (e.g., Goodmark, 2012; Smart, 1989), law continues to be a central feature in the lives of many women who have been abused or continue to be abused. Intimate partner violence is now considered an ordinary part of the work of police (Barlow & Walklate, 2020), and every year many women apply for civil protection orders (Manjoo, 2015, pp. 26–27; Cattaneo, Grossman, & Chapman, 2016).[1] Intimate partner violence also is now routine in the family courts (Kaye, 2019a; Laing, 2017). Sometimes IPV underpins a decision by CPS to remove a child (Radford & Hester, 2006, p. 58),[2] and many sponsored migrant women claim they have experienced IPV when they apply for permanent resident visas under migration legislation (Maher & Segrave, 2018).

Most of the key studies about law and IPV focus on one aspect of the legal process experienced at a moment in time (e.g., Hunter, 2008; Ptacek,

1999).[3] Through interviewing a group of women on three occasions over a period of 2 to 3 years, I hoped to improve understanding of how abused women's experiences of legal processes and legal system actors change over time. Ultimately the women's stories demonstrate how abusers creatively harness multiple aspects of the legal process and its actors, from protection orders, to custody cases, to police and beyond, to continue their abuse over years. Dobash and Dobash (2015, p. 39) have observed that on separation some abusive men "change the project" from one focused on "keeping" a woman in the relationship to an approach of destroying her.

The women's stories highlight the regular failure of legal processes and actors to come to terms with the significance of nonphysical abuse and coercive control (Robinson, Myhill, & Wire, 2018; Stark, 2007) and the negative effects this has on women's experiences of going to law. Women show how legal system actors' common expectation that separation is a single event, rather than a process, has implications for their connections with law and the outcomes they achieve over time. As the interviews progressed, some women did change their approach to law; some withdrew from law, or parts of the law, altogether; and some tried alternative strategies. Their experiences show how they are both constrained and supported by the requirements of law, and they expound on some of the creative approaches they conceive to get what they need from law. They describe their successes and disappointments in achieving their objectives through legal engagement over the period of the interviews.

Over the past 30 years or more there has been extensive law reform across the English-speaking world aimed at improving the legal response to IPV in an effort to improve the safety of victims and to ensure accountability and responsibility among abusers. In Australia, Evan Stark's (2007) concept of coercive control has been highly influential and is now reflected in definitions of IPV in state-based civil protection order legislation and federal family law legislation (see Appendix 2). While the concept of coercive control is not yet mirrored in federal migration law (see Appendix 2), the Australian policy definition for the broader term *domestic violence* does address coercive control:

> While there is no single definition, the central element of domestic violence is behaviour motivated by gendered drivers of violence that can involve controlling a partner through fear, coercion and intimidation—for example by using behaviour that is violent and threatening. In most cases, the violent behaviour is part of a range of tactics to exercise power and control over women and their children, and can be both criminal and non-criminal. (Council of Australian Governments, 2019, p. 56)

Both scholars and policymakers contend that legal interventions can promote victim safety, help to end violence, and have the potential to empower victims and ensure perpetrators are held responsible and accountable (Lewis, Dobash, Dobash, & Cavanagh, 2001; State of Victoria, 2016a; Ursel & Hagyard, 2008). However, it is also well known that IPV presents distinct challenges for the application of the law, and its application may produce unintended consequences (Goodmark, 2012; Hunter, 2008; Lewis et al., 2001). Regardless of whether the woman and her abusive partner begin to live separately or continue to reside together, there are often complex and continuing emotional, financial, and legal ties between them, as well as enduring and complex power dynamics. Financial and care responsibilities and visiting rights to children often remain after separation. Abuse frequently continues despite separation and indeed often becomes heightened (Mahoney, 1991). Sometimes women find the processes themselves too complex and stressful; the legal system experience itself can seem abusive (Herman, 2005). These factors have implications for how women go to law and how and whether they continue to engage with it.

Civil protection orders, family law (custody and property), child protection, immigration law, and criminal law are parts of the legal response to domestic violence; however, the way in which these different parts overlap, conflict, or work together has been an issue of major concern for law and policymakers and for women who use law (Australian Law Reform Commission and New South Wales Law Reform Commission [ALRC/NSWLRC], 2010; Slote et al., 2005). Understanding how women from diverse backgrounds engage with law has important implications for policy development and law reform (Crenshaw, 1989). Many countries, including Australia, continue to struggle with how law can respond to IPV in a way that answers these unique challenges (ALRC/NSWLRC, 2010; Slote et al., 2005).

Many studies have shown that, far from being a set of clear rules that operate in an orderly fashion, the ways that engagements with law proceed, and how they end, are often unpredictable (Holder, 2018; Nancarrow, 2019). In their interviews with people in New Jersey about the everyday experience of law, sociologists Patricia Ewick and Susan Silbey (1998) identified three types of "legal consciousness" to help understand how law was experienced. The first type involves being "before the law," which means that "the law achieves its impartiality and objectivity through a deliberate indifference to the particularities of biography or personality . . . they stand before the law, all persons are treated the same" (Ewick & Silbey, 1998, p. 76). Second, they describe "being within the law," which refers to when the law "is an arena of competitive, tactical maneuvering where the pursuit of self-interest is expected and the skillful and resourceful can make strategic gains" (p. 48). Finally, the third type of legal consciousness involves a sense of being "against the law," where "people exploit the interstices of conventional social practices to forge moments of respite from the power of law. Foot-dragging, omissions, ploys, small deceits, humor and making scenes are typical forms of resistance for those up against the law" (p. 48).

There are clear echoes of these approaches among the women I interviewed both in relation to their own experience of law and in how they describe their abusive partners' use of law. The women's stories show that how they understand and experience law shifts and changes overtime, depending on many factors, including the legal issue they are addressing, what else is going on their lives, and, importantly, the approach their ex-partner takes.

Silbey has emphasized the importance of "getting across the lived experience [of law] not some idealistic, legalistic, theoretical notion of what the law was supposed to be" (Halliday & Schmidt, 2009, p. 215). We need to understand how those legal systems are working on the ground if we want to make them work better for the people they are supposed to serve (Genn, 1997, 1999). The documentation of lived reality, to understand the facts of women's lives, is a part of feminist legal method (Ahmed, 2017, p. 26; Brooks & Hesse-Biber, 2012, p. 4; R. Campbell & Wasco, 2000; Scales, 2006, p. 108; Smart, 1989, p. 68). Influenced particularly by Ewick and Silbey's (1998; similarly, see also Ferraro, 2006; Stark, 2007) approach, I have included longer stories from some of the women who participated in the study. Each chapter tells a handful of women's stories in detail. While shorter illustrative comments are also included from many of the women, it is the longer stories that best capture women's changing and often fraught experience both of law and of themselves in relation to law, over time. Their stories also capture the messiness of the law and the contradictions and unintended consequences of going to law.[4]

The longer stories in this book communicate specific women's lived experience of law in the context of IPV over time. Choosing which stories to present in a fuller way was challenging. I selected a diverse group of women (culturally diverse, employed and not employed, with and without children) who were interviewed for the study on three occasions. I also selected women whose experiences were common among the women interviewed and that highlighted the topics of the specific chapters (see Appendix 1). Their accounts help build our understanding of the diversity of women's experiences of going to law, as well as when, why, and under what conditions they engage and disengage with law as a response to IPV.

As the interviews progressed, it became clear that women's stories often focused on the individuals, or the justice actors, they dealt with in relation to law. Law was about social relations (Ewick & Silbey, 1998, p. 45), in particular, with child protection workers, police, lawyers, and the judges the women interacted with. The women I interviewed identified two issues as being misunderstood by those justice actors time and time again: Nonphysical abuse was regularly downplayed, and separation was overemphasized as a solution. The chapters also draw out these experiences.

After setting out the approach and methodology of the study in Chapter 2, in Chapter 3 I explore women's experiences of nonphysical forms of abuse and also set the scene for Chapters 4 through 8. Most women reported that the most difficult forms of abuse they dealt with were nonphysical abuse, especially emotional abuse. Many stated that nonphysical abuse deeply impacted their sense of self and freedom and often continued to affect them years after separation. Other forms of nonphysical abuse that the women highlighted included abusive tactics targeting their role as a mother, isolation within the relationship, financial abuse, and, for women on insecure visas, threats about their visas.

Chapter 4 maps out women's engagement with different aspects of law over time. It identifies differences in engagements linked to their intersecting identities. In particular, it considers the different legal processes experienced by migrant women with insecure migration status and Aboriginal and Torres Strait Islander women. It also expands on Chapter 3 by highlighting experiences of how the law itself was used by abusive partners as a form of nonphysical abuse to extend control after separation.

Chapter 5 focuses on the women's interaction with CPS workers and the child protection system in the context of IPV. Three key themes are explored in this chapter. First, women felt they were held accountable by CPS workers for their ex-partner's IPV. Second, a number of women reported that their partners made malicious allegations to CPS about them, leading to lengthy and stressful investigations that resulted in no concerns being found about their mothering. Third, some women's experiences highlighted the complex experience of IPV, intergenerational trauma, and CPS involvement.

Women's experiences with police are explored in Chapter 6. Three interrelated themes from the women's experiences are considered: police failing to understand the dynamics of IPV, especially failing to recognize nonphysical forms of IPV; women's sense that the police were aligning with the abuser; and police failing to intervene where there were children in the relationship. Chapter 6 also highlights some of the unexpected safety strategies, involving police, that women developed over time.

In Chapter 7 I examine the women's experience of engaging with lawyers. While women generally had a positive experience with their own lawyers, many women reported difficulties in getting access to and retaining state-funded legal aid. Women who paid privately for legal advice and representation often faced mounting debts at the time of interviews 2 and 3, causing significant anxiety. Some women found their stress and debt were amplified by their ex-partner's abuse of legal processes and, in some cases, the unethical behavior of their ex-partner's lawyer. Many women also reported that their circumstances in relation to legal representation and potential costs contributed to their decisions about going to law. Finally, women also identified a range of strategies and compromises they employed to access legal support but also identified the stresses and challenges they faced when they were only partially represented or unrepresented.

Chapter 8 explores women's interactions with judges. Women commonly described judges who prioritized physical violence and minimized other forms of abuse and also seemed to align with abusers, discounting the women's experiences of abuse. Women recalled that judges often were unprepared for hearings, rubber-stamped witness subpoenas, and failed to stop irrelevant witness examination. They explained how these approaches facilitated their partners' misuse of the legal system as a tactic of abuse. Women also discussed how judges, especially in the family courts, prioritized fathers' rights to contact with children over safety. However, women's stories also demonstrated resistance to their abusers' control over them through the courts, and their efforts to ensure the safety of their children regardless of court orders.

Based on the women's stories, Chapter 9 explores four aspects of the relationship between the law and separation. The chapter considers women's dynamic experiences of leaving in the shadow of static legal understandings of separation and the ongoing dangers women face when they engage with legal systems and processes. Sometimes law is the one thing that brings women back into contact with their abuser when they are trying to separate. Drawing on the experiences of some of the women in the study, the chapter highlights two areas of law where separation underpins the legal response: the migration and visa system and the family law system.

Chapter 10 draws together key themes developed in the foregoing chapters, including the common and continuing failure of many legal system actors to recognize the significance of nonphysical abuse, the persistent misunderstanding of the dynamics of separation, and abusers' use of the legal system to continue abuse.

This is a book about legal system failure from the women's perspective. Ultimately, it shows how legal system actors and the legal system fail to prioritize safety, but there are some bright spots. From time to time, the women in this study achieved what they sought from law, including safety for themselves and their children, being heard and recognized by justice actors, and closure. Sometimes this happened in circular and unexpected ways. This book closes with some suggestions for how safety might be prioritized in the legal system.

NOTES

1. Across Australia, the numbers are likely to be more than 200,000 new orders each year (Magistrates' Court of Victoria, 2019, p. 43; Queensland Courts, 2019, p. 62).
2. In Australia in 2017–2018, emotional abuse was the most commonly substantiated primary abuse type (59%) reported to child protection authorities. This is the category of abuse that most often reflects claims of children being present in a context where there is IPV (Australian Institute of Health and Welfare, 2020, p. 60).
3. For an expanded discussion of the approach taken in the study, see Chapter 2, "The Study Approach and Methodology." Note also that Chapter 2 considers language used throughout the book.
4. Many women will never engage with law as a response to IPV (Hamby, 2014; Kelly, Sharp, & Klein, 2014), and they were not the focus of this study, I recruited women who were already engaged with law; see Chapter 2.

2

The Study Approach and Methodology

In this study, I interviewed 65 women from diverse backgrounds about their experience of engaging with law because of intimate partner violence (IPV). I returned to speak with each woman on at least three occasions over a 3-year period, talking with them about how they made sense of the law and its role in their lives and how this changed over time. In the course of the interviews, the women talked about some of the factors that influenced their connections to and disconnections from different aspects of law at particular times in their journey. They explained how the behavior of others influenced their decisions and experiences and the way they saw their role in the various processes they were involved in. They explained how the particular legal paths they took did not always end up where they expected, or wanted, to go.

WHY THREE INTERVIEWS OVER TIME?

Many studies to date have assessed victims' experiences of IPV and legal engagement from a cross-sectional perspective, or a single point in time (e.g., Laing, 2008; Lewis, Dobash, Dobash, & Cavanagh, 2000; Meyer, 2011; Nancarrow, 2019; Wangmann, 2012). For example, researchers have interviewed victims on a single occasion to consider their experience of

Women, Intimate Partner Violence, and the Law. Heather Douglas, Oxford University Press (2021). © Oxford University Press.
DOI: 10.1093/oso/9780190071783.003.0002

child protection (Dosanjh, Lewis, Mathews, & Bhandari, 2008); family law (Laing, 2017); courts (Bell, Perez, Goodman, & Dutton, 2011; Hunter, 2008; Ptacek, 1999); police (Hirschel & Hutchison, 2003; Hoyle & Sanders, 2000); prosecution (Nichols, 2014); and the criminal justice process (Barata, 2007; Fleury, 2002) in the context of IPV. In her research, Fleury (2002) interviewed 178 survivors of IPV whose assailants were charged with a crime against them. Fleury considered how satisfied victims were with the criminal justice system and what factors about the survivors, their situations, and the criminal legal system impact on their satisfaction with that system. She found the actions of legal personnel (e.g., court staff) were significant in influencing satisfaction. Fleury's findings were similar to those of Ptacek (1999), whose study of women's satisfaction with civil protection orders found that women who experienced empathetic treatment from judges and police also had improved satisfaction with the legal process. In their study, Van Camp and Wemmers (2013) showed that women who are victimized by IPV share with victims of other crimes a desire to be treated with courtesy and fairness. In her interviews with women victims of sexual violence and IPV from diverse backgrounds, Herman (2005) asked the women about the meaning of justice for them. She found that their notion of justice includes social acknowledgment, a sense of control, an opportunity to tell one's story, not having to continually relive the crime, and not being required to confront the perpetrator directly.

The key benefit of "over-time" studies is that they can show patterns of change (Menard, 1991). There have been few over-time studies undertaken with victims of IPV, even though such studies have an important role in social science research. In their study Kelly, Sharp, and Klein (2014) spoke to 100 women over 3 years in England to explore the factors that support long term-settlement after exiting domestic violence, the obstacles to settlement, and the community resources that need to be developed. These researchers were able to explore the different ways women moved on from violence and the resources they used at different times in their journey. A number of studies have tracked the life courses of those who desist from or persist with crime (e.g., Blumstein & Cohen, 1987; Farrington,

Piquero, & Jennings, 2013; Halsey, 2007; Laub & Sampson, 2001; Maruna, 2001; Nagin, Farrington, & Moffitt, 1995). There have been some over-time studies involving perpetrators of IPV. For example, Gondolf and White (2001) investigated the "rehabilitation" of perpetrators of IPV over time, and Sherman and Harris's study (2013) of the Milwaukee Domestic Violence Experiment examined domestic violence perpetrators who were arrested versus warned over 21 years. They found that those suspects arrested were three times more likely than those warned to have died of homicide.

While, as noted, they have been relatively rare, some researchers have undertaken studies focused on victims of IPV and the role of discrete aspects of law in helping them to live free from violence over time. For example, Belknap and Sullivan (2003) examined battered women's experience of the criminal processing system. They interviewed women on three occasions over the course of a year and found that how the women were treated by actors in the system strongly influenced their overall satisfaction with, and their willingness to engage, with the criminal justice process in the future.

In Canada, Ursel and colleagues (Ursel, 2013; Ursel & Hagyard, 2008) conducted a longitudinal study beginning in 2004 involving 222 women from Manitoba who had experienced IPV and engaged with the law. Ursel and her colleagues have conducted interviews with participants approximately once per year since 2004. Their study collected information from women victims of IPV from different cultural groups (including Indigenous women). The researchers asked these women about their experience of the justice system, including courts, police, prosecutors, and judicial officers. Published findings to date show that quick resolution of criminal cases significantly improves the experience of victims over time and, unexpectedly for the researchers, that Indigenous women were more satisfied than others with police and prosecutors.

In the United States, Dutton, Goodman, Lennig, Murphy, and Kaltman (2006) interviewed a group of 406 women on eight occasions (initially face to face and thereafter by telephone) over 4.5 years and made a number of findings around the likelihood of re-abuse and the use of coping strategies.

However, the focus of their study was not on the use of legal interventions. In Australia, Holder and Daly (2017) and Holder (2018) have explored victims' experiences of justice in the criminal justice system. They tracked change, over time, in conceptions of justice for 27 victims of violence (at time 1, decreasing to 14 at time 3) who turned to the criminal law. Holder (2018) interviewed participants on three occasions over 4 years and found that participants experienced engaging with the criminal justice system in different ways depending on their acceptance of the outcome, the quality of their personal treatment, the influence of their voice, and the rights of the offender.

Undertaking three interviews over time with women in the study provided a chance to build on much of this previous work to understand how a diverse group of abused women construct their narratives about their interaction with the legal system and its actors and how this changes over time.[1]

NAMING AND DEFINING

Most Australian legislative and policy documents refer to "domestic violence," "family violence," or "domestic and family violence"; however, terminology has become increasingly fragmented across the policing, legal, and service sectors in Australia. Legal definitions cover a wide range of relationships, including extended family relationships and include "intimate partner violence." Although some of the women in this study did talk about other violent relationships that come under Australian definitions of domestic and family violence, the focus in this study was on violent relationships between intimates. I use the term *intimate partner violence* except where women speak about some other relationships in which they experienced violence. There are long-standing debates about the most appropriate terminology to use (MacDonald, 1998; Radford & Hester, 2006, p. 7), but IPV best reflects the central focus of this study. I assumed a broad definition of IPV throughout the study, encapsulating coercive and controlling behavior perpetrated by an abuser on his intimate partner (Stark,

2007). This definition was generally consistent with the legal definitions of IPV and domestic and family violence at the time and place the research was undertaken.[2] Coercive control includes the microregulation of routine behaviors, the invasion of personal space, isolation, undermining autonomy, and depriving the person of access to resources. Overlapping behaviors that may be part of coercive and controlling behavior often include physical and sexual assaults, stalking, property damage, financial abuse, abuse of pets or service animals, emotional or psychological abuse, humiliation and degradation, or isolation from family and friends; they sometimes also include co-opting others to carry out such abuse or threatening to carry out such abuse. Research has identified that this type of abuse has a cumulative effect not found in individual incidents of assault or property damage (Pence & Paymar, 1993).

Where possible, I have referred to the interviewed woman and the abusive partner or ex-partner she speaks about by name, using pseudonyms. Where I have generalized about women who have experienced IPV and engaged with the legal system, I have used the word *victim*, acknowledging the diversity of their experiences (Goodmark, 2009, p. 41). Use of the word *victim* has been criticized for implying that women who have experienced IPV are powerless, a stereotype that does not resonate with many women (Fine, 1989, p. 553), including some of the women interviewed over the course of this study. While the term *survivor* may suggest empowerment and be preferred, it may minimize the trauma the woman has experienced (Fernandez, 2010, p. 24) or imply that those who do not escape IPV are weak or consented to the behavior (Meyersfeld, 2010, p. xxxiv). Where I have generalized about the men in this study who were abusive or used the legal system in a controlling way toward the women who were interviewed, I have referred to them variously as absuser(s), perpetrator(s), or abusive partners or ex-partners. While I use the terms abusive partner or ex-partner, I recognize that the status of the relationship was not always clear and it often changed over the course of the women's relationships (see Chapter 9).

In terms of what is meant by engaging with law, Scales (2006, p. 24) has identified that "what makes law, law is a big question of jurisprudence," and there is not sufficient space to enter into those debates here. Smart (1989, p. 164) has pointed out that law does not have a single appearance, and it includes at least statue law and judge-made law. While critical of the usefulness of law in advancing women's emancipation (p. 5), she provides a rough definition of law: "Law constitutes a plurality of principles, knowledges, and events . . . it claims a unity through common usage of the term 'law'" (p. 4). Following Smart, I employed a broad definition of legal engagement. For the purposes of recruitment for the study, it included interactions with the people who implement, interpret, and apply the law, including police, prosecutors, lawyers, and judicial decision makers. It also included aspects of, or systems within, the legal process that are most commonly associated with IPV, such as civil protection orders, criminal responses, child protection, family law, and immigration law. As the chapters throughout this book show, however, while women reported on these aspects of legal engagement, they also reported on other forms of engagement with law, such as statutory victim assistance and child support assessments, private contracts and leases, defamation, equity, and civil disputes with banks.

RESEARCHER AND RESEARCH SETTING

I bring my own experiences, perspectives, and background to the research process, and it is important to acknowledge this from the outset (Beuthin, 2014; Hesse-Biber, 2015). To start with, I am white, middle-class, university educated, and a woman. After working as a lawyer in private criminal practice and then at an Aboriginal legal service in other parts of Australia, I moved to Brisbane, where the study was carried out, and I lived and worked there for more than 20 years mainly as an academic. During that period, I was involved in research and in law reform around the legal responses to IPV and other forms of domestic and family violence. For many years I have participated in boards and committees of community organizations that support women escaping violence, and in clinical teaching and qualitative research programs that focus on legal responses to IPV. Needless to say, there are both similarities and real differences between me and all of the participants (Oakley, 2016, p. 197), and these similarities and differences would have resulted in the women participants speaking either more or less freely with me.

The study sample of women is drawn from the southeast corner of the state of Queensland, Australia, with most of the participants based in Queensland's capital city, Brisbane, and its surrounds (see Map 2.1). Given my strong networks in Brisbane with organizations and lawyers that support battered women, it made sense, at least on a practical level, to base the study there. Furthermore, as a sole researcher, limiting the research to one reasonably localized area was important from a resourcing perspective. I needed to be able to reschedule interviews on relatively short notice

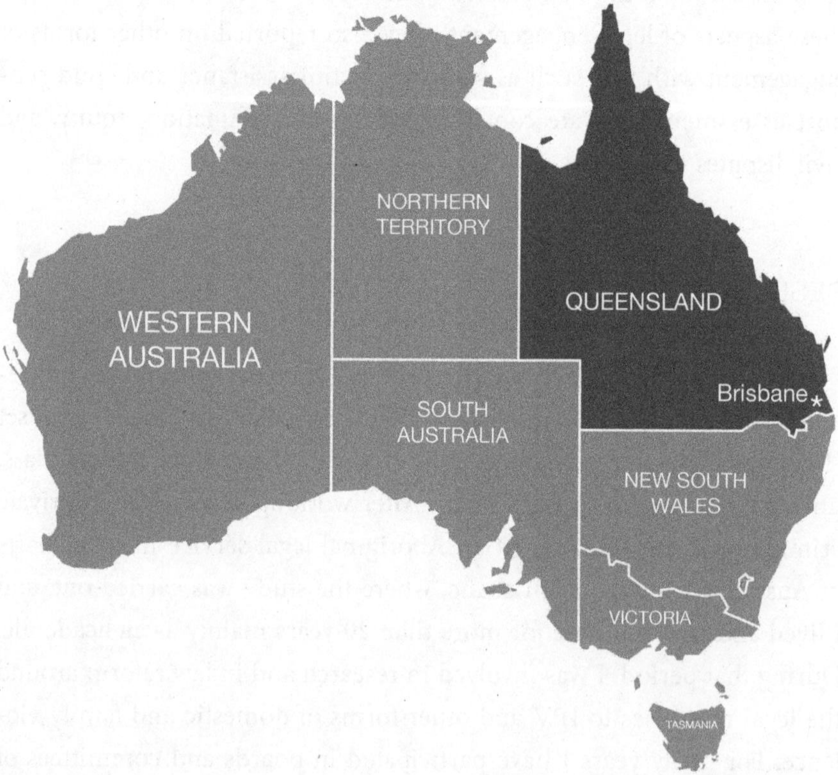

Map 2.1 Location of Brisbane.
Image Ingo Menhard/Shutterstock.

to best suit the women, and, as often as possible, I wanted to carry out interviews in person. Importantly, the Brisbane setting was large enough to ensure the anonymity of the participants could be maintained.

Brisbane and its surrounding region has approximately 3.5 million people. It is the third-largest city in Australia. It is comparatively well resourced to respond to IPV, with a fairly high density of police, courts, various support services, and legal aid services. There has been a significant focus on IPV in Queensland, especially for the past 10 years. State-based legal reforms in 2012 led to a significant expansion of the definition of domestic and family violence to include coercive control and other non-physical forms of IPV. *Not Now, Not Ever*, a report by the Special Taskforce on Domestic and Family Violence in Queensland (2015), recommended a number of changes to how the Queensland legal system should respond to IPV and other forms of domestic and family violence. Several developments occurred in response to the report's recommendations, including the introduction of a criminal offense of strangulation, guidelines for lawyers dealing with cases involving domestic and family violence, and specialist training for magistrates. This study cannot track the effect of these changes, but over the course of the interviews, some of the women did comment on improvements in their treatment and their experiences with justice actors, and this may in part be due to some of the changes recommended in the report.

RECRUITMENT

I decided to recruit women who had experienced IPV from a male intimate partner. In doing this, I excluded male victims of IPV and people in lesbian, gay, or other relationships. This is a limitation of the study. I made this decision for a number of reasons, including that the services I have links to support women and also my own identity as a straight woman. Women who have been abused by men have been a strong focus of many recent inquiries and developments in legal responses in Australia (Australian Law Reform Commission and New South Wales Law Reform

Commission [ALRC/NSWLRC], 2010; Special Taskforce on Domestic and Family Violence in Queensland, 2015; State of Victoria, 2016a) and elsewhere, and they continue to be killed by male intimates in very high numbers in Australia and beyond (Walklate, McCulloch, Fitz-Gibbon, & Maher, 2019, p. 66). However, I recognize there is a need for more research into the experiences of abused men and individuals who identify as lesbian, gay, bisexual, transgender, or intersex and their interactions with the legal system (Australasian Institute of Judicial Administration [AIJA], 2020, [4.4.13]).

Ultimately, I recruited 65 women to the study. They were over 18 years old, had experienced IPV by a male intimate partner in the 12 months preceding the first interview, and had in some way engaged with the legal system in relation to the IPV during those past 12 months. This approach to recruitment required women to be already connected in some way to the legal system. While some did opt out of their engagement with the legal system during the course of the Study, there are of course many women who never turn to law, and their voices are not captured in this study (Meyer, 2011).

The recruitment process occurred over the course of the first 2 years of the project with the assistance of a range of organizations and individuals. Given the links I had established through previous work, I recruited most participants with assistance from domestic and family violence services, community-based legal centers, and private law firms in Brisbane. This approach to recruitment created another limitation of the study, as many battered women never engage with these more public forms of support.

Primarily because of the commitment of a range of organizations to the project, it was not difficult to recruit the first 50 women. After that, however, recruitment was slower. I initially planned to recruit 80 women to the study in expectation of significant attrition to around 60 women for the time 3 interview (Holder, 2018). I discontinued recruitment once I reached 65 women. At this stage, I also found that the group of women I had recruited reflected significant diversity, in terms of their own attributes and also in terms of their engagements with law. Furthermore, as I consider later in this chapter, attrition was not as high as I had anticipated.

I attracted a diverse cohort of women to the study thorough a variety of services, including services working with migrant women and with Aboriginal and Torres Strait Islander women, a service working with women with intellectual disabilities, private lawyers, and a range of other nongovernment organizations that provide support and legal advice to women who have experienced IPV. At least three women were supported by two of the services that assisted with recruitment and were referred to the study by both of the services.

Service providers and lawyers discussed the study with clients who fit the study parameters and explained the consent form; if the women were interested in participating, the service providers and lawyers either arranged initial interviews with the women in consultation with me, provided me with the women's contact details (with the women's consent), or suggested the women email or telephone me directly to arrange an interview. As the study progressed, women heard about it through their own networks, such as from court workers, other women already involved in the study, or news media. Some women emailed me their stories and asked to participate in the study. In response, I sent copies of the information and consent form and answered their questions by email. In five cases women who had discovered the study via these other channels, emailed their interest, and fit the study parameters ultimately took part in interviews. I commenced interviews with the recruited cohort of 65 women at the end of 2014 and concluded in 2017.

I made a decision not to recruit women to the study based on the time that they separated from the perpetrator. As other researchers have shown (DeKeseredy, Dragiewicz, & Schwartz, 2017; Mahoney, 1991), separation may exacerbate or result in the commencement of abuse, leading women to engage with the law. While at time of the study 14 (22%) of the 65 women had separated from their intimate partner in the past 12 months, 18 (28%) had separated 1 to 2 years before the time 1 interview, 12 (19%) had done so in the 2 to 4 years preceding the time 1 interview, and 16 (25%) had been separated for more than 5 years. For most women, the point of separation was not absolutely clear; most of the women had left many times before and returned to their partners, and some left and returned during the study. The women's reflections on separation were an important part of their narrative; I discuss these reflections in Chapter 9.

During the study, five of the participants were living outside of Brisbane at some point. It is common for women who have experienced IPV to be highly mobile due to safety concerns and housing instability, among other reasons (Bowstead, 2016). I continued to contact the participants for interviews even when they were no longer in Brisbane. Although legal resources and processes available to women were similar in the areas they had relocated to, their knowledge of local resources and their networks of support may have been more limited, and these issues may have affected their interactions with law. While a focus on one jurisdiction represents a limitation for the study, it is also strength because it ensures that participants were generally subject to the same legal regimes and had formal access to similar legal resources. Notably, many of the over-time studies that have examined desistence from crime have focused on a cohort from a particular place (e.g., Liverpool [Maruna, 2001]; Adelaide [Halsey, 2007]; Canberra [Holder, 2018]) and have produced results that have been useful beyond the original setting of the study.

Each of the 65 women recruited to time 1 of the study were provided with a pseudonym, which is used consistently throughout the text. At the time 3 interview, women were asked if they wanted to choose a name, and some did; for others I selected a name, including for those women who did not take part in the time 3 interview. When I chose names, I attempted to use names that would not suggest the woman's cultural background to ensure her identity remained confidential.

TIME AND PLACE OF INTERVIEWS

I planned to undertake interviews three times with each woman over a 2-year period, with interviews taking place at approximately 8-month intervals. I selected this time frame on the basis that while some legal processes, such as protection orders, can be finalized within months of application, others can take longer to finalize. The 2-year period would show some change in the processes and in the women's approach and experience of them. I envisaged that undertaking interviews over a 2-year period would ensure that a significant proportion of women would consider that they had completed their interaction with the legal system in relation to IPV. However, as the chapters show, most women still had ongoing legal engagements related to the abuse at time 3.[3]

Interviews often took some weeks to arrange after I made an initial contact; many of the women were busy juggling work, study, children, and court proceedings, especially around the time 1 interview. Depending on women's circumstances, interviews were more or less spaced out. On average, the time gap between the time 1 and time 2 interviews was 10 months, although the time between these interviews ranged from 6 months to 17 months. On average the time gap between the time 2 and time 3 interviews was 8 months, although this time ranged from 4 months to 14 months. The 4-month time gap between interviews was a one-off; the next closest time gap between time 2 and 3 interviews was 6 months.

The time 1 interviews usually took place in person at the service from where women were recruited; some took place in coffee shops where I purchased a drink or something to eat for us, educational facilities where some women were studying, or in public libraries. At times 2 and 3, some interviews were conducted on the phone or, again, in coffee shops or other public places. At times 2 and 3, I interviewed five women in their homes, as this was most convenient for them. Some of these women had baked cakes especially for the occasion. However, I was generally reluctant to go to women's homes, mainly because of safety concerns. In several cases, I drove to women's homes, picked them up, and went with them to a coffee shop or library, driving them home at the end of the interview.

ATTRITION

Given the vulnerability of the group of women I interviewed, I was concerned about significant attrition from the study. Researchers recommend several components to minimize attrition: build trust through confirmation of confidentiality; with the interviewees' consent, obtain detailed information about two or three safe contact persons through whom the interviewee is willing to be followed up; identify safe and unsafe contact times at each interview; provide the researcher's contact details to the participant so that changes in contact details can be communicated by the participant; and compensate participants for participation (Burton, Purvin, & Garrett-Peters, 2009, p. 73; Sullivan, Rumptz, Campbell, Eby, & Davidson, 1996; Ullman, 2011, p. 194). I followed these approaches in the Brisbane study as much as possible. Most women had mobile phones, and this made it easier to keep in touch with them. Most were reluctant to provide more than one follow-up contact, although generally women advised they could be followed up through the services they were supported by. Where the women did provide a follow-up contact, it was usually the victim's mother or sister. I discussed with each woman how she could be contacted and developed an individualized approach to follow up with each woman. My efforts to find women for the second and third interviews were limited to the methods and contacts they had provided at the first interview or contact with the service they were initially recruited from (usually text message, telephone call, email, or posted letter asking them to call me or via the identified alternative contact person). On one occasion, I went outside this approach and asked the child protection agency to pass on a message to one of the women, and she then contacted me. While it would have been possible to "try harder" to contact the six women who could not be contacted at times 2 and 3—for example, by physically attending at their address, tracing through Facebook or social media, or following up through police services or child support agencies—I was conscious to avoid the kind of "sociological stalking" that Sharpe (2017) has warned against and so limited my attempts to the methods I had discussed with the women. Participants were provided with a $40 (USD26) supermarket shopping voucher at time 1 and a $60 (USD42) shopping voucher at times 2 and 3 both as an incentive to participate and as a form of thanks and appreciation for the time and effort involved in taking part in interviews (Head, 2009). No doubt, in some cases the provision of these vouchers facilitated the high retention rate. The retention rate was also probably assisted by the fact that I was a sole researcher contacting and communicating with the women over the three "times" for the interviews and so was able to build a stronger rapport with many of the women than might have been the case if they had been contacted by more than one person (Sharpe, 2017, p. 242). The time 1 interviews included 65 participants, the time 2 interviews included 59 participants, and the time 3 interviews included 54 participants. This represents a 90% retention rate at time 2 and an 83% retention rate at time 3.

It was not possible to interview six of the women at time 2. Two could not be located. In another case, the agency that had initially recruited the woman to the study advised me that she was "in a bad place" and could not continue. A further three women told me they did not want to continue at time 2. Two of these women provided reasons. Angelina, a recent migrant, was contacted by email prior to the time 2 interview and responded that she tried "to forget about it and not to talk about it even with my relatives, hope you understand me. I keep quite busy myself every day . . . but memories from that period of my life are very painful and unfortunately still affect my emotional mood." Hannah reported that her abuser had received a jail sentence for a significant period, and it was her view that she could no longer usefully contribute to the study.

By the time 3 interview, three more women could not be located, and two other women indicated that they did not want to continue with the study; one of these two women who did not want to continue provided an explanation. Lahleh, a recent migrant, explained she was "overwhelmed" and just wanted a "normal life."

Of the 11 women who did not complete the study, 4 were migrant women who had arrived in Australia within the past 5 years. It is possible that one of the migrant women, Tabora, was deported because she was still on an insecure visa at the time of the second interview. Tabora had separated from her partner, who was on a work visa, and her continuing visa relied on her ex-partner gaining a further work permit or permanent residency. Two other participants who did not complete the study were Aboriginal women. Consistent with other studies, marginalized women in particular were less likely to continue on to the time 3 interview. Nevertheless, the retention of women to the third interview in this study was quite high compared with similar studies (Young, Powers, & Bell, 2006).

In his study of desistence from crime, Maruna (2001; see also Logan, Walker, Shannon, & Cole, 2008) also followed up participants with at least one telephone call to see how they were doing between interviews. I did not follow up with women routinely between interviews, although I communicated with them on many occasions between interviews. In some cases, I was in touch to pass along information to a woman that I had committed to providing in the previous interview. This included referrals to housing or income support and links to alternative support agencies when the woman was no longer associated with the organization that originally referred her to the study. Many of the women also contacted me by text, phone, or email between interviews. They updated me on the progress of the cases they were involved in, shared concerns about the perpetrator, and let me know about other developments such as new jobs, housing, and travel difficulties. On a number of occasions, I attended court with women, and I attended a community legal service with one of the women.

In any interview or contact where a woman disclosed concerns for her safety, I sought her consent to let the support agency she was working with know about the issue so it could follow up with her directly or I recommended she contact her support agency or the police. Sometimes women asked questions about legal responses. Usually I arranged referrals for these inquiries, but sometimes I referred women directly to online information or answered their questions. For example, at time 2, when Vera asked about divorce, I referred her to the relevant website where she could download forms and initiate the process. At time 3 Vera reported that she had accessed the website and was now divorced from her abuser. Sometimes women talked about the financial costs that had accrued because of violence, such as paying to have locks changed or walls repaired. In those cases, I referred women to victim assistance services to follow up on the possibility of compensation. I understood my actions as part of the reciprocity of the research process and a form of information and knowledge exchange (Oakley, 1981). To this extent, my involvement in the project also contributed to how women in the study engaged with various legal processes.

I made a decision not to attend "social" events that the women invited me to on the basis that my attendance might endanger myself or the women or that they could disclose information to me based on friendship rather than on the research basis. As Sharpe (2017, p. 234) has identified, there is a fine line between walking alongside research participants "in order to gain a deep understanding of how their lives and narratives develop over time, and reproducing everyday modes of scrutiny and surveillance."

INTERVIEW APPROACH

The time 1 interviews can best be described as semistructured (Adams, 2015), although some aspects of them were more structured. The first part of the time 1 interview was usually fairly structured. I made initial introductions, took the woman through the study information and consent form, and then collected some background information. Sometimes, one of the background questions would lead the woman into telling her story, and I tried not to interrupt this if it happened. On other occasions, once we made it through collecting the background information, I would ask the woman a broad question such as "Tell me about your experience with the legal system." I followed the woman's narrative with a questioning phase in which I sought clarification on some points and asked questions about her involvement with legal processes and actors that had not been mentioned in her narrative. For example, I asked, "Did you have a protection order?" or "Did you have legal representation when you were at the family court?" I would then follow up with something like "Tell me about your experience of the legal representative/of representing yourself." For the time 1 interview, I used a guide with topics I wanted to cover, and I followed up on any of these topics that had not been covered in the woman's story. My aim in taking this approach was to prioritize the woman's perspectives and experiences of events and of legal actors and to understand how she made sense of the legal system and its actors and her relationship to it (Allen, 2011, p. 28; C. Anderson & Kirkpatrick, 2016, p. 631; Maruna, 2001, p. 39; Reissman, 2008; Riger, 1992).

At the time 2 and 3 interviews, I usually began by summarizing the interactions with the legal system and actors that the woman had reported at the previous interview and then asked her to bring me up to date. For example, I might say something like: "Last time your family law matter was adjourned and X [the abuser] was awaiting sentence for the assault. What's been happening since then?" Once the woman had finished their narrative, similar to during the time 1 interview, I asked questions about her involvement with legal processes and actors that she had not mentioned.

Where possible, and with participants' consent, I viewed and obtained copies of some of their court records. Some women provided me with copies of their applications and orders for civil protection, copies of court transcripts, statements, appeal documents, and other orders and applications. Sometimes they provided news media articles; these were always focused on the perpetrator and usually reported on their sentence for a criminal matter related to the IPV. A number of the women also provided me with documents prepared during family law proceedings, including affidavits of both themselves and their abuser, reports written by psychologists and social workers, and mental health reports. It is not possible to refer to these because in Australia, the Family Law Act 1975 (Cth) s 121 prohibits the identification of parties to family law proceedings. Penalties are high and can result in imprisonment. The time 1 interviews lasted around 90 minutes in total; time 2 and 3 interviews were usually shorter, but this depended on what had been happening for the women between interviews.

At the time 1 interview, eight of the women required interpreters, and the agency supporting the women provided them. Only four women required interpreters at the time 2 interviews. Interviews that involved interpreters of necessity took longer. Interpreters also had varying skill levels. Some interrupted the woman's narrative on many occasions so that smaller "chunks" could be interpreted. It is likely this interrupted the flow of the story for some women.

ANALYSIS

The interviews were recorded, transcribed, and thematically analyzed both manually and by using the NVivo qualitative software package (Braun & Clarke, 2006). I carried out initial coding of interview transcripts, and other material that the women provided at each subsequent interview, with assistance from two research assistants, with whom I was in constant communication throughout the first phase of coding. This initial coding or search for themes was deductive, or "top down," in that the codes were generated from the topics I hoped to cover at the time 1 interview. As the research progressed and more interviews were added, broad themes were identified around women's involvement with the legal system; their interaction with other actors, especially the abuser and those connected to legal processes (especially police, prosecutors, lawyers, and judicial officers); and their journey to law and the consequences of this engagement (how it made them feel, what happened, etc.). I repeated the coding process to identify overarching themes that seemed to fit the data. This later phase was more deductive; I looked for repetition of words and concepts and also for metaphors used by the women that seemed to suggest further themes (C. Anderson & Kirkpatrick, 2016, p. 633; Ryan & Bernard, 2003, p. 104). These overarching themes included the minimizing of nonphysical abuse across systems and actors and its significance to women, the focus of justice system actors on separation as a moment in time and women's ambivalence about it, and the use of the legal system by abusers (and legal system actors) to continue abuse. Once all the interviews were completed, I reviewed the coding of the whole data set, reappraising the fit of the already identified themes to the data and looking for women's changing views about the role of the legal system in their lives and their motivations for pursuing or opting out of law.

THE WOMEN

I collected demographic information at the time 1 interview. The mean age of the participants was 39 years (*SD* = 9), ranging from 23 to 68 years. Just over half of the participants were currently married to the abuser or had been married to him in the past (*n* = 35; 54%), and another 26 (40%) women had lived with him. All the abusive partners were identified as men. Women spent between 1 and 29 years in their abusive relationships, with a mean relationship duration of 9.6 years. Most of the women also had children with their abuser (*n* = 48; 74%).

Overall, the participants were highly educated. The highest level of education attained for 28 (43%) women was a university degree (bachelor's degree or higher);[4] 16 (25%) had a diploma or advanced diploma; 10 (15%) had completed high school (year 12 in Australia); and 11 (17%) had finished school at year 11 or earlier. In part, the relatively high education of the women in the sample is explained by the fact that nearly half (*n* = 11 of 24; 45.8%) of the migrant women interviewed had gained a bachelor's degree or higher in their home country prior to migration. Approximately half of the women (*n* = 30; 46%) were employed either part-time or full-time at the first interview. Nearly half of the women (*n* = 32; 49%) relied entirely on social security payments, and, at time 1, 3 women had no employment or access to social security because of their visa status. The majority of participants were Australian-born or had migrated with their families when they were children (*n* = 35; 54%). Six (9%) of the women identified as Aboriginal women, with 2 of these women identifying as having an intellectual disability.[5] Twenty-four (37%) were migrant women who moved to Australia as an adult; all of these women spoke English as a second or third language.[6] Their complex visa pathways are set out in Appendix 3. Of this group 17 (of *n* = 24; 70%) discussed visa issues connected with their experience of IPV at the first interview. Three of the migrant women had been living in Australia for less than 2 years, 13 women for between 2 and 5 years, and 8 women for 5 years or more. Notably only 3 of the 24 migrant women had come to Australia as refugees. The other 21 migrant women had originally come to Australia on tourist, work, study, or partner visas, although most of these women had held a variety of visas. Ten of the women indicated that they had a physical disability, with 6 of these women identifying their disability as an intellectual disability.[7]

All of the participants had experienced multiple forms of abuse, making them representative of the larger population of women who are abused (ALRC/NSWLRC, 2010, pp. 300–301). Most reported that they had experienced physical abuse ($n = 55$; 85%), and all of the women reported some form of emotional or psychological abuse during the relationship (this is discussed further in Chapter 3). For most women, the abuse had continued after separation.

As noted earlier, the interview participants had diverse backgrounds, and this was an important aspect of the study from the outset. The concept of "intersectionality," introduced by Crenshaw (1989, 1991), has become a vital analytical tool to help understand how intersecting aspects of identity, including but not limited to race and gender, influence a person's experience of the world. As Collins and Bilge (2016, p. 11) have identified, people's experience of the world is "better understood as being shaped not by a single axis of social division . . . but by many axes that work together and influence each other." There is of course no single experience of IPV, nor is there one single experience of engaging with the legal system. As Goodmark (2012, p. 4; Matsuda, 1987) points out, "Women stand at the intersection of the various identities that construct them: race, sexual orientation, socioeconomic class, disability, and other defining characteristics," and the subordinated victim should be at the center of feminist analysis. This study speaks to various facets of intersectionality, including how socioeconomic circumstances, the experience of insecure migration, Aboriginal and Torres Strait Islander status, disability, and the presence of children interact with gender to shape legal engagement.

ETHICS APPROVAL

The study received ethics approval from the University of Queensland Human Research Ethics Committee (approval number 2014001243).

NOTES

1. On self-positioning and constructing self through narratives, see Allen (2011), Riger (1992, p. 737), and Jarnkvist and Brannstrom (2019, p. 4688).
2. The Family Law Act 1975 (Cth) s 4AB defines family violence, and the Domestic and Family Violence Protection Act 2012 (Qld) s 8 defines domestic and family violence. The definition of family violence is narrower under Australian immigration law; see Migration Regulations 1994 (Cth) reg 1.21. See Appendix 2.
3. Those who were interviewed at the third interview were asked if, subject to future access to resources, they could be recontacted to discuss their legal engagements at a future time; all agreed that they would be willing to be contacted. In the future, this research may be able to contribute postseparation studies such as the one undertaken by Miller (2018), whose book draws on participant observation, research, and interviews with women, focusing on the resilience of long-term (more than 5-year) survivors of intimate partner violence and abuse.
4. In Australia, around 35% of women hold a bachelor's degree or higher (Australian Bureau of Statistics, 2017).
5. Six is a low number; however, only 4% of Queensland's population identifies as Aboriginal (or Torres Strait Islander) (Australian Bureau of Statistics, 2016a).
6. Approximately 22% of the Queensland population was born overseas (Australian Bureau of Statistics, 2016b).
7. The particular experiences of this group of six women is considered in more detail in Douglas and Harpur (2016).

3

Nonphysical Abuse and Coercive Control

UNDERSTANDING COERCIVE CONTROL

This chapter explores women's experiences of the behaviors and tactics used by their abusive partners. Most women who were interviewed said that the most difficult form of abuse they dealt with was nonphysical abuse, especially emotional abuse. Many stated that nonphysical abuse deeply impacted on their sense of self and freedom and often continued to affect them years after separation. This chapter explores several recurring and interrelated tactics that abusers used to control women. Women's experiences of abuse were complex, and many women reflected explicitly on their sense of being controlled by their partner. Emotional abuse was one of the tactics abusers used to limit women's freedom. Other tactics commonly included targeting a woman's role as a mother, isolation within the relationship, financial abuse, and, for women on insecure visas, threats about their visas. Importantly, most women could also point to incidents of physical violence or threats of physical harm perpetrated by their abusive partner. For many women, these incidents were rare or a one-off and occurred early in the relationship, often years earlier, but showed their partner's capacity and potential for physical violence.

Evan Stark's exploration of intimate partner violence (IPV) as coercive control highlights the importance of nonphysical forms of abuse in

Women, Intimate Partner Violence, and the Law. Heather Douglas, Oxford University Press (2021). © Oxford University Press.
DOI: 10.1093/oso/9780190071783.003.0003

creating conditions of "unfreedom" (2007, p. 204; see also Jeffs, Kelly, & Klein, 2018). Abusers' exercise of coercive control involves using a variety of methods, including physical violence, threats, deprivation of basic needs, surveillance, and degradation, to hurt, degrade, intimidate, exploit, isolate, and control their victims (Crossman & Hardesty, 2018, 203; Stark, 2007, p. 209). The tactics, or technologies, of abuse develop and change over time and are specific to the woman's circumstances, with the abuser testing strategies to see what works best to control the individual woman at a given time. These tactics are often routine, and their effects are cumulative rather than incident-specific. Stark observes that control consists of "structural forms of deprivation, exploitation, and command that compel obedience indirectly by monopolizing vital resources, dictating preferred choices, microregulating a partner's behavior, limiting her options, and depriving her of supports needed to exercise independent judgment" (2007, p. 229).

Coercive control is gendered and relies on vulnerability arising from sexual inequality (Stark, 2007; Stark & Hester, 2019, p. 88). A woman's experiences of mothering and domestic work, insecure immigration status, social isolation, and financial circumstances intersect to ensure a distinct experience of IPV. Her access to private and public resources and support will also vary. The abuser's tactics of abuse will fluctuate and change in response to these different factors, and the effects of IPV are compounded depending on the intersecting social and structural inequalities that the woman faces (Crenshaw, 1991; Ptacek, 1999, p. 10; Sweet, 2019, p. 869; Tolmie, Smith, Short, Wilson, & Sach, 2018, p. 184). An intimate partner who is an abuser has special knowledge of her circumstances and can exploit these vulnerabilities in targeted ways.

Increasingly, the concept of coercive control underpins legislative responses to IPV. The United Kingdom introduced a criminal offense of coercive control in 2015 (McGorrery & McMahon, 2019). In some US states the definition of IPV has been expanded to include emotional and psychological abuse (e.g., Office of the Administrative Rules Coordinator Division of Financial Management, 2020). In Australia, family law legislation and some civil protection order legislation now define IPV to include coercive control (see Appendix 2; Jeffries, Field, & Bond, 2015; Rathus, 2013). Australian policy information, aimed at stakeholders in the legal system such as judges and lawyers, explains IPV as a pattern of behavior involving a perpetrator's exercise of control over the victim, with perpetrators employing a wide range of abusive tactics to control a victim's life (Council of Australian Governments, 2019, p. 56; Australasian Institute of Judicial Administration [AIJA], 2020, [3.3]; Council of Australian Governments, 2019, p. 56). Despite this recognition, as Chapters 5 through 8 demonstrate, the legal system and its actors continue to misunderstand IPV, minimizing nonphysical forms of abuse, expecting women to "just leave" the violence, and assuming a woman will be in a position to negotiate as an equal with her abuser within the legal system. It is important to understand the study women's experiences of IPV in order to appreciate how the legal system and its actors routinely fail in their responses to abused women.

THE COMPLEXITY OF ABUSE

All of the women interviewed experienced a complex pattern of abuse during their relationship that often changed over time and continued after separation. For each woman, the pattern of violence was unique and directly targeted to her circumstances and, in many cases, drawing on knowledge held only by her abusive partner (Stark, 2012a, p. 21). In the course of the second interview I asked women, "When thinking about the abuse you experienced during your relationship with your abusive partner, what abusive behaviors were the most difficult to deal with?" Of the 60 women who answered this question, 44 (73%) identified nonphysical abuse as the most difficult aspect. Most (n = 40) highlighted emotional abuse, including insults, name-calling, and put-downs as the most difficult form of abuse to deal with. Four other women pointed to other types of nonphysical abuse: financial abuse (n = 2), stalking (n = 1), and isolation (n = 1). While 3 women cited threats to kill or cause harm as the most difficult form of abuse to deal, only 14 women identified physical abuse as the most difficult aspect: physical violence ($n = 6$), sexual abuse ($n = 4$), violence toward their child ($n = 3$), and fighting ($n = 1$).[1]

Most of the study women ($n = 55$ out of 65 women; 85%) said they had experienced physical violence from their partner at some stage during their relationship. However, even where women reported serious physical abuse, they often pointed to nonphysical abuse as the worst part of the abuse they had to deal with. For example, 24 women reported being strangled or choked during the relationship, but 18 of them identified nonphysical abuse as the worst form of abuse they had experienced: emotional abuse ($n = 16$), financial abuse ($n = 1$), and stalking ($n = 1$). Sometimes the physical violence had occurred many years previously, frequently in the earliest stages of their relationship; however, incidents of physical abuse or threats of physical harm were important in establishing power dynamics. Even when physical violence had been perpetrated years earlier, women recognized that such incidents demonstrated that physical violence was possible and contributed both to a sense of simmering threat and to a feeling of being trapped in the relationship (Stark, 2007, p. 250).

Yvonne was with her partner, Emir, for almost 14 years, and they had children together. She described the relationship as being extremely controlling after the children were born. Emir determined how each day was organized, what they ate, and how money was spent. Emir did not allow the family to have access to technology, including mobile phones and television. He denied visits from Yvonne's family and friends, making her feel isolated. Yvonne could only remember two incidents of physical violence being directed at her throughout the course of their relationship. She recounted that after one of the children was born, Emir refused a friend's offer to care for the older children. When Yvonne asked why, Emir smacked her twice across the face. He then said to her, "Never question my authority—especially in front of the children." On another occasion, again when the children were present, Yvonne asked why they had to take a train instead of driving, and he had pushed her toward the train tracks. That event was terrifying for Yvonne. Despite being able to recall only two occasions of physical violence, Yvonne said they had a big impact on her. She felt she had to "modify" herself. As she explained, "There was always this threat of violence. . . . I just felt like I had . . . no way to discuss things with him, and I always felt like I would get my head pushed through the wall if I did. . . . We were walking on eggshells." Yvonne said this was a form of "psychological and emotional" abuse that was the worst aspect of the abuse she experienced.

Several women whose partners had never been directly physically violent toward them said that their potential for physical harm was shown through other forms of violence. These other forms rendered threats of physical violence credible, even where the threats were implied or indirect, and credible threats were often an effective control tactic (DeKeseredy, Dragiewicz, & Schwartz, 2017, p. 36; Wilson & Daly, 1992, p. 12). Jane commenced her relationship with her abusive partner when she was a teenager. They had two children and separated after nearly 30 years together. She described her relationship as being characterized by emotional and financial abuse but recalled a particular incident of physical threat early on in the relationship. Jane had a clear memory of how her partner threw a coffee cup at the wall near her head more than 20 years ago and how he broke things she needed or was proud of:

> I remember a coffee cup flying past my head at the age of 20 and smashing—it didn't just thud on the glass lazily, it smashed on the brick wall five meters away. . . . Then he used to break my stuff. So '"I'm angry with you, I'm going to break your squash racket." "I'm angry with you so I'm ripping up your violin exam certificate." So he did do that stuff, early on. So then I basically became worn down. (Jane, interview 1)

For the most part, Francis's partner, Mark, was not physically violent toward her; his abuse was "more verbal than physical." However, Mark punched holes in the walls and doors and broke her things, so when he threatened to push her off a balcony on one occasion, she believed he might do so. The constant sense of threatened violence made Francis feel trapped in the relationship, although she said the emotional abuse was most difficult for her "because you start believing it."

EMOTIONAL ABUSE

Emotional abuse includes verbal abuse such as name-calling and other comments that are aimed to be, and are, experienced as degrading, ridiculing, or humiliating. Such comments are often targeted at women's intelligence, body image, and sexuality (Ahmed, 2017, p. 170; Bagshaw, Chung, Couch, Lilburn, & Wadham, 2000; Stark, 2012a, p. 26). Previous research has highlighted the damaging effects of emotional abuse in both the short term and the longer term (Crossman, Hardesty, & Raffaelii, 2016; Estefan, Coulter, & VendeWeerd, 2016; Follingstad, Rutledge, Berg, Hause, & Polek, 1990, p. 117; Stark, 2007, p. 202). Many of the study participants experienced ridicule as an extremely damaging form of abuse. Thinking back on their relationships, the women explained how emotional abuse impacted on their self-esteem and self-belief: "I don't have faith in my judgment anymore, I'm not open to relationships anymore, I'm closed down" (Lisa); "It made me doubt myself and question myself and continually justify what [I am] doing and why [I am] doing it and cover myself" (Felicity); "It lives on forever" (Teagan); "I died every day" (Pari [culturally and linguistically diverse (CALD) background]).

Alex talked about the roller-coaster effects and power of emotional abuse and how it played into a cycle of abuse and contrition (Pence & Paymar, 1993):

> He was supportive in one way—held me up and then he would so easily just rip that stool out from underneath you. That's how I felt. I felt like a princess at some stage and then he would just go, swoosh. Don't feel too good, I'm going to bring you down. Then I'd question myself and then I'd think, did I do something wrong? I would always be questioning what am I?

An abuser often used emotional abuse as a tactic to shift blame and responsibility for the abuse to the woman, sometimes making her feel crazy—a tactic sometimes referred to as "gaslighting" (Sweet, 2019, p. 853). In many cases, the woman reported that she started to believe the insults and felt that it was her fault her partner was abusive. At interview 1, Bianca said "I probably did push his buttons." Susan said she was blamed for "everything" and she was continually being told by her partner that she "was the crazy one who had to apologize and atone." Milly explained:

> He was manipulative. Really verbally aggressive and controlling. With the manipulation everything would end up being my fault and then he'd just hammer that in verbally, over and over and over again. Your fault this, your fault that, you did this, you did that. . . . Always my fault. My fault that I pushed him . . . to react that way. It was my fault that he ended up having to get angry. I quickly got to know my place.

Mira (CALD) explained that emotional abuse was the worst "because nobody will understand. . . . It's better if you punch me and I know it's already abuse. But with this constantly in your head, it's hard . . . the insults and how you feel responsible for something."

Women provided many examples of how the emotional abuse was intensely personal in the way it was targeted, increasing its impact (Stark, 2012, p. 21). For example, Frieda's childhood was difficult; child protection had been involved, and one of her family members had committed suicide. Her partner repeatedly taunted her about the dysfunctional family life in which she had grown up. He was "super-degrading," "he goes, oh you're a fucked-up family." Ingrid (CALD) also had difficult childhood experiences, and she had confided in her partner about them. She experienced childhood sexual abuse by a relative, and her partner constantly made jokes about sex and rape when she didn't feel like having sex. She felt "triggered" by these comments, and she believed this was his intention. Similarly, Maddy explained that her partner would always focus on her weaknesses, and anything she had shared with her partner that she "wasn't proud of would be brought back." Jacinta said the "verbal abuse was hideous. He'd bring up anything and everything you'd ever told him."

Comments about sexuality, connected to a sense of sexual possessiveness and jealousy, were common and often experienced as demeaning and exhausting. Celina met her Australian-citizen partner online and moved to Australia on a sponsored visa.[2] Her partner called her a whore and a prostitute and, knowing Celina wanted to have children, called her "infertile." Alex found the "ranting and questioning for hours about [her] previous partners, the intrusive questions often sexual in nature, his obsessive behavior and then his remorse" the worst aspect of the abuse. Valeria (CALD) said her partner was extremely jealous and texted her many times a day to check on where she was. As she explained, "It looks like he wants to own you . . . like a thing."

Some women said their partners' repeated insults and comments about weight and appearance had a significant impact on their self-esteem. Bianca said, "He would call me a fat cunt, knowing that I had an eating disorder in the past and all that sort of abuse, verbal abuse." When Kim was pregnant with her partner's baby, the emotional abuse escalated. She explained: "Being pregnant was . . . an abhorrent sort of thing for him. It was an ugly thing. He would put me down about my weight . . . he called me a keg on legs. He hated the fact I was putting on weight." While Skye's partner had punched her, splitting her lip, and "choked" her more than once, she stressed the impact of the emotional violence and control on her selfhood: "Everyday life, you can't be dressing like that, you can't wear makeup. I couldn't experience myself." Teagan had a similar experience:

> Like you can't wear perfume. It stinks. Don't wear makeup. You're ugly, he told me all the time. Then too skinny when I was skinny, too fat when I was fat . . . all that sort of stuff, that I couldn't cook or do anything. It does play in your head years later.

Women who were already more marginalized and isolated as a result of their cultural background described receiving racist taunts from their Australian-born partners. For example, Bisera (CALD) was called a "savage." For many women, the choice of language used by abusers was carefully targeted for maximum effect. Evie described how her partner called her a "cunt all the time . . . he knows I hate it . . . he makes me feel horrible." Rosa said, "He calls me a pig, fat, ugly all the time. In [my country] pig is highly insulting."

Early in the relationship many women tried to deal rationally with the emotional abuse and put in place strategies aimed at ending it, but they often gave up, exhausted by the conflict. Angelina (CALD) explained, "I have to be like very strong woman and I have to argument with him every day, fighting and demonstrate my position. But it destroys me. I was getting empty."

Jacinta dated James off and on for some years. Throughout the relationship, his behavior was erratic, and although he was mostly verbally abusive, sometimes he did hit her. Jacinta tried various strategies to end the abuse. At one point, she determined James was hypoglycemic and made changes to his diet to address this. However, this turned out not to be the cause of his unpredictability. She then tried to set some ground rules in the relationship, for example, that he would only visit when he wasn't "hypo." This didn't help much, as James would still call and text abuse multiple times a day. She also tried abusing James in response:

> I will be honest and say that after 10 or 15 or 20 calls being called an f cunt and this and that and everything else under the sun, everything else, a whore, everything, I have turned around and been verbally abusive back. I've told him to fuck off, I've told him to leave me the fuck alone, I've called him crazy, I've told him he's insane. I have, I've abused him back.

Ultimately Jacinta said she "gave up" and felt "battered" by the verbal abuse. At interview 2, Jacinta said that she and James had separated, gotten back together, and separated again. When we spoke again at interview 3, Jacinta and James were not in a relationship anymore, but he was still harassing her via email, text, constantly calling her, making various threats, and following her. She has blocked his numbers, but he rings from numbers she doesn't recognize. She said:

> I'm not scared of him in that sense because I'm not scared of anyone really because I just don't have a lot of fears. . . . I do get anxious when he drives past my house or rings 50 million times a day. It wrecks my day.

Some women explained how they tried to monitor their own behaviors to navigate around the constant threat of violence, an argument, or emotional abuse. The metaphor of "walking on eggshells" was common. Kirsten said: "It's the lead-up to the outburst. It's the lead-up to the monitoring. It's the walking on eggshells. It's the waiting for the implosion to come. That's the worst part." Faith explained:

> At first I'd get fiery. So when [our first child] was little, I'd just fire back, "You can't do that." By the end of it I was just quiet. So I'd just sit there and say nothing and that would be worse, because he'd be like, "Oh you sit there and you don't say anything, you're just like a robot."

Bianca tried tactics of placation to calm her partner's irrational anger, but this approach made her feel like she was "compromising" herself. She said: "I didn't respect myself at all for that—and I know it's a survival thing, to try and pretend you love someone who at that time, you hate."

FIONA'S EXPERIENCE

Fiona's story illustrates how a complex range of factors underpinned her entrapment in her abusive relationship. While she experienced various types of abuse over many years, including physical abuse, it was emotional abuse that most undermined her sense of self and was for her the worst abuse to deal with. Fiona highlighted the effects of emotional abuse across all three of the interviews and how they impacted on her life years after separation. At the first interview Fiona also identified herself as not "meek and mild" and therefore "not the right kind of victim" in the legal system (Goodmark, 2012, p. 54; Merry, 2003, p. 354).

> ***Fiona, interview 1:*** *I always did what I was told. He always told me that I would never do any better than him and for 20-something years you have that drummed into you, you believe it. I was called fat, ugly, dumb, slut for numerous years, so you believe it. . . . I was always told to cover up. "Fat people should never be seen." . . . Wear jeans, long sleeve shirts. . . . "Cover yourself up." "You don't go to the beach. People don't want to see a fat whale on the beach. They'll call the [animal charity]."*

Fiona found out about the study from a support worker when she was at the courthouse getting a protection order. She contacted me, and we arranged to meet at a local service. She brought a stack of papers with her that summarized her experience.

Fiona was married to Tony for 25 years, and they had separated a year ago. She is taking medication for depression, which she says is a result of the relationship. Fiona met Tony when she was in her early teens and a high school student. He was several years older and her first boyfriend. She became pregnant by Tony while she was still at school, resulting in her estrangement from her father. At the beginning of the relationship, Tony pulled her hair and hit her, sometimes hard in the stomach or across the face, causing her nose to bleed. She points to her crooked nose and some crooked fingers from past injuries. She says Tony was "extremely jealous." In the early days, Fiona fought back, but this made the violence worse. Tony insulted her constantly, but she put up with it because she didn't want him to retaliate physically. In the end, she believed the insults. She tells me, "The verbal abuse [was worst] . . . it was control. Control. That's all he wants. It still is control."

A few years into the relationship, by then with two children, Fiona and Tony moved to a property on the edge of town and Tony gave up work. Until that point, he had held a variety of unskilled jobs. Fiona's workplace supported her to get a diploma, and she worked full-time throughout the relationship, paying all the household expenses. She says: "Everything was my responsibility. Nothing was his. He never washed, he never cooked, he never cleaned, he never took the kids to sporting events, nothing."

Tony was often in trouble for minor criminal offenses and used cannabis. Toward the end of the relationship he started using "ice" (methamphetamine), then dealing it and "moving" people's stolen goods. Fiona didn't think the drug use changed the way he behaved toward her. He had always gotten angry, smashed furniture, and punched holes in the walls. Once she found a hidden recording device in the car that he used to record her trips to work.[3] Tony sometimes threw food she had cooked out the window or fed it to the dog, or threw dirt from pot plants on the floor and demanded that she clean it up. He often took her car keys so she could not leave the property. He routinely told her he could make her death look like an accident and laughed about how her body could end up in a barrel. When he came to bed, he regularly told her to "put out or get out," so she spent a lot of nights sleeping on a lounge chair. When friends came over, he called her names in front of them, so she stopped inviting them. She says no one knew about the abuse because she was ashamed: "You don't want everyone to know that you've put up with someone since you were [young] who hit you." Sometimes she called the police but then would not follow through with complaints as Tony threatened to kill himself if she left. One day, when both the kids were in their late teens, Tony locked her out of the house, and she went and slept at a neighbor's house. Fiona tells me that her neighbor's son said to her

> "You need to do something. You need to sort your shit out." . . . The next morning, I packed my stuff and went home to my parents, went home to my dad. . . . I'd always been planning when the kids were old enough, I would go. I knew that.

Fiona obtained a protection order a few months before our first interview, but Tony has continued to follow her around town. He turns up at the supermarket when she is shopping, and she has seen his car parked near her work. She has reported seven breaches of the protection order to the police, and Tony has been charged with stalking her. She tries to vary her routines, taking different routes to work and avoiding shopping. She believes Tony broke into her current rental house and stole things, including her dog, and that he tampered with her car. She reported these incidents to the police, but they say it is difficult to prove Tony did them.

When Fiona appeared before a family court judge in relation to her property settlement, she was convinced the judge was on her ex-husband's side. Fiona blamed this in part on her not being the right kind of victim "because I didn't walk in all meek and mild and cry. No. He wasn't going to do that to me. . . . You don't fit it—too bad. . . . Just [the judge's] whole demeanor." The judge ordered Fiona and her ex-husband to vacate the property while the matter was being settled. In the interim, Tony and Fiona were allowed to collect personal items. Fiona says Tony returned to the home and, with one of their sons, stole everything, including all the fittings and appliances, even the toilet and shower. She said sarcastically that the judge: "allowed him back into the house because men are victims and a lot of women make this stuff up."

Despite the ongoing abuse, Fiona agrees she is starting her life again: "Like a butterfly, you've been in a cocoon and now you're coming out and you've got wings." She says, "A lot of times it is good but then you still have this stuff playing in your head. . . . You still have to go to court, you've still got to see him, you've still got to write affidavits, summonses, statements, police officers every weekend." The extra stress of legal costs has strained Fiona's financial circumstances. Fiona says the law needs to change, although she is not sure how.

> ***Fiona, interview 2:*** *If [the emotional abuse] doesn't kill you it makes you stronger, but geez I get sick of that. . . . I'd like to [stop seeing a psychologist] but when you've copped abuse since you were [young] it's ingrained in you. That's my self-esteem. . . . That's the bit that sucks.*

Eleven months after our first interview, Fiona and I meet again at the support service. Fiona's property arrangements have been settled in the family court. She feels that she got less than her fair share of the property, but she could not afford to continue with legal proceedings.

Tony pleaded guilty to the stalking charge. As part of the sentence, the court ordered that he be restrained from contacting Fiona for

5 years. Tony was also charged and, at the last minute, pleaded guilty to five breaches of the protection order. Fiona says he was "slapped on the wrist and fined." She still has a protection order in place, but that hasn't stopped Tony from following her. Fiona says she recently saw Tony on her street and had a "meltdown" and could not stop shaking. Her car has been repaired, and this cost a significant sum; it appeared that the brakes had been tampered with. Naturally, she suspects Tony but can't prove it.

A few months ago, Fiona decided to start dating and joined a dating website. On a couple of occasions she was deceived by Tony's fake dating profiles, which was humiliating. She steeled herself and tried a different dating site, meeting her current partner. He is a security guard, and she says he is very protective of her.

Fiona tells me she is getting by: She has gotten a new phone and a new security system for her house and has disconnected from social media because Tony was harassing her via friends on Facebook. She regularly has nightmares and has been diagnosed with post-traumatic stress disorder (PTSD) as well as depression and is seeing a psychologist. She says she is coming to terms with her abuse: "I had to make the admission to myself that I was raped." She asks rhetorically, "When you have sex against your will, and you don't want it—well technically that's rape, isn't it?" Fiona doesn't go out much and doesn't see many people, she is "living day by day."

> ***Fiona, interview 3:*** *I still watch out for his vehicle. . . . Even when we went down the coast, I'm still looking for the vehicle. . . . It's just, you've still got to be wary. I mean this could go on for the next 20 to 30 years. Who knows what's going to happen after the criminal restraining order [ends]? Is he going to start again?*

It is 7 months since Fiona and I met at our second interview, and she hasn't seen Tony since then. She thinks that while the civil protection order was "just a piece of paper" for Tony, the 5-year restraining order made as part of the sentence for stalking has kept him away.

When I ask her about the legal response and how the legal system might have responded differently, she reflects that the legal system is "a mess, it's a joke." She explains:

> You have to actually wait until—you can have all the evidence, I mean I was lucky I was able to chronologically make mine make sense. Even though it was pages and pages long. If someone doesn't have the ability to do that, they haven't got a chance in hell. If you don't keep notes right from way back and tell every incident that's happened you don't have a hope . . . of getting a [civil protection order] on that person, or even getting them off your property . . . he actually breaks in and steals something . . . because it's a marital home and he has the right to do that.

She feels she should have left many years earlier but explains: "I waited until the kids left home. . . . Or he would've taken them. I should have left when I was a teenager, I should've left when it first happened."

Fiona continues to see a psychiatrist for PTSD, but her nightmares are now more sporadic. She still watches out for Tony's car and has recently moved into a new place with her security guard partner. They are having security screens fitted and cameras installed. She explains this is "so I can be safe in my house. It's still [Tony]."

MOTHERING AND DOMESTIC WORK

Fiona's comments in the third interview reflected how the mothering role became part of her entrapment in the abusive relationship (Kelly, Sharp, & Klein, 2014, pp. 88–91; Radford & Hester, 2006). Highlighting the gendered aspect of IPV, Stark (2007, p. 211; 2012a, p. 21) identifies that strategies underpinning coercive control are often linked to women's roles as homemakers and caretakers. Many study participants identified their partner's focus on domestic work and mothering as part of their abuse. For example, Bisera (CALD) described herself as a "slave"; she was required to iron all 40 of her partner's shirts each day, even though he would wear only 1. At one point, Bisera was hit by a car and hurt her leg. Her abusive partner refused to let her visit the doctor for some weeks, and she "had to crawl to the kitchen to eat and do my chores crawling. He laughed at me." Radha (CALD) said she was treated like a maid and had to "cook, wash, and clean every day just so." Roseanna (Aboriginal and Torres Strait Islander [ATSI]) said, "The house had to be spotless, I mean spotless, . . . [or] I'd get bashed up. . . . That's how he had me.' Jarrah (ATSI) said: "If I didn't have his dinner cooked by the time he got home, I was in shit."

Similar to what has been found in other studies (Heward-Belle, 2017; Humphreys, Thiara, Sharp, & Jones, 2015; Radford & Hester, 2001), many abusers exploited and threatened the woman's role as a mother to further abuse and entrap her. It was common for a woman to report that her abusive partner had threatened that if she left, he would take the children. Milly said that her partner often tried to abuse her through the children. He would say "how selfish I am, how pathetic I am, how [I'm] not being child-focused, how I'm ruining [the child's] life, how I'm just thinking about myself and not what [the child] wants."

Felicity's partner, Jason, used the children to dissuade Felicity from leaving: he would say, "You've just ruined your children, Felicity." Sometimes he exploited Felicity's strong Christian faith in criticizing the way she cared for the children, saying "things like the only person you don't disappoint is the devil, Felicity." Jason often said these things in front of their children, who tried to defend Felicity. Many of the women said they attempted to circumvent any tension or abuse because of the stress and pressure it placed on children, who often intervened if they saw or heard abuse. Jane explained that after a round of verbal abuse her children would "come up to me afterward and say, 'are you OK, Mummy?' It happened many times a day."

ISOLATION

Most of the study women (*n* = 49, 75%) indicated that isolation was a key part of the pattern of abuse they experienced. Isolation contributed to their sense of entrapment, underlining their vulnerability, undermining their confidence and independence, and challenging their sense of identity. Women described their partner isolating them socially from their family, friends, and communities. Stark observes that by "inserting themselves between victims and the world outside, controllers become their primary source of information, interpretation and validation" (2012a, p. 27). Some of the women experienced "bans" on seeing friends by themselves. For example, Lyn was never allowed to be with her friends alone. Some women were punished if they saw friends or family members. Julia's social life revolved around competitive sports, but this made her partner jealous, so she stopped going. She told me, "I really didn't have anything that I did for myself or wanted to do for myself." Milly stopped seeing her friends and family because "he'd throw tantrums the day before, the morning of, a couple of hours before. He'd start fights, so I'd end up being a mess and have to cancel. Or have to say . . . some stuff's come up."

Jane recalled that if she went shopping with a girlfriend, her partner would call her several times over the course of each hour. She described how she would get "the fear flood" seeing his number register and knowing he would be angry that she was meeting friends. Francis found that whenever she went out with friends, she "paid for it for a long, long time after that," so she eventually stopped going out with them. Evie recognized that her partner

> was trying to get rid of all my family members one by one. I was at home by myself. I had no job. I had no friends. He kept saying to me that they're trying to run my life and ruin me and interfere with the children so I hadn't spoken to them. . . . Looking back on it now, he was picking them off one by one so virtually I had no one but Simon. . . . I was blind, I stuck up for him. I lost friends and family over him.

Many of the women reported that their partner didn't get along with their family members or their friends and was constantly rude to them. Celina said: "He virtually ruined almost every connection in my life, and he made me all alone." Some abusive partners required women to choose between staying in the relationship or maintaining contact with family and friends. Felicity's partner told her she had some "tough choices" to make, that she either wanted to be with him or spend time with her sister and parents. Felicity said she would choose him each time because she didn't want an argument and was a "peacemaker." Skye found that she lost contact with all of her friends and became friends with all his friends "because for me to be close to him I had to be close to his friends. It was just really hard.... It was just like I don't have anyone to talk to and I just felt so alone."

Sometimes women felt they contributed to their own isolation. If they burdened their friends with their experiences but refused to respond to friends' advice to leave or take other kinds of actions to resist or stop the abuse, maintaining contact often became uncomfortable. Sandra explained: "I could see my networks dwindling out because I wasn't hearing from people as much . . . every time we spoke . . . people were going will you just get out . . . I wouldn't listen . . . I had him threatening to shoot my horse . . . kill my parents . . . but I said I am not safe if I leave."

Some women became more geographically isolated as the relationship progressed. Milly said her abuse was "life-wise, it was a lot of controlling, it was verbal and psychological, he wouldn't let me move back to [hometown] to my family, so he isolated me completely." Vera (CALD) lived with her Australian-born partner, Nigel, for 19 years. She explained that once the children were born, Nigel decided that they should all live on a property out of town. Nigel traded in their car with an automatic transmission for a manual one that she was not able to drive. This meant that she could not leave the property to go into town unless he drove: "Everything [was] controlled." Vera often found herself trapped on the isolated property, alone with small children. Sometimes abusive partners insisted on regular moving. Shelley's partner, for example, moved the family often. She said: "He cut me off from people—I realize now. So that would keep me under his thumb."

Sometimes women were imprisoned in their home and described being locked in rooms and houses. Jarrah (ATSI) explained that she was not allowed outside of the house alone, even to "peg the washing out. . . . I couldn't leave his sight." Similarly, Sara (CALD) said: "He never give me the keys. He always keep the keys with him and lock us in the house." For migrant women settling in Australia, isolation was often intense, and it was a particularly effective method of control. It was sometimes enforced through their partner's prohibition on their speaking to friends and family in their first language (e.g., Bisera, Rosa). Doya (CALD) had originally moved to Australia on a tourist visa, but the visa had lapsed some time ago. Despite her ex-partner's promises to marry her or assist her in renewing her visa, Doya was ultimately living illegally in Australia. She had children with her abuser, and he kept her and the children locked in the house with no external communication. Fearful of deportation and of being separated from her Australian-born children, Doya endured significant physical, emotional, and financial abuse for months before she was so badly beaten she feared she would die. She finally escaped from the house, leaving her children behind. Notably, despite these experiences of violence and imprisonment, Doya said, "Putting me down in front of the kids was the worst."

Leah (CALD) arrived in Australia on a sponsored visa. Both she and her partner Ethan were tertiary-educated in their home country, and their marriage was arranged by family overseas. After arriving in Australia, they soon had young children together. Leah described being badly beaten, sexually abused, and placed under surveillance by Ethan, but she had no one to confide in. Although Leah described emotional abuse as the worst aspect of the abuse, she also found her partner's isolating tactics very hard to bear. She said, "I was very lonely. I didn't know anyone here. . . . It was like a strange land. . . . I was just locked in that house. He would tell me in the morning, when he was going to work, 'just lock yourself in and don't come out.' . . . I was caged." Sometimes Ethan went overseas for weeks at a time, leaving her at home with limited food and without money, a prisoner in the house. It was only after developing a secret alliance with a neighbor that Leah was able to escape with her children.

FINANCIAL ABUSE

Financial abuse contributes to women's isolation and may include controlling access to, or information about, finances and bank accounts, and behaviors that exclude the victim from decisions that affect her (Kelly et al., 2014, pp. 50–51). Sometimes a perpetrator exploits the victim's finances or coerces her to take on debt. Examples include perpetrators taking out credit cards in the victim's name without the victim's knowledge; coercing the victim to sign a contract for the provision of finance, a loan, or credit; or coercing the victim to sign assets over to the perpetrator or to enable access to a line of credit (e.g., associated with a mortgage) (Littwin, 2012). In some cases, victims report that their opportunity to work is sabotaged by their partner who variously refuses to let her attend work, harasses her at work, or causes her to be fired or let go (Anitha, 2019; Fawole, 2008). Financial abuse can have particularly harsh effects on women on sponsored visas who may have no independent access to income and may be totally reliant on their partner to support them (Sanders, 2007). All of these types of financial abuse were reported by the women in the study, and most experienced financial abuse as another significant part of the pattern of abuse during the relationship (n = 42; 65%), but in some cases its effects continued after separation. Notably, by the time of interview 3, many women were still paying off significant legal debt that had resulted from their ex-partner's misuse of, or protracted use of, legal engagement. This can be understood as an aspect of financial abuse (see Chapter 7) and often had long-term implications for family law property settlements (see Chapter 8).

A common story from some of the study women was that at some time during the relationship they had opened up a joint account with their partner. Any family social security money and any money earned by the woman would go into this account. Meanwhile, her partner's income went into a different account that she had no access to. Lisa said that the only money she had access to was the government family allowance, and this was all she had to spend on groceries for the family. Julia said that sometimes when the money came into the account, her partner would withdraw it all before she had a chance to pay the bills. In explaining that she often relied on her mother to buy medications and diapers, she said, "Mum would help us with any grocery stuff, and my bills just wouldn't get paid until things calmed down." Roseanna (ATSI) said her pay would go into the joint account, but her partner would take control of her spending. She said, "He used to control me for my clothes, my money, everything."

Some of the women reported that their partner stole their bank cards or used them without their consent. For example, Janet was pressured to give her partner the personal identifying number of her bank card. He sometimes took money out of her account to pay for gambling. Janet also said she had to leave work a number of times to "rescue" him from bars and clubs, and she felt she lost jobs and pay raises as a result. These experiences contributed to her financial insecurity.

While some women reported pressure and ultimatums to stop work or work in particular jobs, others were required to work or to return to work shortly after childbirth. Hilary's husband, Bruce, told her that if she didn't go back to work shortly after having a baby, Bruce would stop working. She said, "There was a lot of pressure to return to work . . . we didn't have a big mortgage . . . but he was never satisfied with part-time." After Bruce set up a small business, he opened up his own separate bank account while Hilary's wages continued to go into a joint account toward the family expenses. She found it was not enough, and she had to ask for grocery money and was only sometimes provided with it.

Some women, like Mira (CALD) and Jane, were routinely called to account for their spending, often being required to produce receipts. Others would have their wallets checked by their partner regularly. Some women on sponsored visas relied completely on their sponsoring partners for financial support and thus were particularly susceptible to financial abuse (Segrave, 2017). Celina (CALD) explained that her sponsoring partner was suspicious of her spending:

> When I asked him he would give just 10 bucks, 15 bucks, 20 not more than 20 [USD13]. He would count the money left in the purse sometimes. He would question me, OK, what did you do with the money I gave you last week? I gave you this much money. Did you spend all? Did you spend all of that on public transport?

Luciana (CALD) transitioned from a tourist visa to a student visa to a sponsored visa after arriving in Australia. She said that in her home country, "I had my own money, my own life, and if I stay with him I don't." In Australia, she relied on her partner, Mario, also from her home country but a longtime permanent resident in Australia, for money but often ran out for basic things. Luciana told me in interview 1:

> He'd give me some money for the telephone but only just $10, $20 [USD13]. . . . Sometimes he needed to give me money for the bus card. But two or three times I didn't have money. One time the bus driver had to give me a free trip.

At her first interview Luciana said she had left Mario 6 months previously after living with him for nearly 2 years. She said that during their relationship Mario insulted her, calling her stupid, lazy, and dishonest; complained she did insufficient housework; and threatened to have her deported. He also frightened her, kicking doors and walls and yelling often. Eventually Mario physically pushed her out of the house. A friend pointed Luciana to a local specialist service that helped her to connect with a counselor, apply for permanent residency through the IPV exception, and find shelter accommodations.[4] She stayed for 3 months in the shelter before moving in with friends and finding work. When we met for the second interview, Luciana had moved back in with Mario after long discussions with him about how their relationship could work. She was still living with him at the time of the third interview and reflected that her permanent resident status and her financial independence had made it possible to have greater respect from Mario and to negotiate within the relationship: "Now we can talk about the problems just as it happens. Yes, we can talk about the problems."

Dara (CALD) arrived in Australia on a sponsored visa; like Luciana, her partner was also from her home country, but he was already a permanent resident in Australia. Dara had a master's degree in her home country and found work in a fast-food store in Australia, but this was insufficient to pay for all the household expenses. Her partner refused to contribute, and she found she was often hungry and had to go without food. Dara also talked about physical violence and emotional abuse within the relationship. The teacher at her English class noticed she looked unhappy and asked her what was wrong. The teacher referred Dara to a specialist support service that helped her leave, find accommodations, and connect with a community lawyer to apply for a protection order. When we met at the first interview, Dara had been separated from her partner for 9 months. At the second interview Dara said her experience through the court process was positive; referencing her home country, she said, "Here I feel that I am a human being . . . some laws is here who can save me, who can respect me." She said she was living independently, but she was concerned that her ex-partner was sometimes stalking her. By the time of the third interview, Dara had a job and lived in a rented room. She still had a protection order and had recently talked to the police about her ex-partner following her home from work, but she didn't think anything had come of it. For Dara the assistance of the specialist support agency was pivotal. She reflected on her change over the course of the interviews: "I was scared with the world. It is not fake that I am now happy and I'm safe. I can fight." It is notable that neither Valeria nor Dara had children with their partners, and their engagements with legal processes were less complex than those generally experienced by CALD women with children.

Research has identified a lack of financial independence as one of the central reasons that victims stay trapped in abusive relationships (Kim & Gray, 2008). Financial dependence was cited by Melissa (ATSI) as one of the reasons she stayed with her abusive partner for so long. She was with her partner for 20 years and had several children with him. For most of the years of their relationship he was a high-income earner, and so, despite significant physical abuse and control, Melissa remained with him. She said, "I felt financially stable with him." She also felt, for a long time, that the abuse was the price she paid for that stability.

For some women, the level of financial manipulation and concealment of money only became clear at separation or shortly after. When Jarrah (ATSI) left her relationship, she discovered she was in significant debt:

> He got me into a car finance. Now I owe $2,500 [USD1,700] through the car finance. He took the car. I reported it to the police as stolen. . . . I've got the paperwork already saying that I'm full ownership of that car. . . . I knew I was signing up for a car, but I didn't realize that I was getting myself into debt. I didn't want to go for a car loan, (Jarrah, interview 1)

At the third interview, Jarrah said she was still paying off the debt.

Carol was subjected to serious physical abuse, including nonfatal strangulation and other assaults, during her relationship. While her partner was financially controlling during the relationship, once she separated from him, she found herself in serious debt. She explained that when she and her husband took out a mortgage to buy a house, they also established a line of credit up to $180,000 (USD123,000) with the bank. After she separated from her husband, she discovered a joint bank account had been emptied and that he had taken out the entire line of the credit, and she now shared a debt of $180,000 with him. The bank was not willing to waive her share of the debt, and she was still trying to settle this matter 5 years after separation. Carol said simply: "So that was his control."

Martha had shared the costs of house contents and other insurance policies and shared joint accounts with her partner. At separation, she discovered that the insurance policies were all in his name and that a joint account was empty. Martha believed that after they separated, her ex-partner made a concerted effort to waste their joint finances. She reported that soon after they separated, he went to a beach resort and spent thousands of dollars on accommodations. He also transferred $40,000 (USD27,000) out of their accounts, telling Martha the funds were used for living expenses for a 1-month period. Another woman, Jane, discovered only after separation that over the course of their nearly 30-year marriage her partner had made a number of overseas investments that were purchased only in his name. She found out that these investments had to be excluded from the property settlement because they were too difficult and expensive to trace.

MIGRANT WOMEN AND VISA THREAT

The particular vulnerability of migrant women in relation to IPV is well recognized (Anitha, Roy, & Yalamarty, 2016; Ghafournia, 2011; Segrave, 2018). In relationships involving overseas-born women and Australian-born men, or men who have been living in Australia for some time, there is often a significant knowledge differential, and this may be exploited to exert control. While migrant women experience similar forms of abuse, these experiences may be intensified because of certain circumstances, including heightened social isolation in a new country, lack of knowledge of English, financial dependence, and limited information about their legal rights (Ghafournia, 2011; Mitra-Kahn, Newbigin. & Hardefeldt, 2016). As earlier sections of this chapter have shown, these circumstances can be exploited by abusers. Women who rely on their partner's continued sponsorship to remain in the country may be particularly at risk of coercion and control (Segrave, 2017). Threats of deportation or ending sponsorship have been recognized as a tactic of coercive control that is specifically targeted at migrant women with insecure visa status (Pittaway, Muli, & Shteir, 2009; Vaughan et al., 2015). Twelve of the 24 migrant women involved in the study were on sponsored visas at the time of the first interview, and all reported threats to their visa status being used as a tactic of control.

Women on sponsored visas were commonly threatened with withdrawal of their partner's sponsorship if they did not conform to his demands. Celina's partner, David, had sponsored both Celina and her mother to live in Australia. David constantly threatened to send her mother back "home," saying, "I can do that anytime I want." Luciana's partner also used her visa status to underline his power: "Once or twice he said to me about the visa. Like you will stay here for me . . . like I can do something and you can go." Sometimes visa threats were used to stop women from calling the police (e.g., Tabora, Trisha). Demands for sex made alongside visa threats were common. Tabora was threatened with deportation if she refused to comply with such demands:

> He would oblige me to always have sex with him as if nothing was going on . . . he would be threatening me with visa issues all the time, that he was going to cancel it, that he was going to warn the court on me, that he was not my sponsor anymore. . . . Then I was with the fear and then . . . because of the threats and I would accept having sex with him or not have a visa because he was saying he was going to cancel.

Valeria's comment sums up the insecurity and vulnerability experienced by many women on sponsored visas:

> He was threatening me like, I'm going to send you back to [birth country], I'm the Aussie here. So, things like that, it's like make me feel—make you feel like nothing. . . . No one is here. I have no one. . . . Your rights when you are permanent visa provisional, you've got one foot here in Australia, another one in your country.

ROSA'S EXPERIENCE

Rosa (CALD) experienced a pattern of abuse that included tactics such as visa threats, financial abuse, her partner attacking her role as a mother, and some physical abuse. Despite her isolation and visa insecurity, Rosa identified the emotional abuse as the worst aspect of the abuse. Rosa's vulnerability and desperation increased over the period of the three interviews. She had separated from her partner by the time of interview 3 but had no visa security and feared being deported and separated from her child, who had her ex-partner's American citizenship status. By interview 3, Rosa was trying to find a new visa sponsor on the internet in an effort to stay with her child in Australia.

> ***Rosa, interview 1:*** *I have to learn English, not use the [European language]. It was difficult because here, he doesn't like it if I talk in [my language]. He told me I am stupid . . . . He told me I don't want*

you . . . when he fights me and I say I'm going to police, he tell me, "Go to police, run to police, [our child] is an American citizen"

I meet Rosa at the support service she is connected with. Rosa tells me she was living in Europe when she met Ken, an American citizen, on an internet dating website. They married in the European town where Rosa grew up, and she became pregnant. Together they moved to Asia for Ken's work, where their baby was born. Several months after the baby's birth, they moved to Australia. Ken arrived in Australia on a temporary work visa, sponsoring Rosa and their child; thus, Rosa's visa status was dependent on Ken's. Both Rosa and Ken have university degrees, but Rosa hasn't been able to work in Australia.

Rosa says that even before they came to Australia, Ken would sometimes become "upset." He verbally abused her and once smashed a computer in front of her. When the family arrived in Australia, the emotional abuse intensified. Rosa knew no one and felt isolated. She describes angry rages in which Ken would slap himself in the face or smash his own head into a cupboard. These rages scared her. Her struggles with English made Ken angry.

The baby was only 6 months old and still breast fed when Ken and Rosa separated. Rosa advised the immigration department of the separation and the IPV she had experienced and was granted a visa extension.[5] A few weeks after they separated, Ken visited the apartment where Rosa was staying, saying he missed the baby. Rosa handed Ken the baby, and minutes later she realized that Ken had left the apartment with the child. Rosa called Ken on his cell phone. Ken told her he wanted a divorce, he had paid a year's rent on the apartment, and he was taking the baby. Rosa called the police, who attended and told her the child would be OK and could have a bottle. Rosa was distressed, and rang the police a second and third time, and throughout the following day and night, pleading with them to find the child. She also tried to find Ken without success.

Eventually, 3 days later, a police officer advised Rosa to go to the family court and seek an order authorizing that the child be placed on the airport watch list so that he could not be removed from Australia.[6] A lawyer assisted Rosa and discovered that the child has US citizenship, something that was news to Rosa. The lawyer found that Ken had already filed an application for divorce and for the child to live with him, claiming Rosa was abusing the child. The child protection authority ordered that the child should stay with Ken while they investigated.

Rosa saw the child for the first time 1.5 months after Ken had taken him from her care. Ultimately the family court found that Ken's allegations about child abuse were unsubstantiated and ordered that the child should live with Rosa and for Ken to have contact with him on weekends. Rosa is entirely financially dependent on Ken as she is unable to receive social security benefits and cannot find appropriate work given her limited English and her childcare responsibilities. Rosa has to text Ken weekly to ask for money to cover her living expenses. She says Ken constantly manipulates her, saying that "he'll just cancel my visa, and then he'll take the child."

> ***Rosa, interview 2***: *We're dependent people here, of him. We can't apply to [become] permanent residents. Just he have to be apply. If he no want, we don't get nothing. We just dependents.*

For the second interview with Rosa, 8 months after our first interview, we meet in a children's playground, where Rosa's son plays in the sand while we talk. Ken still has a work visa, so for now Rosa can stay in Australia as his dependent. Despite being separated from him, she is still completely reliant on Ken to pay her rent and provide money for food. Ken often pays the rent late and sometimes gives her very little money for food. The weekend handovers of the child are very stressful, and Ken abuses Rosa each time, sometimes physically pushing her. She tried to get a protection order, but Ken had a lawyer while she represented herself, and her application was not successful. Rosa says Ken is using the family court orders to "manipulate" her, and he routinely comes late to pick up their child or is late to return him. She says she is very worried about her visa situation: "If I have to go and I cannot take [my son] from Australia, yes, I'm afraid."

> ***Rosa, interview 3****: We have no support. We applied to [the social security office] to get support because we're dependent . . . but nothing . . . I don't know what will happen. I want to live because I have a child.*

Eight months after our second interview, I meet Rosa in a car she has borrowed. I sit in the passenger seat and she is in the driver's seat, with her son in the back seat. Rosa is distressed and crying. Ken's work visa has run out, and Rosa has been told by the immigration authorities that she must leave Australia. She has been told she will be separated from her son. She is desperate to stay in Australia with her son. Two months before this interview, she met a man named Leo on Facebook, and he has been staying with her and the child sometimes. Leo has been paying Rosa's rent and has provided her with some money. Initially Leo said he would sponsor Rosa on a spousal visa so she and her son could stay in Australia. However, Rosa is worried that Leo no longer wants to do that because it would be expensive. Rosa says Leo has been pressuring her for sex; he has pushed her bedroom door open, and she has had to call the police a couple of times. Rosa is tearful and says that she has no support—any support she had from her ex-husband or the government is "finished." She says she feels like she is "pushed down."

CONCLUSION

Understanding women's entrapment in abusive relationships requires an appreciation of the complex dynamics of coercive control and the pivotal role of nonphysical forms of abuse within this dynamic (Ptacek, 1999, p. 10; Tolmie et al., 2018). When asked about the most difficult abusive behaviors they have dealt with, most of the study women highlighted nonphysical forms of abuse. In particular, women emphasized emotional abuse and its deep impact on their sense of self. This is similar to other studies that show emotional abuse is common within relationships of IPV and generally more difficult for victims to cope with than physical abuse (Follingstad et al., 1990; Bennett, Goodman, & Dutton, 2000, p. 1192; Stark, 2007, pp. 258–259). There is a significant literature highlighting the long-term damage that emotional abuse can have (A. L. Coker et al., 2002). However, studies have found that, despite its recognized harm, many people still fail to acknowledge its effects (Capezza & Arriaga, 2008). Of potential relevance in the legal context is research that has indicated that victims of IPV who have experienced emotional abuse may have increased worry about contact with the abuser after the relationship has ended (Estefan et al., 2016, p. 1410). This specific effect of emotional abuse may have particular relevance in the legal context in determining appropriate protection order conditions and child contact arrangements.

Other routinized forms of nonphysical abuse highlighted by the study women included tactics focused on domestic work and mothering, isolation, financial abuse, and, for migrant women, visa threats. It is important to recognize, and re-emphasize, how these tactics contribute to women's entrapment in abusive relationships (Kelly et al., 2014, p. 7). Such recognition helps to address the question often posed by legal actors: Why didn't she leave (Hanna, 2009, p. 1471)? While physical violence and threats of such violence were also common for the participants, for many of them they were not a routine occurrence, and for some they had only occurred a few times and/or very early in the relationship. Such incidents did contribute to women's entrapment in the relationship; however, older claims of violence are likely to be invisible or "irrelevant" to law (Smart, 1989, p. 21). Despite the study women's focus on the role of nonphysical forms of abuse in their entrapment, as Chapters 6 through 8 show, legal system actors continue to privilege physical violence and in so doing often fail to support women to reach safe legal outcomes (Robinson, Myhill, &Wire, 2018; Wiener, 2017, p. 512).

NOTES

1. Cassie, an Aboriginal woman with an Aboriginal partner said "fighting" was the worst; for more of her story, see Chapter 5. Some scholars have argued that IPV may be experienced differently between Aboriginal people (Nancarrow, 2019, p. 167). None of the four other ATSI women who answered this question had Aboriginal partners and answered variously that sexual abuse, economic abuse, emotional abuse, or abuse of the children was the most difficult aspect of abuse they dealt with.
2. An Australian citizen or permanent resident can apply to sponsor his or her partner, spouse, or prospective spouse to obtain a temporary or permanent visa to live in Australia (Borges Jelenic, 2020).
3. The study women's experiences of technology-facilitated abuse are considered in more detail in Douglas, Harris, & Dragiewicz, 2019.
4. Those women who have experienced IPV and separated from their sponsor before the 2-year period has expired may be able to ultimately transition to permanent resident status by virtue of what is known as the *IPV exception* (Gray, Easteal, & Bartels, 2014; Maher & Segrave, 2018).
5. Bridging visas allow a "noncitizen"—for example, a citizen whose visa has expired or been canceled—to stay in Australia until a substantive visa is granted or to give the person time to leave the country (Crock & Berg, 2011, pp. 495–496).
6. The family court can make an order (a watch list order) that prevents an adult from removing the child of a relationship from Australia without a court order or the consent of both parents (Harland, Cooper, Rathus, & Alexander, 2015, p. 296).

4

Using Law

INTRODUCTION

This chapter maps women's engagement with different aspects of law over time. In particular, it considers the different legal processes experienced by migrant women, particularly those with insecure migration status, and Aboriginal and Torres Strait Islander women. Mapping women's engagement indicates how long women are caught up in legal processes, especially when they are involved in child and property matters in the family law system. It demonstrates the complexity and variety of women's interactions with the law as a result of intimate partner violence (IPV) and, for some, their deepening enmeshment in legal processes over time. Building on literature that has identified that abusers sometimes use legal processes to extend their control over victims after separation (e.g., DeKeseredy, Dragiewicz, & Schwartz, 2017; Laing, 2017; Douglas, 2018), and focusing on the experiences of Sandra and Ingrid, this chapter considers how abusers' multiple applications, appeals, and other legal actions contribute to and amplify women's enmeshment with both their abusive partner and the legal system over time. For some women the courthouse provides the only opportunity for her abuser to see her after separation so his attention shifts to this arena as one of the only remaining spaces where he can continue to exert control. Some women referred to their abusive ex-partner's use of the legal system and processes as, variously, a

Women, Intimate Partner Violence, and the Law. Heather Douglas, Oxford University Press (2021). © Oxford University Press.
DOI: 10.1093/oso/9780190071783.003.0004

"fight," "battle," "hunt," "game," or "playground" underlying the tactics and maneuvering employed.

LEGAL ENGAGEMENT OVER TIME

As outlined in Chapter 2, Smart's (1989, p. 5) definition of law sets the broad parameters for how I have understood women's engagement with law in the study: "a plurality of principles, knowledges, and events . . . it claims a unity through common usage of the term 'law'" (p. 4; see also Silbey, 2005, p. 331). Law includes interactions with child protection workers, police, lawyers and judicial decision-makers. It encapsulates engagement with child protection services (CPS), civil protection orders, the family law system, criminal processes, and immigration law via the visa system. It also includes victim assistance, private contracts and leases, defamation, equity, and civil disputes with banks.

As I explore further in Chapters 5 through 9, separation rarely marked the end of women's contact with their abusive partners. For many women it signaled the beginning of a long, arduous, and complex journey through the legal system. At the first interview, most women (n = 57) reported that they had interacted with at least three aspects of the law over the preceding 12 months. Most commonly, women had contact with police (n = 54), had attended court at least once about protection orders (n = 55), said their protection orders had been breached (n = 33), or had attended court about family law custody and property matters at least once (n = 31).

Of the 59 women who were interviewed in the study for the second time, nearly all (n = 56) were still involved in some kind of legal process associated with their experience of IPV. By the third interview, of the 54 women interviewed, almost all (n = 47) were still involved in a legal process associated with their experience of IPV, and most (n = 31) were involved in more than three aspects of the legal process (Table 4.1).

At interview 3, some women (n = 15) reported they had been in contact with the police between the second and third interviews, and some reported they were still involved in ongoing matters about child protection (n = 7),

Table 4.1 WOMEN AND IPV-RELATED LEGAL ENGAGEMENT OVER TIME

Interview	**1** **Past 12 Months**	**2** **Between Interviews 1 and 2**	**3** **Between Interviews 2 and 3**
Number of women interviewed	65	59	54
Involved in at least one legal process associated with their experience of IPV	65	56	47
Involved in three or more legal processes associated with their experience of IPV	57	41	31
Had contact with police at least once	54	18	15
Had attended court about protection order application at least once	55	16	8
Reported at interview that protection order/undertaking breached at least once	33	20	14
Criminal matters (excluding breach of protection order)	25	15	12
Had contact with child protection service at least once	15	14	7
Had attended court about custody or property matter (family law) at least once	31	27	14
Visa issues*	12	5	2
Other legal matters	22	23	24

*See Table 4.2.

protection orders ($n = 8$), or family court matters ($n = 14$). For some women the relative stability they started to experience by the time of interview 3 gave them an opportunity to deal with outstanding legal issues, including applying for victim's compensation ($n = 7$) and making formal complaints about police ($n = 2$). At the third interview, 16 women also reported that they continued to struggle with debt associated with lawyer's fees. This "counting" shows that many women continued to be involved in a variety of legal processes throughout the study and suggests that over time their interactions decreased in number and variety, but it gives only a broad-brush indication of the time and energy women spent engaging with law. This counting fails to reflect just how many times some women contacted police or other justice actors or returned to court for specific matters between each interview. Like IPV itself (Walby, Towers, & Francis, 2016, p. 1204), the repetitive nature of women's legal engagements make them hard to measure. Some women had so much contact with police or went to court so many times it was difficult for them to keep count. Sometimes women could not be sure if they had reported a specific breach of a protection order to the police or if they had actually attended court for a particular matter or simply that their lawyer or a police officer had told them about it.

This counting also does not reflect all the time women spent on the more "invisible" work of engaging with law, including organizing witnesses or filling in forms for legal aid and protection order applications, and the time they spent drafting, checking, and completing court documents. It fails to account for all the time spent photocopying and writing notes and diary entries; logging recordings, emails, and texts; and generally keeping a record for potential use as evidence.

Alex was one of the few women who kept a careful count of her court appearances. Over the 6-month period immediately before our first interview Alex had been required, largely as a result of her ex-partner, Gordan's, applications, to attend courts on 31 occasions. These included Gordan's applications to vary conditions on protection orders, his various appeals of the protection order, Alex's attendance in court as a witness in charges of Gordan's breaching the protection order, his challenge to custody matters in the family courts, his civil applications about various debts Alex supposedly owed him, defamation, and so on. Alex had a no-contact protection order, and their son was protected under the order; as a result of his previous violence toward Alex, Gordan had no contact with their child. At the first interview, Alex said:

> His purpose is to keep me engaged by going to court . . . it's the only way he has access to me. He's using the law as a tool to abuse me and

> how do you get out of that, because you can't just not turn up—I'm not at the stage where I can't just not turn up, because we haven't had final orders yet.

At the time of interview 1, Alex, in her 40s, had moved in with her parents so that they could help her with childcare of her preschool-aged son. Ten months later, at interview 2, Alex reported that Gordan's abuse of legal processes continued. While the family court ordered that Gordan could have supervised contact with their child at a contact center, he refused to exercise it.[1] Alex only saw Gordan when she had to go to court, but this happened at least twice a month. In order to maintain her eligibility for legal aid, she had to limit her working hours. The legal processes activated by Gordan constrained how much she could work, where she could live, and her movements (Sharp-Jeffs, Kelly, & Klein, 2018; Stark, 2007). Alex said: "I live in—not a debilitating fear where I don't go out, but it's a conscious awareness. . . . It's a consciousness not to be fearful, but it's also a consciousness that I am fearful. So it's like the balance." By the time of interview 3, which took place 8 months after our second interview, Alex said things had improved; she was working again and living with her child independently of her parents. She had spent a lot less time in court over the past 8 months, but she expected more legal processes in the following months. She told me, "I'm frustrated that I still feel scared . . . and I have to turn up. I'm not at that point now where I can say, 'hasta la vista.'"

Some women experienced a significant break in their involvement with legal systems, only for their engagement to start again at the time of interview 2 or 3. For example, Bianca reported a period of quiet at interview 2, and her legal issues seemed largely resolved, but they restarted when she was reported to child protection authorities by her ex-partner in between interviews 2 and 3. Similarly, while Shelley believed she had finalized custody arrangements sometime before our first interview, new issues had emerged by the time we met, and she was starting her legal journey all over again. Bianca's and Shelley's experiences are discussed more fully in Chapter 5.

For Carol, her partner's use of the legal process in an attempt to control her seemed to continue indefinitely, long after separation and long after their children became adults. Carol had separated from her partner, Rod, 12 years before our first interview, and yet she was still involved in legal processes associated with his continued stalking, harassment, and threats. She had applied to renew her protection order every few years, Rod always resisted the renewal, adjourning hearings often. Once the order was made each time, Rod breached it regularly. Carol feared for her life. At interview 3, Carol said it was now 14 years since she had separated:

> [Rod] has contacted me . . . and other people on my behalf and death threats and all of that . . . we had death threats [2 months ago] . . . it was an email sent to me saying that he's finally going to [kill me]. . . . We went to the police about that. . . . But I honestly do believe—and I tell the police this—I honestly do believe that he will do this in the end. He will kill me in the end.

Carol was still married to Rod at the time of interview 3. She can't afford to divorce him because the house they co-own carries a significant mortgage, which resulted from Rod's use of a line of credit attached to the mortgage years earlier. Divorce required a property settlement. Carol dreaded the prospect of litigation about this and feared being forced into debt and made homeless if she tried for a property settlement.

In interviews, women generally focused on their interactions with child protection workers and the CPS and their experiences with judges about civil protection orders and family law property and custody. These issues are considered in Chapters 5 and 8, respectively. While women had a lot to say about their interactions with police in terms of police attitudes, a topic that is considered in Chapter 6, overall they were less focused on whether or not criminal offenses (other than breach of protection order offenses) had been charged in the context of their experience of IPV.

CRIMINAL LAW

Most women in the study felt they had very little information about the criminal charges their partners faced and how the charges progressed or were resolved or what punishment their partner received.[2] When they did have information, they were often dissatisfied with the final result (Douglas, 2012; Merry, 2003, pp. 352–353), as criminalization often had mixed consequences. Bianca, for example, was disappointed that a charge of deprivation of liberty was downgraded to a much less serious offense of assault via a plea negotiation process (Flynn & Freiberg, 2018, pp. 37–40), resulting in no recorded conviction and her ex-partner placed on a good behavior bond. As was common for women in this study, Bianca could not recall playing a role in the negotiation. Ingrid, whose experience is detailed later in this chapter, struggled to understand why her ex-partner was not charged with stalking (McMahon, McGorrery, & Burton, 2019). An exception to this general experience of lack of information was Fiona, whose experience is detailed in Chapter 3. She was advised by police that her ex-partner had been charged with stalking. He received a sentence that included a 5-year order that he not contact Fiona. The type of sentence he received may explain why she was provided with the information.

For Tabora (CALD), the consequences of her ex-partner being charged with assault were mixed. She received information about her ex-partner's plea hearing for assault and was initially pleased with the outcome. At interview 1 she reported her ex-partner was charged with assault, after breaking her nose. She attended court to hear him sentenced to 2 months in prison. Speaking through an interpreter, she said that this response had implications not just for her but for her community: "[He] is more angry now that he's been to jail but for me it helped. Also I used to hear quite a lot about men [in my community] hitting their women and now [they] are keeping pretty quiet because they understand. I think they know that in Australia the law means business, so they're getting quite worried about hitting their women." When I spoke to Tabora at interview 2, she talked about her fear that she and the children might be forced to return to their birth country. Because her ex-partner had been charged with a criminal offense, there was a danger his work visa would be terminated and he would be ordered to return to his home country (Bagaric, Alexander, & Bagaric, 2019, pp. 8–10). Tabora, on a dependent spouse visa, would have to return too. As she told me, "We have a fear that we have to go away because of the visa. . . . So this is very difficult for me."[3] She described how her young son wanted to buy a dog, and she told him: "We're going to move to another house and then we're going to buy a dog. But it depends on the government." I could not contact Tabora at the time of interview 3, and she may have been deported.

Monica and Cassie (ATSI), whose partners were in custody throughout the period of the interviews awaiting their ex-partners' trials, chose to attend the court to hear the progress of the criminal charges. While Cassie's partner was charged with violence and sex offenses against people other than Cassie and the offenses were not connected to IPV, the outcomes were important for Cassie because they would potentially impact on the child protection orders placed on her children. Cassie's experience is explored in Chapter 5. Both Monica and Cassie were usually informed of court dates by the detectives involved in their ex-partners' cases, but the procedures were not explained to them. I attended the court hearings involving Monica's ex-partner, who, by the time of interview 3, had been sentenced for the murder of someone close to her. Monica often asked me to explain things because there was no one else available. The progress of the murder case was Monica's focus throughout all three of the times we spoke.

Jennifer also attended court to hear how a charge of criminal damage against her ex-partner was concluded (this charge resulted from her ex-partner kicking in her garage door). She was frustrated with how the matter proceeded, ultimately being dropped. Jennifer felt the prosecutor was unprepared and the judge in the case didn't have "the slightest idea that it was domestic violence. . . . I think he just thought it was two people that had split up and were acrimonious." Melissa and Anna both had partners who had long criminal records, and throughout the interview period they said their partners had warrants out for their arrest.

While some women were charged with breaches of protection orders (e.g., see Shuang's story in Chapter 9) only four women (Chi [CALD], Shelley, Vera [CALD], and Janet) were charged with other types of IPV-related criminal matters, other than breach of protection orders. The charges were withdrawn by police for three of the women (Shelley, Vera, and Janet) before their respective prosecutions began.

At interview 1, Chi laid out her story. Chi pleaded guilty to receiving stolen goods after she accepted delivery of a package of illicit drugs on behalf of her abusive partner, Jason. In her sentencing hearing she was represented by a legal aid lawyer, the history of IPV was taken into account, and she received a good-behavior bond. Meanwhile, Jason was sent to prison for drug-related offenses. Chi explained through an interpreter, "After I met him I stay home all the time. I don't have much social network, I don't have any friends . . . I only listened to him." Chi said she knew Jason had a methamphetamine ("ice") problem and was in and out of prison for criminal offenses associated with his drug use. Whenever Jason came home from prison, he was violent. He pushed and punched her, causing significant bruising. When they had a child together, Jason encouraged her to become more involved in his ice supply business so that the baby could be properly looked after. Chi said, "He just kept saying that you're doing it for your baby . . . sometimes he was talking very softly asking me to do it, and then sometimes he's just very, very angry at me." In the end, fearing violence from Jason, and believing it was the best way to care for the baby, Chi agreed to help. She collected a parcel for him. The parcel contained ice, and Chi was arrested and convicted of an offense. Chi had been a permanent resident in Australia for some years, but when Jason was jailed, she decided to go and live with her family in her birth country. When Jason was released, he successfully applied for a return of the child under the terms of the Hague Convention, and Chi traveled back to Australia with their baby under police guard. On her arrival at the airport, Jason assaulted her, and she spent some months in a women's shelter before moving interstate with police support. When I met Chi, she said Jason was seeking child contact through the family court. By the time of interview 3, Jason was seeing their child at a contact center, but the family court matter was not finalized. Chi said it is "so hard and takes a very long time."

In contrast to the United States (Goodmark, 2012, pp. 107–113), in Australia there is no policy of mandatory arrest and charge in response to IPV, and police have the power to apply for a protection order on the woman's behalf. Often this is the preferred approach of police, followed by charges of breach of protection order if necessary. Breaches of protection orders, including breach of no-contact conditions, can result in severe sentences, including imprisonment (Australasian Institute of Judicial Administration [AIJA], 2020, [9.3.1]). In general, women in this study were able to relate limited information about charges of breach of protection orders and the sentences their abusers received. Despite reporting breaches of orders to police on numerous occasions, it was common for plea negotiations to involve "rolling up" multiple protection order breaches into one charge, resulting in a plea of guilty (Flynn & Freiberg, 2018, pp. 37–40) and a reduced sentence, often a monetary fine.[4] In other cases police were reported as being reluctant to charge where there were family law orders in place or where the alleged breaches were nonphysical (this is explored further in Chapter 6). Women generally did not attend court to hear about breach of protection order charges. Most often this was because they were not required as witnesses, probably because pleas of guilty were negotiated, and thus women usually were not advised by prosecution services about court dates. In many cases, despite reporting breaches of protection orders to police, women received no information about whether charges would go ahead. As a result, women were rarely able to comment on the approach of judges in criminal law matters.

Sandra's Experience

Sandra reported her experiences with police failures to prosecute breaches of protection orders. Sandra saw herself as part of a community of abused women who share expertise about their experience of IPV. She refers to this community through her use of the word *we* in her interviews. Sandra describes the "court system" as a "battle" and her engagement through the various legal systems as a "journey" on which she is becoming "smarter" and more "confident" over time. While Sandra sees neither winners nor losers through engaging with law, she sees her engagement as necessary both for her children's safety and to demonstrate that she won't be controlled by Gary anymore. As she said, she "won't back down."

> ***Sandra, interview 1:*** *There's no winners in the court system, but this man has a control issue. If he hasn't worked out that every single court that he's been to, he has not won a battle yet. He's got to give in somewhere.*

Sandra and Gary are both in their late 30s. They were in a relationship for about 6 years and have two children, both of whom are now school-aged. One of the children has a serious disability. Sandra finished high school and makes ends meet with a mixture of social security and money she earns from selling products online. At this time she lives with her children in rented accommodations. Gary receives a disability pension as a result of a chronic illness. She says Gary has sometimes used illicit drugs like amphetamines. Sandra and Gary separated nearly 4 years ago, but they have been involved with police, the courts, and CPS since they separated.

I got lost on my way to meet Sandra, so we had to sort out an alternative meeting place over the phone. She knew it was usually a quiet day at one of the courthouses she is familiar with and suggested we meet there. Sandra seems confident. She has a small suitcase on wheels that she trundles into the courthouse and a dog-eared diary with numerous colored sticky notes poking out of it. The suitcase is full of legal documents. Sandra has become an expert on IPV, she says: "The IPV cycle doesn't stop when you leave that and hence why some females prefer to stay in the situation. We know that when we get out it's going to be bad. . . . I moved away six times in 9 years. Each location that I went to, to start afresh . . . he would track me down."

Gary's violence toward Sandra began around 6 months into their relationship. He physically and emotionally abused her and "was forceful with sex." Sandra has kept a horse for many years, and Gary often threatened to shoot the horse or slit its throat; he also threatened to kill Sandra's parents. Sandra provided me with a copy of a newspaper report detailing Gary's conviction for assaulting her 7 years ago. He was fined. The newspaper report says that Gary kicked her, choked her, and threatened serious harm. Police and ambulance attended. Gary was removed to the watch-house and Sandra to the hospital. On another occasion Gary karate kicked Sandra in the leg while she was holding one of their children. CPS intervened and arranged for shelter accommodations for Sandra and the children. Sandra has not ever fully recovered from her leg injury; she needs surgery but can't afford it.

When she and the children "finally" left, Sandra obtained a temporary protection order against Gary stipulating only email contact between them. She also got a family court order requiring the children to live with Sandra and have contact with Gary every second weekend, with child handovers at a contact center. Six months before our first interview, Gary failed to return one of the children, keeping him for 28 days. Sandra called police, but they told her they had no power because of the family court order. Sandra was able to get a legal aid lawyer to represent her to get a child recovery order in the family court and the child was returned to her.[5]

Two months before this interview, Gary applied for a change in the family court orders to move child handovers to a public place, and Sandra has agreed to the change. The travel to the contact center was long and the cost high, and she hoped the new handover arrangements would help the children feel "more normal" moving between parents. Gary repeatedly adjourned the final protection order hearing and then he applied for a protection order against Sandra. Eventually, after several adjournments, Sandra and Gary consented to mutual protection orders.[6] She would like to have other people, like her father, listed as protected under the protection order, but, she asks rhetorically, "The thing is, do I really want to keep coming back to court?"

Sandra has legal support from a local community legal center and some legal aid, but sometimes she represents herself.[7] She identifies significant costs and effort in the legal process: "You need to . . . print stuff off the computer as well . . . try and read up on stuff, printing out all the phone logs." Sandra says, "It's a long process and I understand that it's—I understand that there's money involved, that judges need jobs and barristers. . . . That's what it feels like to me." Sandra says she has been supported "pretty well" by police, although recently police told her she should be leaving the community. She says:

> I've got big chains and padlocks on my front gates, a 6-foot-high fence. I have my surveillance cameras all in position . . . police [said]: "It's time to move out of this community." I said, "No, I'm not moving. You do something with him and I'm prepared to die in this house with two children to prove to you police that running away from him is empowering him. Get rid of him out of the community. The children and I are not—they're established."

> ***Sandra, interview 2:*** *I could have had a great house deposit by now, but the court system and . . . everything else. No one has benefited out of it . . . Gary hasn't even benefited out of it. So it's a silly, silly process that we go through. But we do what we have to for our children and for our safety. It's worth every single cent. But now I'm being a lot smarter and savvier. . . . So you have a little court account set a little bit there. Sometimes it's not about the court cost. It's the parking fees and it's the printing costs and all that sort of thing.*

Seven months after our first meeting, Sandra says there is another year to go on the mutual protection orders. Gary has breached the protection order many times. He has contacted her with denigrating emails and texts. Sandra feels like the police are looking after her; they have "downloaded the phone," taking a record of Gary's messages and calls, and told her they plan to charge him with three breach of protection order offenses. She feels that magistrates never have the whole backstory of the perpetrator, which they need to make the right decisions, and she thinks the police and magistrates need specialist training. She says: "You are on alert. You are on the lookout. Watching who might be in disguise for him, looking and watching your whereabouts and all that stuff." Gary is having contact with one of the children every second weekend but refuses to see the child who has a disability. Sandra is still receiving social security and a little bit of money from an online sales business. She is living in community housing and says she has a bag ready so she can "pick it up and run. I have places that are marked, that are reasonably priced all ready, for accommodation."

Sandra, telephone calls between interview 2 and 3:

Telephone call 1: *Sandra called to say the breaches of the protection order are "piling up" and the police aren't doing anything. The breaches relate to Gary attending the children's school or contacting her by text or phone. Sandra asked me to call the police on her behalf. I called the police and described my role as a researcher. I was surprised when the police officer openly discussed Sandra's case with me on the phone. The police officer told me, "There are two sides to every story" and "we can't go behind the family court order" and insisted that Sandra's breach claims were being investigated. The police officer told me she had suggested Sandra go back to the family court to change the family court order. When I relayed these messages to Sandra, she said, "It's a cop-out, it has happened many times before . . . it's time I go to the media. . . . I will be calling [CPS]."*

Telephone call 2: *Two weeks later Sandra called me again, distressed. Gary reported to her to the CPS and she was investigated, although CPS found the report unsubstantiated and closed the case. She has called support services, but they are too busy. She says the police sound "cranky" on the phone. I referred her to a support service.*

Telephone call 3: *Sandra called to report that Gary has applied to the family court for shared 50-50 care of the children. She has received a 200-plus-page affidavit from Gary, and they have to attend mediation. Legal aid has refused to assist her, so she is relying on a community legal service.*

> ***Telephone call 4:*** *Gary is now contesting his parenthood of her son with a disability. He made a further report to CPS, but the complaint was unsubstantiated. Sandra says CPS "have been great!"*
>
> ***Sandra, interview 3:*** *His purpose is to bully me; the courtroom is his playground.*

Gary's application for joint care of the children and DNA testing of one of them is still under consideration, and Sandra is waiting for the judgments. Gary has filed a "notice of risk with the family court claiming that Sandra is harming the children."[8] Until any new order is made, the family court order is very clear about the children's contact arrangements with their father. Despite this clarity, Sandra says that Gary keeps withholding the children from school and keeps them from returning home to Sandra. She has called the police regularly to intervene. Because Sandra is not eligible for legal aid, she is still relying on a community legal service to help her prepare for court. She feels they are not helping as much as in the past as she has gotten more "confident on her journey." The house she is living in is to be demolished, so her housing is insecure, and in the midst of this she is trying to set up a new business. She says:

> The more resilient I get on the journey, knowing that he's a power player and he's a control freak and all that sort of stuff. I know what the system is like and I don't see it as protecting victims as they should. I don't see it as that because there's been too many loopholes . . . I won't back down, I'll keep going to these courts . . . I know that 10 years—long time.
>
> ***Sandra, telephone call 2 weeks after interview 3:*** *Sandra called to tell me that the family court delivered its response to Gary's application. The order was unchanged, and the children to continue to live with Sandra and spend every second weekend with Gary. Gary was found to be the father of both the children after DNA testing. Gary has continued to contact Sandra in breach of the protection order, and she continues to report these incidents to police. She has obtained a new 2-year protection order and has state housing.*

WOMEN FROM CULTURALLY AND LINGUISTICALLY DIVERSE BACKGROUNDS

The group of women interviewed in the study who were from culturally and linguistically diverse (CALD) backgrounds held a variety of visas, and for many their visa status changed over the period of the interviews (see Appendix 3). Ten of the women in the study had a partner who was Australian-born. These women met their Australian partners in a variety of ways, through online dating websites (n = 4),[9] while their partner was overseas for work or travel (n = 4),[10] or while the women were in Australia as tourists or students (n = 7).[11] Some women came to Australia through an arranged marriage (n = 2) to marry a man from their birth country who was already an Australian permanent resident. Some came to Australia with their partner from their birth country, either as a spouse on his work visa (n = 2) or vice versa (n = 1). Three women came to Australia as refugees, with a partner they had met in their home country (n = 2) or with a partner they had met in a refugee camp (n = 1). One woman, Bisera, arrived in Australia on a visa sponsored by her daughter, but on her arrival her daughter refused to provide for her. Bisera then moved in with an Australian man, who offered her a place to stay in exchange for housework. He was abusive. The common link between all of the CALD women was that on arrival in Australia they had few close contacts beyond their partner, they all spoke English as a second or subsequent language, and they had limited or no independent financial resources. While there is extraordinary diversity in the experiences of CALD women, including those interviewed in this study, these common factors have been identified as contributing to the higher risk of IPV experienced by CALD women (Ghafournia, 2011; Maher & Segrave, 2018, p. 505). For women on insecure visas it is common for an abusive partner to use threats about her visa (including deportation) as part of a pattern of coercive control (Segrave, 2017; Vaughan et al., 2015). This issue was experienced by many of the CALD women in the study and is explored further in Chapter 3.

Individuals who are in Australia on a sponsored spouse visa must be financially supported by their spouse. Assuming they remain in the relationship with their spouse for 2 years, they can apply to transition to permanent resident status. Those women who have experienced IPV and separated from their sponsor before the 2-year period has expired may be able to successfully apply for permanent resident status by virtue of what is known as the *IPV exception* (Gray, Easteal, & Bartels, 2014; Maher & Segrave, 2018). This requires an application to the relevant department and evidence that the relationship was "real" and that there was IPV (Borges Jelenic, 2019). The need to provide evidence of a real relationship can sometimes be an obstacle, but assuming that can be shown, the requirement for evidence of IPV may be satisfied by the prosecution of the spouse with an IPV-related criminal offense, a court-ordered protection order, and/or a statement about the IPV from a service provider (Borges Jelenic, 2020; and see Appendix 2). At interview 1, three women whose most recent visa was a sponsored spouse visa already had permanent resident status as a result of the IPV exception, and eight others had obtained a bridging visa and were applying for permanent resident status on the basis of the exception under Australian migration law. By the second or third interviews, all of the eight women had been able to demonstrate both that they had a real relationship and that they had experienced IPV and had obtained permanent residency. All of the eight women who transitioned to permanent resident status over the course of the interviews were assisted by a specialist support service and had court-ordered protection orders at interview 1.

Two women, Rosa and Tabora, were sponsored by their overseas-born partner on his work visa. This meant they did not have access to the IPV exception. While both women had separated from their violent partners when I met them at interview 1, their visa status remained insecure, and both were facing deportation once their partner's work visas expired. Rosa's rising desperation about this is explored in her extended narrative in Chapter 3. Tabora, mentioned earlier in the chapter, was unable to be contacted at interview 3 and was possibly deported.

A number of studies have pointed to the reluctance of women on insecure visas to engage with formal systems (Ghafournia, 2011; InTouch, 2010, p. 28; Mitra-Kahn, Newbigin, & Hadefeldt, 2016; Vaughan et al.,

2015, p. 36). Most of the CALD women interviewed for this study were recruited from a specialist service that works with CALD women who have experienced IPV. This helps to explain their relatively high level of engagement with legal systems and legal actors.

Of the 24 CALD women interviewed, 16 (66%) had children with their abusive partner, and most of them (n = 13) engaged with the family law system about custody of the children. None of the CALD women interviewed had property matters being dealt with in the family court, and

Table 4.2 Culturally and Linguistically Diverse (CALD) Women and IPV-Related Legal Engagement Over Time

Interview	**1 Past 12 Months**	**2 Between Interviews 1 and 2**	**3 Between Interviews 2 and 3**
Number of CALD women interviewed	24	23	20
Continued visa uncertainty*#	12	5	2
Had contact with police at least once	17	13	3
Had attended court about protection order application at least once	20	18	8
Reported at interview that protection order/undertaking breached at least once	10	9	2
Criminal matters (excluding breach of protection order)	6	3	0
Had contact with child protection service at least once	3	4	0
Had attended court about custody or property matter (family law) at least once	11	12	9
Other legal matters	5	9	11

*At the time of interview.

#See also Appendix 3.

all but 2 of them relied on social security after separation, highlighting their financial insecurity (Ghafournia, 2011).

Some of the CALD women who had obtained permanent residency after a period of uncertainty could turn their minds to traveling to their birth country to visit extended family at interview 2 or 3. In some cases this provided a fresh opportunity for their ex-partner to reignite litigation in an attempt to obstruct the woman's application for the child's passport. Six of the CALD women reported that their partner contested their application for children's passports at either interview 2 or 3. This obstruction may have reflected a real concern that the child would not be returned to Australia; however, in each case courts granted children's passports, underlining the courts' views that the woman and child's failure to return was unlikely. Certainly the obstruction often created significant stress, cost, and delay, sometimes retraumatizing the women. This was part of Ingrid's experience.

Ingrid's Experience

Echoing the findings of Dobash and Dobash (2015, p. 39), Ingrid found her ex-partner, Scott, "changed the project" after separation, trying different ways of using the legal system to control her and obstruct her freedom (Sharp-Jeffs et al., 2018). Ingrid felt that the justice system actors—police, her ex-partner's lawyer, and judges—often facilitated Scott's continued efforts to "hunt" her via the legal system, through their failure to appreciate the continued IPV and future risk manifested in Scott's previous sexual assault and his threatening text messages, stalking, and suicide threats (J. Campbell et al., 2003). It was not until the third interview that Ingrid felt justice system actors had begun to understand her experience of abuse. At the third interview she reflected on Scott's use of the legal system to "hunt" her.

> ***Ingrid, interview 1:*** *So I'm like, what, is he going to make an order now trying to get an order against me every year with something else . . . but he's trying it different ways with the control, that's the thing.*

I meet Ingrid at a support service she is familiar with. Ingrid and Scott met overseas in Ingrid's home city and had separated around 16 months before our interview. Ingrid has postgraduate qualifications and was working in a well-paid position in her birth country at the time they met. Scott is Australian. When they met, he was taking a break from work as he had health issues and self-medicated with marijuana and prescription painkillers. Ingrid describes Scott as "the strong alpha male kind of thing," but he also "seemed pretty considerate." She says she got pregnant straightaway, and they resolved to keep the child. After their child, Kelsey, was born, they decided to return to Australia. Ingrid and Kelsey arrived in Australia after Scott and found he wasn't working. Ingrid found a job and childcare and, with some pressure from Scott, she paid off his credit cards, and soon her maternity leave money from her home country ran out.

After just a few months in Australia, Scott began to verbally and emotionally abuse Ingrid and was easily enraged. She tells me, "One time he was so mad he started . . . yelling at us and then he kicked his computer, then he threw the computer around on the ground." Another time "he took the baby gate and just threw it around in the kitchen, so I took Kelsey, locked the door, and sat in the bedroom." Ingrid says, "He did raise his hand once out of anger, but he didn't follow through. But you still have that image." Scott was also sexually violent. He injured Ingrid on at least one occasion during sex.

One day at work Ingrid disclosed the violence to her boss, who referred her to a support service, and Ingrid started to receive some counseling from a psychologist. For a while Scott and Ingrid lived separately under one roof. A woman moved into the house and was sleeping with Scott. Around this stage Ingrid met someone and went out with him. Scott discovered this through reading Ingrid's emails, and "he blew," sending her a number of abusive text messages demanding she leave and threatening to kill himself. He told her he had found his weapons license, and Ingrid wasn't sure if that was a threat. Ingrid didn't know what to do because she had no family in Australia and little money.

Eventually Ingrid contacted a support service, which arranged for a motel for a few days and then shelter accommodations for her and Kelsey.

Ingrid was on a spousal visa sponsored by Scott, and the support service assisted her to apply under the IPV exemption to gain permanent residency. Her psychologist was able to provide a statement in support of permanent residency. At this time she is awaiting the outcome.

Ingrid prepared an application for a protection order by herself, setting out the emotional, financial, and sexual abuse she had experienced. She went to the court hearing on her own. Scott was legally represented and denied her allegations. She was cross-examined by Scott's lawyer, and she says the court "threw out the sexual violence; can't prove it because it's not going to happen anymore" because they are separated. She says, "The barrister just kept yelling at me . . . there was no physical violence as such," and the text messages taken out of the context of the abuse "did not look so bad." The magistrate refused the order.

Ingrid stayed at the shelter with Kelsey, who visited Scott every second weekend. At one of the handovers at MacDonald's, Scott told Ingrid he knew her address. This was a breach of the shelter security policy, so she had to move to a different shelter. Scott's disclosures that he knew two subsequent addresses made Ingrid suspicious. Scott had given Kelsey a doll, and Ingrid found a GPS device sewn into the back of the doll. Scott had been tracking her movements. With a shelter worker, Ingrid went to the police to report this. Police said they could not charge Scott with stalking because it was her child's doll, and they refused to assist with a protection order application. Ingrid was determined to get a protection order, and with the assistance of a community legal center lawyer, she was able to get a temporary protection order.

Scott then sought a protection order against Ingrid, "fabricating evidence" of her beating and raping him. Scott eventually withdrew his application. Ingrid had evidence. She had taken recordings of his abuse on her phone and had taken screenshots of his online abuse. Ingrid is also very small, around 100 pounds, whereas Scott is twice her size, making Scott's claims difficult to believe. She was granted a final protection order, but she was disappointed that the judge refused to list Kelsey as protected on the order.

Scott refused to allow Ingrid to remove herself from the rental lease they shared. Worried she would be pursued by the landlord for a portion of the rent, even though she did not live in the house, she made an application to a tribunal to have her name removed from the lease. Scott failed to attend the tribunal on the day the matter was to be heard, and the case was adjourned. The lease eventually ran out before the matter was returned to the tribunal.

Ingrid was not able to get legal aid for her family law application and agreed to settle on some parenting arrangements with Scott to avoid a trial. In these negotiations Scott was represented by his privately funded lawyer, and Ingrid was unrepresented. Scott has Kelsey every second weekend and once in the middle of the week for a few hours. Kelsey is not allowed to be removed from the country and is on the "airport watch list."[12] Ingrid and Scott must attend mediation to sort out any parenting issues that arise.[13] Ingrid finds handovers distressing and demeaning. She records all her interactions with Scott on her phone. She has also been having a "continuous fight" about child support. Scott is not paying any child support and indeed says Ingrid owes him child support.

Scott continues to breach the good-behavior provision of the protection order and the terms of the parenting order but has never been charged with breach, or with any criminal offenses relating to the stalking and monitoring or the false affidavit evidence. Ingrid says, "It was . . . psychological kind of like terror. That is something that he's doing to this day, though. Like he kept doing it after separation, so it never—it's nothing that stops."

> ***Ingrid, interview 2:*** *You can't communicate, you can't get anything done with him, and it will be always a fight. . . . clearly all the stuff, what he put me through with the courts, that's all still domestic violence.*

A year has passed since we last met, and Ingrid says there have been many issues about the care of Kelsey. Ingrid bought plane tickets because she wanted to take Kelsey back to her birth country to visit family. However, because Kelsey is on the airport watch list, Ingrid needs Scott's consent, and Scott has refused to grant it. She tried to arrange mediation to negotiate about this, and in the end, because of the history of IPV, this did not happen. The application to travel was then listed before a judge at the family court. Ingrid was unrepresented while Scott was represented by a lawyer, who had prepared a 200-page statement outlining his objections to the overseas travel, including that there was a risk of abuse and Ingrid was a flight risk.[14] Also buried within this statement was an application for a change in custody arrangements to equal shared time. Scott filed five further affidavits from his family members and associates, some of whom Ingrid had never met, who supported his objections to travel. Eventually the judge issued a travel order requiring Ingrid to pay a bond of $4,400 to the court. The judge adjourned the question about parenting arrangements and ordered a family court report.[15]

Ingrid enjoyed a few weeks overseas and returned to have interviews associated with the family court report. The report ultimately recommended that the same arrangements regarding Kelsey continue—she should live with Ingrid and have alternate weekends and an afternoon each week with Scott. Ingrid was able to secure legal aid and representation for the hearings, while Scott changed his legal representation several times. The hearing was set down at least three times, with Scott adjourning proceedings at the last minute each time. Eventually a request for an adjournment was refused, and Scott was unrepresented. Ingrid found the case tense and stressful, although in the end she did get all the orders she wanted. Ingrid got the travel bond back from the court, but she is due back in the family court next month about Kelsey's school arrangements.

Ingrid has a protection order in place for another 2 months but doesn't plan to apply for a new one. She explains, "Like I don't even want to go back to court to get another extension of the protection order because even my lawyer . . . she's like, 'He's just going to be excited to do more paperwork.'"

Ingrid is not receiving any child support, and Scott is in arrears on his payments. Her lawyer has told her she should apply for a property settlement so she can access his superannuation, but Ingrid says, "It's so expensive. Then I have to go back to court for that as well," so she is not planning on doing that.

> ***Ingrid, interview 3:*** *I really felt hunted by him. Wherever I turn, you kind of get used to looking over your shoulder kind of at everything. . . . It was really like a hunting thing. Like there's the stalking and then I got the [protection order] so he took the [protection order] against me. Then I wanted to go to [home country] so he said no. Then he did the thing in that court and then bringing all these people along that I didn't even know and it was really like a manhunt kind of. I mean, it was a literal hunt in between as well with the stalking.*

It has been around 6 months since I last caught up with Ingrid. In the interim she has had another family court case about Kelsey's schooling. Both Scott and Ingrid represented themselves, and schooling was resolved in a way that Ingrid is happy with, and the custody arrangements are unchanged—Kelsey lives with Ingrid, with Scott having regular contact. Ingrid feels like, after starting off "more on his side," the family court finally understands her situation:

> It was really interesting when we went back to the [court] like it was also good to see the change in the system once we had to go back. There's always the same people right that kind of dealt with that. So it was the same family reporter and it was the same judge to just have the progression [to] when they finally got it, [and understood] what was actually happening, from not seeing it to, OK, clearly there's something wrong with this man.

The judge ordered Scott to pay Ingrid's legal costs ($6,700 [USD4,200]) because he had unnecessarily reopened the custody arrangements issue.[16] She is planning to start enforcement proceedings, to get divorced, and then to make an application to access Scott's superannuation.

Ingrid says the child handovers are a lot better, although "there is no communication whatever." Scott only takes Kelsey every second weekend.

He doesn't bother with the midweek contact, saying that "it's not worth it." All of Scott's emails are first filtered by a friend of Ingrid's, "so I don't sit there and just worry about having to see his emails." Scott didn't pay child support for a while because he reported to the agency that he didn't earn a taxable income. However, Ingrid found his profile on LinkedIn, where he stated his current employment. Ingrid alerted the child support authorities, who investigated, and now he pays some child support. She has let her protection order lapse. Ingrid is in a new relationship that is going well; she and her new partner rent a house together, and she is working full-time. When I ask her if she feels she has moved on from the relationship, she responds:

> Oh from the relationship, for sure. But . . . it's like it's always there. Like I still have these nightmares whenever [Kelsey] goes to him . . . you have dreams about having to go back to court or I have to listen to the court thing again or like this general kind of threat kind of feeling sometimes.

ABORIGINAL AND TORRES STRAIT ISLANDER WOMEN

With only six Aboriginal and Torres Strait Islander (ATSI) women interviewed in this study, and two of them withdrawing, one after the first interview and one after the second interview, it is not possible to draw out clear patterns about their interaction with legal processes in response to IPV over time. Only Roseanna (ATSI) and Cassie (ATSI) had an ATSI partner. Three of the ATSI women described their partner as white, and one woman's partner was from a Pacific Island. All of the ATSI women had been involved with the police on many occasions, although, unlike the majority of women involved in the study, this group of women had usually not called them; rather, the police had been called by neighbors and other bystanders. Some research has found that ATSI women may be reluctant to call police to avoid child protection involvement or retributive action against them or their families by police (Blagg, Bluett-Boyd, & Williams, 2015; Willis, 2011). Fear of CPS involvement was clearly expressed by Roseanna, Cassie (whose story is explored in Chapter 5), and Melissa (whose story is explored in Chapter 9).

At the first interview, all six of the ATSI women had, or had previously had, a protection order in place and reported that it had been breached by their partner at least once. For Cassie and Roseanna the protection orders were no longer relevant because their partners were in custody for non-IPV-related matters, throughout the time of the three interviews. All of the ATSI women described severe physical abuse, including broken bones, as part of their experience of IPV. This level of injury is consistent with findings from other studies. Hospitalization statistics show that in Australia, ATSI women are hospitalized for family violence–related assaults at a rate of 530 females per 100,000 female population, which is 32 times the rate for non-Aboriginal and non–Torres Strait Islander women (Productivity Commission Steering Committee for the Review of Government Service Provision, 2016, [4.98]). Notably, two of the ATSI women (Kristy and Jarrah) had an intellectual disability and were not literate. Their partners had exploited their lack of literacy to carry out financial abuse. Jarrah was signed up by her partner for a car loan for a car she never saw. She paid off this loan over the course of the three interviews. Kristy was interviewed only once, but she said she was unable to read the instructions on the automatic teller machine. She gave her partner her personal identification number, resulting in his taking money from her.

Of the three ATSI women who had children with their abusive partner (Cassie, Roseanna, and Melissa), only Melissa described any involvement with the family law system, at one stage registering a parenting plan[17] with the family court.[18] Both Cassie's and Roseanna's children were under child protection orders and living with others. The child protection orders were the most important legal issue for these women, and despite their efforts they had not had their children returned to their care by the time of the third interview. Their experiences are considered further in Chapter 5.

CONCLUSION

Not surprisingly, no two women in this study had the same experience of interacting with law in the aftermath of IPV (Silbey, 2005, p. 357). Their different circumstances, including financial circumstances and employment, education, language facility, visa status, racial and cultural background, social support, whether they had children, and so on, helped to determine which legal processes and systems they interacted with and impacted on their experiences of them (Crenshaw, 1991). Overall, women's interactions across different legal systems did decrease over time, although most women were still involved with three or more legal processes at the time of the third interview. For many women, their partner either used legal processes or engaged with those processes in a way that was experienced as a continuing form of IPV. In a study exploring welfare recipients' perspectives on their engagement with law, Sarat observed, "Law is not a distant abstraction; it is a web-like enclosure in which they are 'caught' . . . a space which is not their own and which allows them only a 'tactical' presence" (1990, p. 345). Similar perspectives about law are reflected in the experiences of Sandra, Ingrid, and many other women in this study whose stories are presented in the following chapters. Their engagement with law was often extended, and sometimes driven, by their abusers, who hunted, battled and played with them through law. While women were rarely passive and often resisted, there were significant costs to women in those efforts of resistance.

NOTES

1. Children's contact services aim to provide safe, neutral, and child-focused venues for facilitated contact and handovers between children and their parents. There is some evidence that there are increasing numbers of long-term orders being made in the family courts that require supervision at a contact center (Schindeler, 2019).
2. Although there is a victim charter in relevant legislation in Queensland, where this study took place, and police are required to communicate with victims about plea negotiation, lack of information being provided to victims has been identified as a concern in other studies (e.g., Holder, 2018).

3. Because Tabora's partner was on a work visa and his status in Australia was also temporary, the IPV exception to claim permanent resident independent of her ex-partner was not available to her (Borges Jelenic, 2020).
4. There has been significant debate about the use of fines as the penalty response to breaches of protection orders (Douglas, 2008), but they remain the most common sentencing response (Sentencing Advisory Council, 2019, p. viii).
5. A child recovery order is a family court order that allows the federal police to recover the child and return him to Rosa (Harland, Cooper, Rathus, & Alexander, 2015, p. 296).
6. When both parties make an application against each other or have a protection order against each other, these are referred to as *cross* or *mutual applications* or *orders* (Douglas & Fitzgerald, 2013; Durfee & Goodmark, 2019).
7. See Chapter 7, Table 7.1.
8. The notice of risk is a form required by the family court in relation to child-related proceedings. It requires answers to specific questions directed at eliciting information about child abuse, family violence, and a range of other risks (AIJA, 2020, [10.6]).
9. See Trisha's experience in Chapter 7.
10. See Rosa's experience in Chapter 3 and Doya's experience in Chapter 6.
11. See Shuang's experience in Chapter 9.
12. The family court can make an order (a watch list order) that prevents an adult from removing the child of a relationship from Australia without a court order or the consent of both parents (Harland et al., 2015, p. 296).
13. For a discussion of mediation within the Australian family law process, see Harland et al., 2015, pp. 90–95.
14. The Hague Convention on the Civil Aspects of International Child Abduction entered into force in 1983, with both Australia and the United States among the signatories. It applies to children under 16 years of age and aims to provide an expeditious way of returning a child who is abducted internationally from one member country to another (Harland et al., 2015, pp. 604–605; Malhotra, 2014).
15. Depending on the facts and circumstances of the particular case, the family court may order that the parties to child-related proceedings take part in an assessment conducted by a family consultant. This will result in the production of a family report (AIJA, 2020, [10.4]; Field, Jeffries, Rathus, & Lynch, 2016).
16. Note that in Australia, if one party is ordered to pay the other party's costs, this order will be made once the litigation is finalized (Littrich & Murray, 2019, p. 229).
17. Where parents can agree on parenting arrangements after separation, they can make a parenting plan. Although these are not legally enforceable, they can be used as evidence in court of agreement between the parties at a particular point in time (Harland et al., 2015, pp. 133–155).
18. Aboriginal and Torres Strait Islander people have a generally low level of involvement with the family law system in Australia (Schwartz & Cunneen, 2009).

5

Interacting With the Child Protection Service

INTRODUCTION

Child protection laws allow the state to intervene into family life to protect the safety of children. Across Australia and in many other countries, legislation provides powers for child protection officers to investigate allegations of neglect, abuse, and other risk factors, such as children's exposure to intimate partner violence (IPV) (Titterton, 2017, p. 155). Similar to other countries, after investigating complaints, Australian child protection officers may decide that the complaint is unsubstantiated. Alternatively, there may be sufficient concern that child protection officers decide to monitor the situation, and they may recommend or direct that carers engage in a variety of courses to deal with any identified issues. In some cases, child protection services (CPS) may determine that the carer is not "willing or able" to keep the child safe and may remove the child and place him or her with an alternative caregiver (Douglas & Walsh, 2010).[1] Of the 48 study women who had children with their abusive partner, almost half ($n = 23$) reported that they had some contact with CPS, and most of those who had contact said that they were also investigated by CPS ($n = 20$). Ten women said they had initiated contact with the CPS seeking support, although none of those women received the support they hoped for. Nine women reported that their children had been removed from their care,

Women, Intimate Partner Violence, and the Law. Heather Douglas, Oxford University Press (2021). © Oxford University Press.
DOI: 10.1093/oso/9780190071783.003.0005

and only 4 of them had their children returned to their care by the end of the study (Table 5.1).

The reasons for CPS investigation are not routinely disclosed to women, so it was often not clear to them who made the complaint or what the complaint was about. Lyn explained at interview 1 that she did not understand why her children had been removed from her care: "I'm totally confused with it, because one minute it was violence. One minute it was the hygiene. One minute was this. One minute was that. It's like . . . I'm a bit confused with it at the moment."

For many women, CPS was just one of the legal systems they were involved in as a result of their experience of IPV. Often, the CPS investigation came as a shock, and women reported a sense that CPS seemed to hold them accountable for their abusive partner's behavior rather than providing them with the support they needed. Bianca's experience, outlined in this chapter, reflects these experiences.

The identity of the complainant is not usually disclosed when CPS investigates. However, of the 20 women who were investigated by CPS, 11 said the investigation resulted from a complaint that they believed was maliciously made by their abusive partner. For Shelley, whose story is also included in this chapter, her partner's malicious complaint led to the

Table 5.1 Engagement With Child Protection Services (CPS)

Interview	No. of Women	% of Women
Women interviewed at time 1	65	100
Women with children with their abuser	48	74
Any contact with CPS	23	35
Contacted CPS for support	10	15
Woman's mothering investigated by CPS	20	31
Mothers who had children removed into state care by CPS	9	14
Malicious false reports to CPS made or threatened by abuser	11	17

temporary removal of her children from her care, with deeply negative long-term consequences.

Most of the nine study women whose children were removed from their care were particularly vulnerable.[2] Two women, Doya and Rosa, were from CALD communities and were on insecure visas. Three were ATSI women, and 3, including one of the ATSI women, identified as having an intellectual disability. The traumatic experience of child removal in the shadow of IPV and intergenerational trauma was also highlighted in some of the women's stories.

These three key themes—women feeling they were being held to account for their partner's IPV; partners making malicious allegations to CPS; and the complex experience of vulnerability, intergenerational trauma, and CPS involvement—are explored in this chapter.

WOMEN HELD TO ACCOUNT FOR THEIR PARTNER'S VIOLENCE

Previous research has identified the pressure placed on women who have experienced IPV to "act protectively," often demanding women remove themselves and their children from the abuser or risk having their children removed from their care (Hughes & Chau, 2012, p. 690; Laing, Heward-Belle, & Toivonen, 2018, p. 221; Radford & Hester, 2006). At least 5 women in this study experienced an ultimatum from CPS workers to leave the abuser or their children would be removed. For example, Francis and Mark had separated several times because of Mark's abuse but then got back together each time. Mark was charged with a range of criminal offenses and was granted bail to live at the family home. In response, CPS determined that it was not safe for the children to live with Mark. Francis explained:

> At first I had to be removed from the home because Mark [was on bail]. So when [CPS] found that out they said, "Well, you're not allowed to stay there, we'll remove the kids." Luckily I already had

> accommodation booked with my caravan . . . I stayed there. . . . So I had 2 weeks down at [the beach].

By the time of interview 3, Francis had separated from Mark, and she was keeping the children away from him. She reported that CPS was "happy with her," but she was worried that the family courts would order some contact for the children with Mark, placing her in conflict with the CPS.

Similar to other studies (Buckley, Whelan, & Carr, 2011, pp. 128, 130; Heward-Belle, Laing, Humphreys, & Toivonen, 2018, p. 142; S. Johnson & Sullivan, 2008), most of the study women who had contact with CPS reported that their interaction was unsupportive or punitive. Sandra was one of the exceptions. She was investigated by CPS, probably, she says, because of a complaint by her ex-partner. CPS gave her an ultimatum that either she leave or they would remove the children. Sandra found this empowering and felt supported in implementing a "solid plan" to leave:

> [CPS] said, well, if you continue to keep seeing him with the children in your presence, then we will remove your children. So it was that heavy advice by [CPS]. It was choose the love of your children or the love of this man. . . . It was just—I was lost in how to get out, away. But [CPS] gave me that strict guideline, which empowered [me]. There was a really great turnaround for me that [CPS] came in with that solid plan. (Sandra, interview 1)

However, when women reached out to CPS for support, they were overwhelmingly disappointed with the response and generally felt they were not listened to. Ten of the women contacted CPS seeking support or advice or to record their concerns. Hannah said she thought it was "sad" that CPS did not help her: "I've reported [children's father] to the child authorities a couple of times, and . . . I've had no one come and see me. I've had no one speak to me about it. Nothing." At interview 1, Milly said she has called CPS a couple of times because she was "really worried about the emotional abuse." She said her daughter came back from contact visits upset, and Milly was worried: "They said they'd record it, they'd put it on a file and to contact us if anything came up again." On one occasion, Milly called CPS about her concerns and ironically, while this did not result in investigation of the abuser, it did result in an investigation of the telephone operator. Milly recounted that when she called to report emotional abuse, she was told by the telephone operator:

> "This is a waste of time; go and sort it out." My response to her was like, "I beg your pardon. This is verbal and emotional and psychological abuse. This is why I'm ringing." She hung up on me. . . . I rang back and I had all the details of who she was and they went into a full investigation. Imagine if I was someone who was really disempowered at that stage. Luckily I was like, no, I'm not taking this shit. (Milly, interview 1)

Although the altercation with the phone operator was investigated, Milly says her concerns about her daughter were not. At interview 2, Milly recalled she was "ringing up to get advice and to say, look this is bad, but I don't know how bad *bad* is for you guys. It's not super bad but I'm worried and I feel like I need to tell someone and have this recorded in case it gets worse, as a track record." By the time of interview 3, Milly felt she was "healing" and that things were going well with contact arrangements.

In one case in the study, the lack of CPS response may have contributed to a fatality. Monica telephoned CPS 3 weeks prior to one of her family members being killed by her ex-partner. One of her school-aged sons had been staying at her ex-partner's (the child's father) place on weekends. Monica was concerned about the downward-spiraling condition of his house. She called CPS

> because I was worried. . . . The house was just disgusting, there's holes in the walls, the walls are probably asbestos—you know, new holes. Just like an alcoholic's house, they all look the same . . . there was rat bait just out on the floor. It was just . . . horrible. I rang [CPS] about it and they got a bit of information, but nothing really came of that. (Monica, interview 1)

The experience of not being heard can be contrasted with women's sense that they were often investigated if their male partners made complaints about them to CPS. In their interviews with CPS professionals, Heward-Belle and colleagues (2018, p. 141) found that many believed the child protection field continued to be influenced by "patriarchal attitudes, providing violent men an advantage over their female victims." The experiences of both Bianca and Shelley highlight the trauma of malicious complaints, legal system inconsistency, and the ongoing negative effects of child removal.

Bianca's Experience

Bianca was held to account for Tom's abuse. Initially, when she sought assistance from a support service, she was challenged about her ability to act protectively toward her children and threatened with a report to CPS. Then, just when she thought that she had finalized her contact with multiple legal systems, including police, protection orders,[3] family law, and criminal law, she had to deal with the trauma and humiliation of multiple CPS investigations. Tom was able to use the CPS to continue his abuse.

> ***Bianca, interview 1:*** *He said he was going to shoot himself in the head, in front of the children, and [the telephone counselor] interpreted that to mean he said he was going to shoot himself in the head while the children were physically present. What I actually meant was he made the statement in front of the children. So this launched this whole "Oh, we're going to call [CPS] about that if you don't act protectively," and I was like, "Oh, God, I'm just trying to help."*

Bianca was referred to the study by a local support service, but because she is currently living in a country town, we talk on the phone. Bianca and Tom are in their 30s and separated last year after more than 10 years together. Bianca has a good job as a teacher, but Tom, although tertiary educated, has had trouble maintaining work, and he receives social security.

Bianca is studying for a law degree. "It's a cheap way to get legal advice," she laughs. They have school-aged children together. At this time, the children live with Bianca and see Tom on weekends. Tom lives in the family home, and Bianca and the children live with friends.

There were only a few occasions during the relationship when Tom was physically violent. However, Bianca says, "From my point of view, I felt like I had to walk on eggshells around him, even prior to the first violent incident . . . he doesn't have a great way of managing his anger. . . . When he lashes out, anyone in the way gets hurt." He was often verbally abusive, and he called Bianca a "fat cunt," knowing she had had an eating disorder. She knew Tom was tracking her internet use. She discovered a keylogger on her computer and confronted Tom about it. He told her he was trying to keep her safe. He kept guns for hunting, read books about snipers and serial killers, and often said things that Bianca interpreted as veiled threats. Bianca's frustration with Tom not doing the household chores sometimes resulted in violence. Once he threw her across a room. Another time he pushed her into a bookcase.

Tom threatened to commit suicide a few weeks before their separation. Bianca telephoned the ambulance, and both police and ambulance attended. While Tom was in the hospital, Bianca contacted a telephone counselor and talked through her options. When she explained her circumstances and Tom's suicide threat, the operator threatened to call CPS if Bianca didn't act protectively.[4] Bianca found herself explaining how she was being protective: "I really don't need that complication." Bianca was starting to think about leaving because she "could feel this buildup and . . . was feeling even more unsafe." She initiated what turned out to be a final conversation with Tom about improving the relationship. In response to her concerns, Tom started to talk about his failed relationships and how he could understand how murder-suicides happen. He had been drinking heavily through the evening and punched her and gripped her hands. She recalls:

> It was horrible. At one point he released my hands and put his hands around my throat, and after I'd said something about "please don't

> kill me" and he was sort of shaking with his hands around my throat, saying, "You stupid woman, I'm not going to kill you. The only reason I haven't killed you yet is because I don't want to," and for some reason he thought that that would make me feel better.

When Tom fell asleep, Bianca escaped to a neighbor's home, where the police were called, and she was able to collect the children and leave.

Police obtained a temporary protection order for Bianca that also named the children as protected. Tom consented to the final order without making admissions about previous violence and on the condition that the children were removed from the order. At the time, Bianca was glad to get the protection order by consent, but this had implications for her later in her custody hearing. Because there was no evidence of IPV given in the protection order case, the family court judge felt that he had "permission to say, well, it's not serious, we don't know if it happened . . . you can't make decisions without testing all the evidence."

The custody matter is ongoing, and child handovers happen at school, so Bianca and Tom don't need to see each other. Bianca has already incurred significant legal fees.[5] The property division was settled by consent. Tom argued he had sacrificed his career to care for the children while Bianca worked full-time. Bianca says: "I walked away with $85,000 [USD58,000], all of the debt of the marriage, and no assets except some furniture that I had. He's got a whole house in his sole name," apparently paid off by his wealthy mother.

Recently Bianca applied for her protection order to be renewed, and Tom took the opportunity to apply for an order against her at the same time.[6] Bianca's lawyer asked that she be dealt with as a protected witness, which would have meant she could give her evidence behind a screen, but this was refused by the magistrate. He found that Bianca was articulate and intelligent enough to manage. Tom was unrepresented and cross-examined her for several hours.[7] After all this, Tom's application was dismissed while the magistrate renewed the protection order for Bianca.

Tom was later charged with serious offenses (including deprivation of liberty) but negotiated a guilty plea to a less serious charge of assault.

He was placed on a good-behavior bond with no conviction recorded. Bianca was glad she didn't have to attend the court for this. Recently, Bianca has unfriended Tom on Facebook, since he made a comment that the law can't stop people from killing their partners and children. Understood in the context of the abuse, this threat seems credible, but it would be too vague and indirect for police to act on, so Bianca didn't report it.

> ***Bianca, interview 2:*** *So really I got what I wanted by default, not because the legal system works in particular.*

I catch up with Bianca 12 months after our first interview. The final family law orders reflect the arrangement that Bianca offered even before the court hearings began, that the children live with her and spend several weekends a month with Tom. Bianca and Tom were both represented by lawyers at the family court trial. Tom was cross-examined by Bianca's lawyer and admitted he had told lies in his statement. Tom then proceeded to blame his lawyer, telling the court that his lawyer made him sign the document even though he knew it was incorrect. Bianca says Tom "wouldn't have understood the gravity of that . . . totally dropped his legal team in it." Bianca says she got the custody orders she was hoping for "by default." She tells me that she has named her cat after the family court judge: "It was just symbolic—I'm allowed to move on. [The judge] was part of that." Bianca says she thought of letting the judge know but decided against it: "I've got nothing to lose now while there's no matter on foot, but when there is again, you never know."

Bianca regularly drops off the children for their contact visits with Tom. She says, "It's still just that being subjected to that fear sometimes. . . . Sometimes I'll text him just to say, you there yet . . . to test the waters, to see if I get back a chatty, friendly-type response. . . . I'll worry if it's just a yes, full stop . . . it was never a good relationship, in the sense of feeling and being safe."

She is struggling to get on top of the debt and had to give up her law studies. She lives with her new partner, which is going well, but she says,

"We've got a house that we're trying to run, and even though I earn really good money and I work really hard, I just can't get ahead." She has received some victim assistance money, which has helped pay for the move and for a security system.

> ***Bianca, interview 3:*** *I find it hard to be objective about that because of how I felt through the process. Feeling you're being a bit persecuted and difficulty separating out whether that belongs to Tom or the [CPS] or the [CPS officers] that investigated us. I mean, fundamentally, they did their job. I think it was dragged out for a long time, but I think that's a lot of people's experience of [CPS].*

Since our last interview 6 months ago, Tom reported Bianca to the CPS. He later admitted this to her, saying he had "genuine concerns," but Bianca believes it was "vexatious":

> We got a visit from the [CPS] officer from [town] one Saturday morning. He rocked up early. I was having a sleep-in, and my partner was just sitting reading on the front deck when he arrived and we had all the children at home. He wanted to talk to us about all the allegations that Tom had made about us, all of which were untrue and vexatious.

The report must have been serious as the children's safety was fully investigated. Bianca says: "I found [CPS workers] a bit critical, but that's because that's how they have to be. I wasn't expecting . . . someone to be 'there, there, it's OK, I'm looking out for you,' because that's not their job." She describes the impact of the false allegations:

> Just when I think everything has calmed down and I'm able to move on and it's all OK, he goes and does that. I just hit the deck and just crumbled, and I really struggled to keep going at work and to function. I felt embarrassed too because I thought, you know, like a lot of [people] will know about this.

Ultimately, the complaint was unsubstantiated, but because of the nature of her employment, Bianca had to step down from work for a few months. All her children were interviewed by CPS investigators along with some of her relatives and friends. She found the whole process humiliating, and the children were angry and upset.

Since that first complaint, Tom has made regular complaints to police and CPS about the children being "unsafe." Bianca always cooperates with the investigations, and Tom's claims are always unsubstantiated. She says it is "humiliating and I don't know how to make him stop using these systems to continue his campaign of harassment and control." Recently, over 2 weeks, there were four visits by police for welfare checks of the children. Since the separation, Bianca has been taking antidepressants and would like to stop but says: "When I get stable enough he just pulls the rug out from under me again and then I'm back to square one . . . and then I have to work through it." She's paying down her debt with some of her superannuation and long service leave payments, but, she says, it's "revolving credit."

MALICIOUS ALLEGATIONS AND COERCIVE CONTROL

Research suggests that false allegations to CPS are mostly made in good faith (Jaffe, Johnston, Crooks, & Bala, 2008, p. 508; Trocmé & Bala, 2005, p. 1338). However, 11 women in this study, including Bianca, claimed that malicious complaints had been made about them to CPS by violent ex-partners (see Table 5.1). This equates to 16% of women in the study experiencing a malicious complaint. This figure is consistent with research from Saini and colleagues (2013, p. 125; see also Saini, Black, Godbout, & Deljavan, 2019), who analyzed data from more than 11,000 child maltreatment investigations and found 13% involved a malicious referral.

In the current study, only Evie reported that malicious allegations were made while she was still living with her abuser. Mostly, complaints were made after separation, and this experience is also reflected in research by

Saini and colleagues (2013, p. 125). At least 7 of the women who believed they were the subject of malicious complaints from their ex-partner had been, or were currently, engaged in custody disputes, a connection found in research by Moloney and colleagues (2007, p. 5). Certainly for some women, false reports to CPS are a feature of IPV, part of their abuser's coercive and controlling behavior, and an aspect of legal systems abuse (Bancroft, Silverman, & Ritchie, 2012; Rumney & McCartan, 2017, p. 517; Ward, 2016, p. 443).

Sandra saw her ex-partner's actions of reporting her to CPS as a form of abuse, stating that he "has been using these children to get at me." Lahleh (CALD) said her partner falsely reported her to CPS "again and again and again." She was investigated, but she says CPS workers didn't believe him and told her she was a "protective mother." Rosa (CALD) explained that her ex-partner had taken their child from her care, contrary to their family law agreement. When police intervened to return the child to Rosa, her partner made various allegations against her, including "that I wasn't feeding the child and that I tied the child up." Rosa was investigated, the allegations were unsubstantiated, and her child was returned, but not until a month and a half later. In Evie's case, her partner made multiple false allegations to CPS. She knew this because she found a letter cautioning her partner about his aggressive behavior with the CPS workers he had reported her to.

Similarly, Alex stated that her ex-partner had reported her to CPS "on numerous occasions"; she mentioned new false reports at each of the three interviews. She was aware she was investigated once, and the complaint was not substantiated. He also reported Alex's elderly parents to CPS; they were also investigated, and that complaint was also unsubstantiated.

Roseanna (ATSI) reported she first became involved with CPS when her ex-partner reported her. She says, "He made the call to [CPS] . . . it was all because of jealousy, he wanted me back in his life and I stood up and said 'no.' Roseanna's children were removed from her care, and for the past few years she has been trying to show that the younger ones should be returned to her. I provide more of her story later in this Chapter.

Shelley's Experience

Like Bianca, Shelley thought she had concluded her interactions with the legal system as a result of IPV. However, Shelley's ex-partner, Pete, used the CPS system to reactivate her engagement with the legal system and to demonstrate his control to devastating effect. For Shelley, the disconnections between legal systems served to magnify the abuse she experienced as a result of the CPS complaint.

> ***Shelley, interview 1:*** *So you get [to] the family law court and they won't make a decision because [CPS] is in the room. [CPS] doesn't seem to think they influence family law. But family law seems to be influenced by [CPS]. So who actually does influence who and who knows they do or it's—my solicitor makes me believe that it's—it depends on how that judge is feeling that day.*

Shelley's story is complex and hard to follow. Her story comes tumbling out, as she mixes up times and the order of events. She is very stressed and nervous, and she cries often during the interview, which goes for nearly 2 hours. The past year has been very difficult for her. Most distressing is that she has been charged with assault, and one of her teenage children is the complainant. She is currently on bail but had to go back to court last week to make sure her bail conditions don't conflict with family court orders and child protection concerns. She is absolutely humiliated by this process, but she says:

> I don't think of myself as a victim. I guess I am in some ways the definition of victim. But to be the victim won't help me mentally through this. If I stay in that mindset, I won't . . . be able to rise up above it because it keeps you in that mode.

Shelley has postgraduate qualifications and only a few years ago received awards for her work in developing a business. Her partner, Pete, was in the same business. They are both in their 40s and have school-aged children together. They lived together for more than 15 years before separating several years ago. Shelley's business fell apart after her separation, and currently she is relying on social security while she tries to establish a new business. She has a house that was fully paid off as part of the property settlement but is now borrowing against it to pay her legal fees for her current court cases. Her costs already exceed $25,000 (USD17,000).

During the relationship, the abuse began when Pete had an accident and then found it difficult to get well-paid work. Shelley became the primary earner in the family, and she feels Pete began to deliberately try to humiliate her and isolate her from her professional and personal networks to deal with his own insecurities: "He moved us [around] so much. He was isolating me all the time because I'm a people person. Whatever he did, he cut me off from people—I realize now. So that would keep me under his thumb." He often called her bipolar and claimed she was crazy. Shelley also experienced negative, controlling interference from her own family and Pete's extended family, including verbal and physical abuse in the presence of the children.

Pete and Shelley separated at Pete's instigation. They engaged solicitors and made a parenting plan a couple of years before our first interview. Under the first parenting plan, the children lived Shelley and spent regular time with Pete. Pete never followed these arrangements. After their separation, Pete's abuse toward Shelley escalated, and she believes he recruited the children as participants in denigrating her. Contact arrangements for the children became more difficult to navigate, and 2 months prior to our first interview, Pete instigated an application to the family court for the children to live with him. They tried mediation but could not agree, and a family report was ordered.[8] Shelley says she has become increasingly fearful of her two older children, especially her son:

> I was having conversations with . . . counselors and my own doctor of how to navigate that space . . . my older two were treating me . . . they'd become Pete's weapons. I had mini-hims . . . he's infiltrated my home. Twenty-four seven he would call them on their mobiles, and I would

see a change in their behavior. I knew exactly when they'd had a phone call.

Things came to a head when Pete physically assaulted Shelley during a child handover. The police were called, but Pete was allowed to take the children with him. Shelley says that Pete's "whole argument was trying to say the children were afraid of me, I was psycho and all this." The family report found that if the children lived with Shelley, they would have contact with both parents but expressed concern that if they lived with Pete, they may not see their mother. Since then, the family court has made temporary orders that the children live with Shelley and spend some weekends with Pete.

Six months ago, Pete handed the children back to Shelley at their usual handover place—a service station especially selected by Shelley because it had security cameras. She says her teenage son got back in the car "and proceeded to talk about how I could be killed and how I could be buried. . . . He goes, 'Oh, a car accident would probably be a good way.'" Shelley explains that in the past her son "had smashed in all the controls of my car at times to try and show me who was in charge." Once they got home, Shelley felt upset by the interactions and sent Pete a text about it. Her son grabbed the phone, and she tried to take it back from him. At this point she says her daughter yelled, "That's assault." The older children then called the police. The police attended and took statements from Shelley and the children. They then called Pete and told him the family needed to sort things out. Pete collected the children the next day, and Shelley believes he reported the matter to CPS.

The next day, Shelley was also charged with assault. She says the police and CPS officers worked together and "I'm DNA tested, fingerprinted, and treated like a criminal. I'm out on bail. Not allowed to ring my children because I'm on bail and they're the supposed witnesses." Someone also applied for an order so that Shelley could be examined by a mental health practitioner.[9] She suspected Pete, but wasn't sure. She was placed under house arrest and examined but was found not to be suffering from a mental illness: "The report actually says it'd be a deprivation of my liberty to continue this." Shelley said she had difficulty communicating her experience of IPV to the CPS workers and police and felt that they did not believe her.

Recently the child contact matter was mentioned in the family court. The child custody order has been flipped in favor of Pete until the criminal matter is resolved. Shelley believes the judge deferred to the CPS worker in the court and did not read any of the material. She says she's "not 100% sure" of what the current orders are: "I get 2-hour visits that are monitored in a safe house. . . . We negotiate phone calls on speakerphone."

> ***Shelley, interview 2:*** *The accusations the [CPS] were given were just so ridiculous that they shouldn't have even been given oxygen, you know what I mean?*

Ten months later, when we next meet, Shelley says she now has more than \$100,000 (USD69,000) in legal debts secured against her home. She points out that somehow Pete has managed to get legal aid, so he does not have to struggle with debt.

The criminal charge was withdrawn because there was no evidence to support it. This took several months to resolve, and meanwhile the family court matters and child protection investigations were put on hold. After the criminal charge was withdrawn, CPS looked into the matter and found the allegations unsubstantiated. Shelley is very upset that CPS took the matter seriously given the history of Pete committing IPV against her.

Last month, nearly 9 months after our first interview, the family court trial took place. Throughout this time, Shelley was having only limited supervised contact with the children. In the end, the new orders followed the recommendations of the family court report, essentially putting back in place the agreement that had operated after Pete and Shelley first separated, except now the teenage children are old enough to determine where they should live.[10] Under the most recent family court orders, the youngest child has been ordered to live with Shelley, but there are no limitations on where the older ones live. The judge recommended the children receive counseling to help rebuild their relationships with their mother.

Shelley is frustrated there was never any acknowledgment of the IPV, specifically the emotional and financial abuse she experienced.

She feels that Pete and other family members have tried everything possible to exhaust her emotionally and financially. She says:

> I have two children that I don't even get a word out of and financial debt, so emotionally and financially we're now heaps worse off than we ever were. No, it's a road that I wouldn't want anyone to travel. . . . The judge actually said that. He said this is an absolute nightmare and the family have been destroyed in every direction.

> ***Shelley, interview 3:*** *What I've learned, because of the state system versus the federal, I was in the [federal] family law court, and [CPS] is in state, because they don't actually work together.*

Six months after our second interview, Shelley has some work, but she also has the maximum loan possible against her property ($150,000 [USD103,000]) and has used the loan to pay legal fees. She still has an outstanding debt of $18,000 [USD12,000] to the lawyer. Shelley continues to have a limited relationship with her older children. She says, "You know, it's just pretty hard to digest that you have to lose your children's childhood basically." She believes that Pete continues to manipulate the older children against her. They do not spend time with her and rarely call her. The youngest child lives with her, and Pete has contact with him every second weekend. Shelley says the handovers are difficult, and she is considering getting a friend to do this but realizes it's a lot to ask. She says, "Any chance that Pete'll get, if you leave a crack in the door, he will try to control or put you down." She feels like she had a bit more hope at the second interview because she thought her older children might reconnect with her if there was support in place, but this hasn't happened. She is disappointed in CPS, saying, "It seems that they're in a rut, they just follow certain routines." She thinks the family court should have ordered counseling for the children to make sure it happened.

ATSI PEOPLE, VULNERABILITY, AND CHILD REMOVAL

In Australia, Aboriginal and Torres Strait Islander (ATSI) children are overrepresented in the child protection system. They are eight times more likely than other children to receive services from CPS and seven times more likely to be the subject of a substantiated complaint than other children (Australian Institute of Health and Welfare [AIHW], 2019, pp. 17, 30). Similar experiences have been identified among Indigenous peoples and people of color in the United States, Canada, and New Zealand (Ball, 2009; Gordon, 2006; Trocmé, Knoke, & Blackstock, 2004). A mixture of reasons have been posited for these figures. The legacy of past policies under which Indigenous children were forcibly removed from their families and often placed with white families or in institutions (Swain, 2014, p. 156) has led to intergenerational trauma (Day, Jones, Nakata, & Mcdermott, 2013). The higher likelihood of low socioeconomic status among ATSI people and cultural differences in childrearing have also contributed to these high rates (AIHW, 2019, p. 30; Human Rights and Equal Opportunity Commission, 1997).

In this study, 3 of the 6 ATSI women (Cassie, Jarrah, and Roseanna) had their children removed from their care by CPS. Notably, 2 Aboriginal women in the study (Geraldine and Cheryl) did not have children with their abusive partner. Thus, of the 4 ATSI women with children, only Melissa did not experience removal of her children. Melissa was, however, very fearful that her children could be removed and was reluctant to call the police to respond to her violent ex-partner. Melissa's comments underlined her deep fears about CPS: "As soon as you hear [CPS] you think, right, no, I don't want any involvement. You think, you automatically—well, I thought kids taken away, that's it, no." She believed at one stage that CPS were keeping an eye on her:

> When I had my second child, that's when [CPS] were put on alert, I think by the police. . . . I thought I'm a good mother . . . when I was in that situation I was thinking, oh, my kids get fed, they get this and, you know. So I wouldn't make the call [to the police]

anymore because I was scared that my kids were going to get taken off me . . . I wouldn't call the police because I was on [CPS's] radar. (Melissa, interview 1)

Melissa managed to retain the care of her children throughout the three interviews and, to her knowledge, was not further investigated by CPS.[11] Jarrah (ATSI) had been removed from her mother's care when she was young and grew up in various out-of-home placements. Jarrah's children were also removed from her care for a period of time because of IPV. She separated from the abuser and felt very lucky to receive significant assistance from a support agency and eventually had her children returned to her care. When I asked her about her involvement with CPS at interview 1, the removal and return of her children was a recent memory, and she was wary: "My kids do not go anywhere near [CPS]. . . . Unless I'm dead. I'd ring [support worker] first, I would." In both the second and third interviews, Jarrah said she managed to avoid CPS interest in her situation.

Roseanna, an ATSI woman, has had children with several violent men, and all her children have ended up in CPS placements with different families, several of which are not ATSI families.[12] At interview 1, Roseanna said that CPS "use my kids against me, they're trying to break me, but they're not going to do it because I wouldn't let them." Roseanna says she feels like "I'm the victim with [CPS], I've been punished." Most recently, her baby was removed from her care when the child was a couple of months old. The baby's father had returned to live with Roseanna after the baby was born but soon after began to hit Roseanna again. Someone reported her to CPS, and the baby was removed, even though her abuser had left by the time she was investigated. When I met Roseanna, she was trying to hang on to her public housing so she had space for the baby to live when she was returned to Roseanna's care. Roseanna says she knows she has to "fix myself up inside," and over the course of all three interviews she continued to do courses recommended by CPS. At the time of interview 3, Roseanna's 16-year-old daughter, Mialla, was brutally bashed by Mialla's violent boyfriend. Mialla is back living with

Roseanna. Mialla has been under CPS orders for years and Roseanna feels that when "something goes tough [CPS] are always chucking her straight at me." Roseanna is worried that Mialla's presence in her home may influence CPS workers' willingness to return the baby to Roseanna's care. Mialla and the baby have different CPS workers who are attached to different offices, and Roseanna says the workers aren't communicating with each other.

Like Cassie, whose story is told later in this chapter, Roseanna has worked with many different CPS workers over the years and feels that many of them have lacked the necessary experience and did not respect her. At interview 1, Roseanna told me:

> Sometimes the workers have changed, and these are young girls that don't even have children. I don't mean to be rude, but when they're coming up to me and they're saying to me, I'm not supposed to be doing this and that. I say, hang on, these are my children, I was the one that laid back and I pushed this kid out. . . . I said, you wouldn't even know what it's like to give birth to a child, so don't even stand there and tell me how to bring my child up, I said, because that's wrong. I don't mean to disrespect them like that, but I just tell them how it is.

For black women, the experience of being told how to parent by young, white, childless women is often particularly galling; black women have often identified white women's actions as part of colonization and oppression (Huggins, 1998).

Most of the study women, including non-ATSI women, reported that when their children were removed, it was without the mother's consent. However, when Terri was at a very low point, she was encouraged by CPS workers to agree to the removal of her children. I interviewed Terri on only one occasion. Terri's partner, Julian, broke her ribs, split her eye, and scratched her face, but mostly he hit her on the body "so nobody would see the bruises." There were holes in the furniture and walls of their house. Terri called the police and help lines many times, got protection orders, and tried to separate, but Julian would always come back, sometimes climbing in the windows. If she stayed somewhere else, he would find her. She told me, "He knows everywhere, everyone." Although Julian "didn't touch the kids," they feared him. Ultimately, Terri agreed to relinquish the children to CPS until they are 18 years old, but she told me that she now has deep regrets about this:

> I signed them over because of domestic violence I left them there because you get so scared . . . there's just that feeling inside you want your kids to be safe, different to what you never had. I don't want to see Dad hit Mum, broken stuff; we can't go to school because we don't have no food because Dad took the money. So I did that for them . . . someone just came around with a piece of paper and just sat down and talked to me about the kids being with the carers until they're 18. . . . [Julian] wasn't there at all. I breached him and charged him but [CPS workers] still came in and took the kids for it. It's quite confusing. . . . I think about it every day because I miss my kids like really, really bad and we've got like photos of them all over my house. I want them back.

Women tried to protect their children from harm; several of the women felt that there were real safety concerns for their children and understood why they were removed. But even when there were good reasons for CPS intervention, women often expressed frustration with how they were treated by workers and the uncertainty they experienced. Lyn's children were removed from her care because of IPV. Lyn has an intellectual disability and struggles with reading and writing. At the time of interview 1, she had separated from her abuser and was taking a number of courses directed by CPS workers. By the time of interview 3, Lyn felt she had done everything that had been asked of her, and yet her children had still not been returned to her care. At interview 3, she said she had a court hearing coming up and that CPS planned to seek another 1-year care order. Lyn remained hopeful and tried to hang on to her three-bedroom social housing in case the kids came back.

Cassie's Experience

There is a multifaceted relationship between IPV, intergenerational trauma, and CPS intervention experienced by ATSI people (Blagg et al., 2018). Cassie's story highlights this complexity. Her experience illustrates the pressures placed on women to leave a violent abuser, the complicated relationship women have with CPS workers, and the effects of intergenerational trauma. Her comments in interview 3 in relation to not wanting to give up on her abusive ATSI partner, Glen, because "in his whole life, he's always had people give up on him," are particularly compelling in their reflection of the marginalization of ATSI people in Australia in all aspects of their lives (Blagg et al., 2018). Like many women in this study, Cassie felt uncertain about what she was expected to do to ensure her children were returned and felt she was not respected by some of the CPS workers she interacted with.

> ***Cassie, interview 1:*** *All of the new [CPS workers] that don't have any experience . . . and walk around thinking they know everything and . . . telling you how to work out of a textbook.*

Cassie is guarded when I meet her at a service that provides her with support. She seems to huddle in her chair. Gradually, as the interview progresses, her voice becomes more forceful and her posture opens up. Cassie met Glen about 5 years earlier, and they separated 6 months before our first interview. Both Cassie and Glen are Aboriginal people. They are both in their 20s and have several children together. All their children are on CPS orders and living with Cassie's family members. Cassie currently relies on social security benefits.

Cassie and Glen met when Cassie was buying cannabis from him. She has had a habit since her teens but hasn't used it in a while. During their relationship, Glen sporadically used amphetamines. On paydays he would go on a bender. At first, his drug use wasn't an issue in their relationship, but after about a year he began to hit Cassie, once breaking her nose. The neighbors called the police on that occasion and the police took out a protection order, even though Cassie didn't want one.[13] Police and social workers visited Cassie in the hospital and encouraged her to follow through on criminal charges, but she didn't want Glen to be charged. She says: "I always thought I could change him. That was my biggest thing is that, I thought I could change him . . . I'm sorted, I can deal with this."

After this hospital stay, Cassie took a short break from Glen, but they soon got back together. He continued to hit her sometimes. She says the protection order didn't really make any difference: "Most of the time when he went off it was . . . he reckons I pushed him to the point where he just lost it. Sometimes he couldn't even . . . remember doing it, blanked out . . . as soon as he'd realize what he'd done, he'd be, 'Oh, I'm so sorry.'" I ask Cassie if she felt Glen controlled her. She is visibly annoyed by the suggestion and says, "Everyone keeps saying that he was doing this to me, he was doing that to me. . . . I'm not sticking up for him. He wasn't trying to make me stay at home. He wasn't making me do everything with him." She describes Glen's violence as "fighting."[14]

The police were called by neighbors and bystanders many times, and police often wanted to charge Glen with breaches of the protection order, but Cassie resisted this. On another occassion when Cassie went to hospital, after being injured by Glen, she took the children with her to the hospital. This time Glen was charged with breach of the protection order and placed on a good-behavior order. He later breached this order when he was charged with drug possession. After this, CPS started to visit Cassie and the kids:

> just to make sure the kids were safe. . . . I always said to them that we didn't do [drugs] in front of the kids; it was always done away from the kids. . . . We tried not to fight in front of the kids. If we were fighting my oldest daughter would always take the youngest ones in the room with them and she'd go and play with them in her room.

Late last year there was a complaint about Glen being violent to one of the children. Cassie denies this happened, but, as a result, all the children have been removed from Cassie's care. They are on temporary CPS orders. Cassie says there are several months of the orders to go.

Glen was charged with violent offenses against other people a couple of months after the children were removed, and his bail was refused and so he is on remand. Cassie has had another child while Glen has been in custody, and this child was removed into care three days after the birth. Cassie says she doesn't know why, given that Glen is in jail. She has supervised visits with all the children once a week. Cassie has also found out Glen was unfaithful to her. For Cassie, this was the last straw. She says:

> I've accepted phone calls [from jail] because I want closure, I want to be able to say to him it's over, that you've done the wrong thing and it's over. Because I always said to him I don't give a shit what you do to me but if I find out that you've ever cheated on me . . . then it's over. I will not take you back.

Cassie's CPS workers are all very young and inexperienced with parenting. But Cassie is doing the parenting programs and counseling they recommend. She says the counseling "shows you what my relationship with Glen looked like and what a good relationship should look like." Cassie says she has learned a lot:

> Especially since I've stopped smoking pot. My head is that clear it's not funny. I think to myself I'm a fucking idiot for staying with him. Why did I put up with this shit for so long? I think to myself, I think the biggest reason was I thought that I could change him. Now I realize that I couldn't change him. I'm never going to be able to change him. If he wants to change, he has to change for himself, no one else.

She says she will never have him back. At this time, she takes antidepressants and other medication to help her sleep. She spends two days a week visiting her children in various placements. The travel on public transport takes a lot of time and is expensive.

> ***Cassie, interview 2:*** *The workers are younger than me. They don't even have kids. The one that I just had before was just having her first kid. I said to her, ". . . have fun. Seriously, now you're going to find out why." They have to do everything by the book. I said, "You raise a kid out of a book. You can't. Every single day you are learning something new about each other."*

At our second interview, 9 months later, Cassie and I meet at a cafe. I buy a Coke for her and a coffee for me. Cassie is in the mood for talking and wants to explain how her children were removed from her care. She says the family were sitting down for lunch together when CPS workers came to the house with the police. She says they forced open the door, and two police held her on the sofa while CPS workers took the children out to a waiting taxi. Glen was handcuffed to the fence, but the police released him briefly so he could give the children a hug. Cassie says the children were gone before she could say goodbye.

Four different CPS workers have worked with Cassie over the past 3 years. She finds it frustrating that they are all so young, don't have children, and want to rely on textbooks in telling her how to parent. But she is glad the children have been placed with family members so she can see them.

Glen is still on remand awaiting trial, and Cassie has been visiting him She says: "If he gets a guilty verdict . . . no matter what, I'm walking away. Because I have to. Because if I don't walk away from him, I'm never going to get my kids back. . . . If he gets acquitted then we'll work on getting our kids back together." She says she never feared Glen, but the worst thing in their life was "us fighting all the time. Usually it was about money and not having what we needed. Most of it was because we both had a drug habit."

Cassie says she is taking her antidepressants and continuing with her counseling. She smokes cannabis now and then and tells me she had a smoke before meeting me, but she is trying to stop. When she is at home, she is bored and doesn't like being alone, so the cannabis helps her sleep. Cassie has social housing and still receives social security, and after all her bills are paid, she manages to live on about $100 (USD69) a week. Her big expense is public transport to visit the children and jail and attend her CPS-ordered appointments. She gets no help with these expenses.

> ***Cassie, interview 3:*** *So we're up for another [case plan] in about a month or so. Because I didn't have my lawyer there with me [at the last one]. Definitely with the next one, I'm definitely taking my lawyer . . . because they're sitting there and they're asking me what do I want. I say to them what's the point of asking me. . . . You know what I want and you haven't done anything—like I keep saying I want my kids at home on the weekends.*

It is 8 months since our second interview when we meet again. Cassie is still taking antidepressants and says she "was up and down with the pipe. I quit again for 3 weeks and I'm afraid I started smoking again." The housing department is trying to get her to move into a small apartment, but she is resisting. Cassie is trying to hang on to her house so that she has space for her children when they come back.

Cassie has a new CPS worker who talks down to her and always tells her "to prioritize." She says: "I do understand where [CPS] is coming from taking the kids." But taking them for this long and seeing that Glen in jail, it doesn't make sense to her. She feels that at her recent case plan meeting, because she didn't have a lawyer present, she might have missed out on getting more contact time with the kids. Despite this, her contact with the children is increasing, and some of the children now have short periods of unsupervised contact with her. The current CPS worker has said she will work with Cassie and Glen together when he gets out of jail. Cassie feels she struggles to be heard by CPS workers, and her telephone calls to them are often not returned.

Glen was sentenced to a prison term for the violent offenses. Cassie was ready to give character evidence, but in the end she wasn't called. Glen has already served almost 2 years and is due for parole soon. Cassie says he has a lot of courses to do, including domestic violence and drug courses, before he can be released. She tells me:

> Like I keep saying, I don't want to give up on him because everybody is—in his whole life, he's always had people give up on him. I keep saying I don't want to do that. But then I sit down and I think to myself, if I didn't have him on the back burner . . . I'd have my kids back now . . . I just hope he's a changed person. He hasn't got anyone else. I don't want my kids' father to be out on the street.

CONCLUSIONS: IMPROVING THE CHILD PROTECTION RESPONSE IN IPV CASES

It is now well recognized that children are often harmed where there is IPV, even when they are not directly in the line of violence (Broady & Gray, 2018; Langenderfer-Magruder, Alven, Wilke, & Spinelli, 2019, p. 2), and in some circumstances there may be good reasons to remove children into alternative care when there is IPV. Relatedly, it is important that complaints about child abuse are taken seriously and appropriately investigated. Although these issues are not disputed, the women's stories outlined in this chapter identify significant shortcomings in how CPS workers understood IPV and responded to the women's experiences.

Many of the study women highlighted disconnections and overlaps between legal systems and how those disconnections contributed to issues of safety and secondary trauma. Some felt blamed and held to account by service providers for their partner's abuse. Abusive partners' misuse of the CPS complaints process was identified by several women, with some reporting that malicious complaints led to lengthy and intrusive investigations in which complaints were, ultimately, unsubstantiated. Malicious complaints to CPS by an abusive ex-partner can be an example of systems abuse (S. L. Miller & Smolter, 2011, pp. 637–638) and an extension of coercive control (Stark, 2007). In circumstances where there is a known history of the reporting party engaging in IPV against the person he or she is reporting, it may be appropriate for both parties to be investigated. The knowledge that the complainant will also be subjected to scrutiny may discourage some perpetrators from making malicious complaints. This approach may lead to additional or extended investigation, but overall it may be in the best interests of the children and the person who has experienced IPV (Douglas & Fell, 2020). Certainly, CPS workers need to be educated about the kinds of coercive control tactics that might be harnessed by an abuser, including tactics like false reporting that may appear to be benign.

The women's stories show, again (Human Rights and Equal Opportunity Commission, 1997; Tilbury, 2009; Trocmé et al., 2004), that particularly vulnerable women, and especially ATSI women, present significant challenges that CPS workers are often ill-equipped to respond to. Finally, even when women appreciated there were dangers for their children, they sometimes were confronted with CPS workers who were disrespectful and demeaning in their treatment. This kind of treatment can be experienced as a form of secondary abuse, amplifying the experience of IPV.

Many of the experiences relayed by interviewees identified shortcomings in the response that may be due, in part, to insufficient IPV training (Fusco, 2013). When women get the help or referrals they need, they are much more likely to be able to keep their children safe (Mandel, 2010). When Sandra received an ultimatum from CPS that she should leave or risk having her children removed, CPS workers assisted her with a "solid plan" that connected her to the services and support she needed to maintain her own safety and that of the children. Most of the women who participated in the study did not have such a positive experience.

Some of the issues women, and consequently their children, faced when coming into contact with CPS can be attributed to the disconnections and overlaps between legal systems (Hester, 2012). These concerns were exemplified in Shelley's story. Shelley was concurrently involved in the child protection, family law, and criminal justice systems. Each system carried out a discrete examination. For the criminal law system, the question was whether an assault could be proved; in the child protection system, the question was whether there was a parent willing and able to protect the children from harm; and for the family law system, the question was what was in the best interests of the children (Australian Law Reform Commission and New South Wales Law Reform Commission,

2010). Yet if a consideration of IPV had been placed at the center of all three investigations in a coordinated way from the outset, as Shelley requested, this may have significantly affected the findings of all three systems, and the conclusions (withdrawal of the criminal matter, unsubstantiated child protection concerns, and a custody determination that it was in the best interests of the children to remain with Shelley) may have been reached much more quickly. Shelley's story highlights the pivotal need for collaboration between systems, including police, CPS workers, and the parties' lawyers and support workers (Humphreys, Healey, Kirkwood, & Nicholson, 2018; Laing et al., 2018).

As many of the chapters in this book show, women experience not only direct physical harm from their partners but also "injuries that come from the bureaucracies within institutions that do not respond to their needs and instead disrespect and mistreat them and further exacerbate their marginalization" (Montesanti & Thurston, 2015, p. 11). This experience of marginalization through the child protection system is clearly reflected in the women's stories in this chapter, but perhaps most keenly by ATSI women who must navigate child removal not only in the context of IPV but within a complex and continuing experience of colonization, oppression, and ongoing trauma (Purske, 2019).

NOTES

1. The relevant legislation in Queensland, where the study took place, is the Child Protection Act 1999 (Qld).
2. At the time of interview 3, Shelley, Rosa (CALD), and Doya (CALD) had their children returned to their care; Jarrah (ATSI) had her children returned to her care shortly prior to the first interview.
3. Civil IPV protection orders obtained via the Domestic and Family Violence Protection Act 2012 (Qld) (Australasian Institute of Judicial Administration [AIJA], 2020, [7]).
4. The CPS operator's response suggests she was well aware of the links between an abuser's suicide threats and the high risk of future harm to his partner (J. Campbell et al., 2003).
5. See Chapter 6 for further discussion of lawyers.

6. Such applications or orders are called cross or mutual orders or applications (Douglas & Fitzgerald, 2013; Durfee & Goodmark, 2019).
7. Since these interviews were conducted, legislation has been introduced that makes it possible for a party to be required to cross-examine the other party through a lawyer in these circumstances (AIJA, 2020, [6]; Corbett & Summerfield, 2017; Kaye, Wangmann, & Booth, 2017).
8. Depending on the facts and circumstances of the particular case, the family court may order that the parties to child-related proceedings take part in an assessment conducted by a family consultant. This will result in the production of a family report (AIJA, 2020, [10.4]; Field, Jeffries, Rathus, & Lynch, 2016).
9. This was a justice examination order. A member of the community can ask for a such an order if they believe a person is suffering from a mental illness and should be examined by a mental health practitioner. A justice of the peace or magistrate issues the order (Shanahan et al., 2018, [161,120C.5]).
10. Depending on the child's maturity and level of understanding, the child's views may be taken into account (Parkinson & Cashmore, 2009).
11. For more about Melissa's experience, see Chapter 9.
12. Pursuant to the Aboriginal and Torres Strait Islander Child Placement Principle, ATSI children should remain connected to their family, community, and culture (AIHW, 2019, p. 54).
13. In Australia, police can apply for protection orders on behalf of a person (AIJA, 2020, [7.1]).
14. Some scholars have argued that IPV may be experienced differently between some Aboriginal people, who may experience it as fighting (Nancarrow, 2019).

Policing Intimate Partner Violence

INTRODUCTION

Police are recognized as key front-line responders to intimate partner violence (IPV), and they are often the first on the scene (Morgan, 2011). Responding to IPV is such a common part of police efforts that it is now understood as "ordinary" and "pervasive" in police work (Barlow & Walklate, 2020). How police respond can have important ramifications for the ongoing safety of women and their children, including underpinning women's decisions to call police for future incidents (Barrett, Peirone, Cheung, & Habibov, 2017; Goodman-Delahunty & Corbo Crehan, 2015). Research worldwide indicates that positive and appropriate police responses may save the lives of those who have experienced IPV (Dowling, Morgan, Boyd, & Voce, 2018; Felson, Ackerman, & Gallagher, 2005; Leisenring, 2012).

This chapter begins with a consideration of study women's decisions to call police. Similar to other research (Leisenring, 2012; Stewart, Langan, & Hannem, 2013, pp. 278–281), the women in this study highlight some frustration and disappointment with police intervention in their cases. Several researchers have linked this negative experience to a masculine police culture (Hoyle & Sanders, 2000; Meyer, 2011; Westmarland, 2001) that is reflected in the study women's common experiences of their interactions with police. Three interrelated themes were identified and are discussed in this chapter: police failing to understand the dynamics of IPV, often

Women, Intimate Partner Violence, and the Law. Heather Douglas, Oxford University Press (2021). © Oxford University Press.
DOI: 10.1093/oso/9780190071783.003.0006

failing to recognize nonphysical forms of IPV; a sense that the police were aligning with the abuser; and police failing to intervene where there were children in the relationship. These themes point to the continued need for cultural change in policing. The women in this study did have some positive experiences with police, and some women drew on some unexpected safety strategies involving police, which are considered in the final section of the chapter. The chapter concludes with suggestions about how to encourage cultural change in the police response to IPV.

CONTACT WITH POLICE

Most of the study women reported at the first interview that they had had contact with police in response to IPV ($n = 59$ of 65; 91%) at some stage in their relationship with their partner or after separation. A slightly smaller number ($n = 54$; 83%) had had contact with police in the 12 months before the first interview. Although contacting police has been identified as the most common type of help-seeking for women who have experienced IPV, most women who have experienced IPV never contact the police (Meyer, 2011). However, most of the study women were engaged with support services, had experienced multiple forms and instances of abuse, had protection orders, or reported fear of death, and all of these factors increase the likelihood of calling police (Birdsey & Snowball, 2013, p. 7; Dowling et al., 2018, p. 19; MacQueen & Norris, 2016). At the second interview, 18 of 59 women (30%) said they had had contact with the police in response to IPV between the first and second interviews, and 15 of 54 women (28%) reported they had had contact with police between the second and third interviews.

Most women ($n = 49$ of 54; 91%) who reported having contact with the police in the 12 months preceding the first interview said that they had called the police at least once over that period. When asked who had called them the most recent time in the past 12 months before the first interview, 15 women reported that others had alerted the police on their behalf. Three said their abusive partner had called the police, 1 reported her new partner had called them, 1 said her child had called, and 2 reported that a neighbor or friend had called the police. Several women ($n = 7$) reported that a service (IPV support worker, ambulance worker, student counselor, child protection officer, or hospital staff) had contacted police on the most recent occasion, and on one occasion the police contact was the result of a drug investigation. In some instances, women reported that more than one person had called the police on their behalf.

Aboriginal and Torres Strait Islander (ATSI) women may be less likely than other women to call the police in response to IPV. Research in Australia suggests that ATSI people have a distrust of police, the criminal justice system, and mainstream services (Birdsey & Snowball, 2013). As in other postcolonial societies, police have been and continue to be implicated in dispossession, deaths in custody, and child removal (Bluett-Boyd, 2005). Although there was only a small sample of 6 ATSI women in this study, all of them had had contact with the police over the course of their relationship, although only one woman had called them herself. Perhaps exemplifying the lack of trust many ATSI people have in the police, Roseanna (ATSI), explained that although she wasn't the one to call the police, they came around all the time to her place. In response to IPV, Roseanna believed police intervention had underpinned decisions by child protection services (CPS) to remove most of her children from her care. She said: "I've got no trust in them. I don't trust the police, I don't."

Women identified many reasons for not calling the police, including that the IPV they experienced was not "enough" for police. Yvonne, who had never called the police, explained:

> I guess there was a lot of psychological stuff, and they were more threats than actual actions. But there was that point where I felt like I was treading a very thin line, so I think that's why. I didn't think the threat was real enough or tangible enough for someone else to take seriously, like the police.

Similar to findings in other studies (Dowling et al., 2018, p. 19), women's reasons for calling the police varied. They included wanting the police to stop the violence, provide protection or protect the children. More than half of the women who had contacted the police believed they were at risk of very serious injury when they called them. Research by Barrett and colleagues shows that the biggest predictor for a woman seeking assistance from police is that she believes her life is in danger (Barrett et al., 2017, p. 16; Barrett & St. Pierre, 2011, p. 58; see also Ackerman & Love, 2014).

In circumstances where a protection order was in place with a "no-contact" condition, it was common for women in the study to call the police when there was an incident of contact, including verbal abuse and threats (Kothari et al., 2012). To begin with, women often expected that the perpetrator would be charged with a breach offense. Over time, however, women generally came to see police responses to such complaints as inadequate. In their second and third interviews, some women reported that they had given up reporting breaches of protection orders because it was futile or, if they did report, they often did not expect action to be taken (Goodman-Delahunty & Corbo Crehan, 2015, p. 1020). For example, at interview 3, Jennifer said: "Who's going to help me? There is nobody out there to help me. I mean, you hear me but can you help me? No. The police take note of what I say, but what do they do? Nothing. Nothing sticks to him."

Jacinta was in a relationship with James for a couple of years before his controlling and stalking intensified. Jacinta left him, but the incessant text messages, phone calls, and following continued. He would often be parked on her street. Although Jacinta called the police several times to report the behavior, each time the police determined that it was not threatening or dangerous. She said, "The police don't do anything. They just gather things will get better." At interview 3 Jacinta said that James's stalking and obsessive contact continued, but she had given up calling the police. When I asked why, she said, "I don't believe in the system. I don't believe it's a system that really works."

UNDERSTANDING THE DYNAMICS OF IPV

A common issue raised by the study women was that police sometimes misunderstand the context of IPV and minimize women's experiences of abuse, especially when the abuse is not physical (see also Gover, Paul, & Dodge, 2011; Li, Levick, Eichman, & Chang, 2015; Myhill, 2019, p. 60). This concern was identified by several women who said that police rarely charged breaches of protection orders in the context of nonphysical violence or contact.

All protection orders in Queensland include a condition that stipulates that the responding party must not commit IPV; in Queensland, this encapsulates coercive and controlling behavior and emotional and psychological abuse. Often protection orders also include a no-contact condition (Australasian Institute of Judicial Administration [AIJA], 2020, [7.4]). One of the reasons underlying the introduction of protection orders was to ensure that survivors of IPV and police would have a legal option that could respond to aspects of IPV that are difficult to prosecute as a criminal offense (Cattaneo, Grossman, & Chapman, 2016; Douglas & Fitzgerald, 2013). Reviews of IPV-related deaths have identified the importance of taking nonphysical abuse seriously, pointing to cases where there was obsessive contact with the victim after separation, leading to a fatality (C. Walsh, McIntyre, Brodie, Bugeja, & Hauge, 2012).

Despite the growing evidence of links between nonphysical abuse and serious harm, some of the study women's narratives show that many police they had contact with did not understand the dynamics of IPV, especially the serious impact and danger of nonphysical abuse. For example, Monica was recently separated after a long relationship of 15 years and had several children with her ex-partner. Monica's ex-partner sent numerous text messages to her on the day he killed someone close to her. The messages mentioned a range of topics, including his love for their children, and they breached the no-contact condition of her temporary protection order. Monica had showed the messages to police throughout the day of the murder, but they had failed to act. She said: "I'd show them the text messages. They'd read them and go, 'Well, they're not threatening.' [They] don't understand this bloke."

Some women researched police manuals and policy documents and challenged police inaction. Kim described the "selective practices of police" in responding to breaches of protection orders that did not involve physical violence. She had reported many incidents where her ex-partner contacted her in contravention of her protection order. Kim said that the police described these breaches as "soft breaches," but she said "Breaches are breaches. There is nothing in the policy and procedure of police that mentions soft breaches. It's like being a little bit pregnant—either it's a breach or it isn't."

Kim's comment, alluding to the need for physical abuse and injury to engage a police response, was repeated by other study women. Anna asked rhetorically, "Do I have to let him physically harm me for them to do something?" Ingrid (CALD) reported that her partner had breached the protection order with calls, emails, and following her. She had reported this to the police, "but because it's not violence, the police don't bother to do anything." Similarly, Shuang (CALD) said that in her experience the police "couldn't do much unless very, very violent stuff happened." While Shuang's comment suggests that police did not have the necessary power to respond to nonphysical behaviors that were in breach of protection order conditions, in most cases contact breaches of noncontact conditions in protection orders are well within police power to enforce.

In any event, and worryingly, physical abuse may not even be enough to ensure police engagement when the threat of future imminent abuse appears to have dissipated. For example, Faith said that her ex-partner, Ryan, had come to her house "screaming abuse," threatening to kill her, and banging on the front and back doors to get in. He then went under the house and started to bang a broom on the floor of Faith's bedroom. Faith explained:

> I had locked myself and the children in my bedroom and pushed the drawers against my door. The children and I were very scared. The police took 2 hours to turn up. When they did [turn up,] we noticed

> that he had snapped a key into the lock of my front door. Ryan had fallen asleep downstairs. The police left him there.

When they attended, the police spoke to Faith about taking out a protection order but did not offer to assist her or investigate possible criminal charges, even though there was a damaged lock and threats to kill.

Although a police focus on physical abuse was reported to be common, Evie's positive experience with police on reporting nonphysical violence was encouraging, at least initially. At the time of the first interview, she had been separated for about 2 months from a violent partner with whom she had lived for 3 years. They had a young child together, and she had a protection order with a no-contact condition. She told me:

> He sent a message Friday morning at half past two in the morning. I went to the police and I breached him on it. They took a photo of it, then I made a statement and then I signed it and then they said they would go pick him up . . . [the police officer] was listening to what I had to say. Because I didn't want to waste his time over a text message but he said, "No, that's what the order is for." . . . Because I think that if I let it go, he's going to think that he can keep doing it, so I've got to show that, no, I'm not going to put up with it anymore.

Notably, Evie's abuser had a long criminal history for many violent offenses unrelated to IPV and had served time in custody. It's possible that police identified him as a "true" or "real" criminal and therefore worth their attention (Gover, Paul, & Dodge, 2011, p. 627).

A number of the interviewees recounted that their IPV complaints were not taken as seriously as allegations that their abuser had been driving under the influence of alcohol, watching child pornography, or growing cannabis. Some said that while assaults on the woman might not be investigated, it was a different story when the abuser assaulted a police officer. Terri reported her abuser's IPV to the police several times, but "the crunch came when he assaulted police . . . and child safety came around then." Hannah reported an incident of physical violence to the police but was told she couldn't get a protection order. She later told the police about her abuser's erratic and drunken driving with the children in the car. She said, "They were more interested in the fact that he was drink-driving, to be honest, than in him hitting me." Her partner was charged with driving under the influence.

Susan's Experience

Susan's story highlights the strategic and tactical approach her ex-partner used to continue his abuse after separation, within ambiguously lawful boundaries. Susan said that Neil sent "veiled" threats embedded in messages that at face value appeared to be about their child, he seemed to turn up everywhere for reasons that might be explicable, and wore a men's rights T-shirt to handovers as a tactic of intimidation. Susan experienced these behaviors as a continuation of abuse, but when she reported them to police, she worried that police considered her "crazy" or a "nut job." Susan's experience of police not charging breaches of protection orders in the context of nonphysical violence also reflects a common experience of women in the Study.

> ***Susan, interview 1:*** *It's [the] police service that is throwing up barriers to me. . . . Completely ignoring me. I'm on the brink of lodging a formal complaint. . . . Every single time he's done something, I've reported it to the police. Every single time nothing has happened. . . . I really want to make a statement but in my experience with police, even getting someone to take a statement from me is like drawing blood from a stone.*

Susan meets me in my office for the interview. She studied at the university where I work, and she was curious to return. Susan was born in Australia, but her parents were born overseas. She brings a big folder of documents that she checks often during the interview. She speaks quickly and urgently and is keen to get started. The first thing she wants to talk about is how frustrated and angry she is about the police. We backtrack a little and talk about her relationship with her ex-partner, Neil. They started out as friends, then dated on and off for a while before moving in together. They have a 2-year-old child, Hugo, and separated about a year ago. On the day she decided to "finally" leave Neil, she took Hugo and some of her things with her and went to live with her parents. Susan earns enough to live independently and take care of her child; she has a university degree and a full-time job in a professional role, but her parents are worried about her. Susan experienced some physical violence and stalking during the relationship, but since she separated from Neil, his threats of violence, stalking, and intimidation have intensified. A few months ago, with assistance from a private lawyer, she got a protection order. She was able to show copies of many abusive and threatening text messages to the court as evidence. Conditions of the protection order state that Neil must have no contact with her unless it's about their child, and he must not commit IPV. She also has an interim order from the family court that orders their child, Hugo, live with Susan and that Neil has contact a few times a week.

Neil has breached the protection order often, and Susan is scared. "I think he is going to kill me," she says. "He is really clever and calculating. He thinks carefully about everything he does, and he's been very calculating in the way that he'll breach the order." After the last contact visit, he slipped her wedding and engagement rings into the child's bag after a contact visit along with a message that read, "We should all be happy together." He sprayed his fragrance over Hugo and his belongings—a fragrance Susan bought for Neil when they were together. She believes he hacked her email and follows her, although she can't be sure and wonders if she is being paranoid. She says "he is still obsessed" with her, and he is always "there." Neil sends Susan many text messages every day; to stay within the conditions of the protection order, they always mention their child, but the messages also include "veiled" threats referring to her taking "one-way trips" and doing things "too late." Susan thinks the messages are threatening and breach the no-contact condition under her protection order because they go beyond talking about Hugo. She has reported them to the police on numerous occasions—too many to remember them all—but the police have not charged Neil. On one occasion when she reported text messages to police, a male police officer laughed at her and asked if she was serious.

> ***Susan, interview 2:*** *They [abusers] need to be held accountable, and it's not happening. I cannot put it down to anything else, other than the failure of police . . . just being completely inept and lazy, and not being trained on what constitutes domestic violence. Maybe they're jaded and they see my situation as relative to other women, who do come in stabbed. They're not actually doing their job. . . . They cannot turn you away, but that's what they've done.*

I meet Susan 11 months after our first interview, and she is now working her way through child custody processes. The family court has ordered a family report and reports about Neil's and her mental health.[1] Their child, Hugo, still lives with Susan and has regular contact with Neil, but the contact handovers are tense. Susan says she takes prescription medication before a child handover to "take the edge off the situational anxiety." She thinks Neil has joined a father's rights group because he always wears a black T-shirt with the insignia of one of these groups. He only wears it to handovers, not to the court, "for intimidation purposes." He usually takes it off as he drives away. Susan passed him in the supermarket the other day, and he said, "You know I'm going to get you."

She still has a protection order, and Neil continues to send messages and photographs to her all the time. She has made many more complaints to police but is always told she doesn't have enough evidence. She says, "I have recordings of him making statements—there's innuendo. It's threatening, but it's a veiled threat, which could be interpreted different ways. So, of course, when he gets interviewed by police, he'll say, oh, I didn't mean it like that, I meant it like this." Susan continues to report these incidents to the police, but they sometimes refuse to take her statement or tell her to come back another time. She recalls, "I said, 'Do I have to show up here black and blue? He's too smart for that, he's not going to lay a hand on me. I'll show up here dead before I show up black and blue.' . . . He laughed at me."

On one occasion, to make it easier for police, Susan wrote her own statement. She says this seemed to annoy the police, and Neil has still not been charged with breaching the protection order. A few months ago, Susan started a new relationship with a police officer. She says it is complicated, but he gives her lots of advice about police powers, although she is careful not to drop his name when she engages with the police on her case. She says, "The fact that he's a cop isn't the only reason I'm with him, obviously . . . it helps. Obviously, I feel very secure with him . . . he's really angry and embarrassed that I'm getting treated this way by police." Susan says, "I hate to use the term, but I feel I'm just getting cock-blocked everywhere . . . it's been all men."

> ***Susan, interview 3:*** *Maybe with my history of constantly reporting breaches they might think, oh, she's a bit of a nut job. But I've actually not reported a lot of them because I've just become so disenchanted by the Police Service, what's the point, they don't even take my statement.*

It is 7 months since I last met with Susan. She says her car was damaged the previous week. The tires were let down while it was parked in her driveway, and there are key marks along the side of the vehicle. She thinks Neil was responsible, but she can't prove it. She thinks Neil has been following her to the supermarket, to her work, and to her new partner's house. He seems to turn up everywhere. He's continued to send many texts and emails to her and members of her family that are "veiled threats." He has also been posting photos and messages about their son, Hugo, Susan, and her police officer partner on Facebook. She's blocked Neil, but her friends have told her about the posts. Susan was able to get a new protection order after the old one ran out. She has started reporting the most recent breaches to a different police station where she says the police treat her with dignity and take her statements. A few months ago, police charged Neil with three breaches of the protection order, and although he contested the charges, he was found guilty and fined. The breaches all related to Neil contacting Susan in breach of the protection order conditions. Susan is pleased about this, but she feels "disenchanted" with the police service and says she continues to "meet with resistance." She has read the police procedures manual, and she sends a compliment to any police officer who does his or her job in line with the manual. She says, "I hate to think what women who aren't literate or just can't stand up for themselves do. The police tell them to go away and they go away. I'm not going away." Her family court matter is ongoing; for now their child still lives with Susan, with weekly contact with Neil. She has managed to continue working full-time and is living with her parents.

ALIGNING WITH ABUSERS

There is a long history of feminist research showing how law is culturally masculine and how this culture is entwined with assumptions about women's lack of credibility (Tuerkheimer, 2017) and lack of rationality (Smart, 1989, p. 91). A number of the women's stories suggest police skepticism about women's credibility and provide examples of police negating women's expressions of fear and anger as irrational and dangerous. In turn, this leads women to believe that police take sides with their abuser and privilege his versions of events and even his life.

Study women who called the police often did so in a state of distress while, from their perspective, their abusive partner appeared to present as rational and in control of himself and the situation. Several women stated that their abusive partner had manipulated the police when they arrived on the scene, and this sometimes led to blame for the violence being shifted to the woman. For example, Frieda called the police for the first time when her partner physically assaulted her. When police attended, an officer spoke to Frieda's abuser privately. The police officer then told Frieda, "He feels very nagged in the relationship, and you really need to think about, are you putting too much pressure on him," Frieda summed up how this statement made her feel: "So she was just like basically placing all the blame on me and completely downplaying or dismissing or agreeing with him that he didn't do it." Monica related a similar experience. She remembered police attending on numerous occasions when she was still living with her partner. She said, "As soon as he would see the police, he would act like the perfect gentleman. I was usually, by that stage, upset. I was always, like I was a mess. . . . He promised he'll stop, he'll do this . . . he'd be totally violent, and then he'd see the police turn up and his whole demeanor would change, like, instantly."

Many women reported their fear of being perceived as irrational ("crazy," "a nut case," "overreacting") when compared with their apparently rational abuser. Colleen said her experience with police had been "awful" because she felt they did not take her seriously. She said, "One thing a woman fears more than anything is she's coming across as the hysterical one. The men are really good at this. They're really good at saying, 'Look how crazy she is.' Because I poked her with sticks for 5 years and look how angry she is."

Bianca reported her partner's suicide threat to the police. The police attended to check out the situation and found her partner, Tom, sitting in a car with his guns (he planned to go hunting the next day). The police took Tom to a health service, and he returned home later in the evening, but they didn't ask Bianca about what had preceded the suicide threat, so she didn't tell them about the violence he had committed leading up to it. Bianca said that she thought the police "were pleasant enough," but she "got the impression" that they thought she was "overreacting" to the situation. Yet, research has been available for many years that establishes that the abusive partner's suicide threats and access to weapons are both significant risks for future harm (J. Campbell et al., 2003), suggesting that Bianca's call was far from an overreaction.

Anna had the experience of being made to feel as if she was overreacting and being blamed for placing herself in a situation where she was fearful. She went to the police station to report a breach of the protection order, and her abusive ex-partner was there being questioned about a previous breach of the protection order. Terrified, Anna hid in the women's bathroom, and when she eventually came out the police told her, " 'He won't do anything.' [They said] ' . . . the situation would have been avoided if you'd just gone somewhere else,' and I was like, 'I was told to attend my local police station.' That was my local police station."

Women "underreacting" can be a problem, too. Lisa called the police late one night to report that her abuser was on her property in contravention of a protection order. He threw rocks through the windows, smashing glass, and the paws of one of her dogs were cut. Despite feeling terrified, Lisa said, "I didn't scream, I didn't cry, I didn't make a noise, I was not going to give that person standing on the other side of my window any satisfaction knowing that they had scared me." She thinks her failure to react appropriately on the phone explained why no police turned up that night. Lisa said they were too busy, but a police photographer visited the following day.

Simply stated, women felt it was often a struggle to get police to believe their version of events. Julia's extended story (told later in this chapter) is a good example: The police believed her partner's claim that he did not make the handprint on her face. Cassie (ATSI) had a lot of contact with police, although it was usually bystanders who called them. She relates one incident when the police attended after her partner, Glen, punched her in the face, breaking her nose:

> The copper comes up to me and says, "Oh, OK, what happened?" I said, "Well that fuckhead just punched me in the nose." He goes, "Well, the story is that you were the one that was being violent and you're the one that had—you were the one that had the attitude." I said, "Excuse me? Can you see my face? Do you see the blood running out of my nose? If you want to talk to me like that, I'll just go."

Although Cassie wasn't charged or arrested, some of the study women were. Vera (CALD) said that her Australian-born partner, Nigel, assaulted her, but he called the police. By the time police arrived, Vera was distressed. Vera and Nigel gave conflicting accounts of who had assaulted whom. Vera said when the police arrived at the house, "He's pretending—he's using crutch for the police that day. He never used crutch. He cry and cry to the police, and he's using a crutch so the police will not charge him. He pretends that he is a cripple man." Ultimately, Vera was arrested, charged with assault, and kept in a police cell overnight; the charge was later withdrawn. Janet had a similar experience. One night, Janet's ex-partner strangled her. She "pulled a knife out to try to defend" herself. The police arrived to see Janet with the knife, and although she tried to explain that she was trying to protect herself, "it wasn't good enough." The police made cross-protection orders against both Janet and her partner (Douglas & Fitzgerald, 2013; Durfee & Goodmark, 2019).

Sandra provided another example of being "incredible." She was in hiding from her abuser, Gary, and had a protection order in place with a no-contact condition. One night at midnight, when she was home with her two children, Gary came around to the house and banged on the door. She called the police, but Gary fled before they arrived. Sandra recalled:

> This police officer turns around and says to me, 'So how do you know it was him?" I said, "Because I've got my curtain and I was looking through the crevice of the curtain. I know his voice. I know it was him. I don't have people coming here . . . I don't have any other enemies. It's him." The police officer said, "Why didn't you get a photo?" Well, that mortified me. I am not into picture taking while someone's bashing in my front screen door . . . [he said], "Well, how do we know that you're not making this up."

In her second interview, Sandra related a more positive experience of police engagement. She had received "horrible, denigrating, and intimidating" emails, and her abuser called her on the phone regularly in breach of her protection order. Police had downloaded her phone messages and emails and used this evidence to charge her partner with breaches of the protection order. By the time of the third interview, Sandra was still routinely contacting police, mainly now about Gary's child contact breaches. Although she was generally happy with the police response, they said they were not able to help with her child contact issues.

Suggestions that women were somehow "incredible" were common and were not limited to nonphysical abuse. Several women related experiences of police challenging them about available evidence for claims of assault even where they had resulted in visible injuries. Frieda felt blamed by a police officer for causing the abuse because she "nagged" her abuser. She took it upon herself to take photographs of her injuries, including scratch marks and bruises, and she took these to the police, demanding they charge her abuser with assault. Eventually he was charged and convicted.

When their stories were challenged by police, it was common for women to feel that police were aligned with their abusers. This experience may help to explain the pressures placed on women to collect their own evidence about IPV. Women reported that they collected text messages, photo footage, and voice recordings in their efforts to convince police to support them to apply for a protection order, activate a breach of the order, or charge a criminal offense. Both Susan's and Julia's experiences, outlined earlier, describe their efforts to collect evidence of abusive messages to prove breach of the protection order.

Women who stayed with a violent abuser often felt police blamed them for the continuation of the violence. Melissa (ATSI) said her partner was physically violent to her whenever he was taking drugs and drinking alcohol. Over a long relationship they had separated and reunited several times. She recalled one occasion in which a police officer attending the house said, "I think we've seen you in your last house and you're still with him. What do you expect?" Sally also called the police on a number of occasions during her violent relationship, and the only advice she can recall from police is "Don't go back, silly." Lisa said, "I was wanting a bit more respect. [Police would say,] 'Well, we've been here before, you know, didn't we see you 3 years ago at that house down there?' I don't want a reminder. You feel silly enough." Monica asked why she should be the one to leave:

> I just thought, I don't know, I was a bit stubborn, I suppose. I just thought, why should I be—you know, it's always like—the police had come around so many times, and they're always saying, you need to go to a shelter and stuff. I was like, why should I be the one leaving,

he's the one doing the wrong thing, I'm not taking my kids, my dog—you know what I mean?

Julia's Experience

Julia reported a consistent pattern of police aligning with her abuser over nearly 3 years during the study. At the time of interview 1, Adam's behavior was excused by a police officer as "frustrated" rather than abusive. At the time of interview 2, police appeared to accept Adam's story that Julia's injury was self-inflicted despite evidence to the contrary, and at the time of interview 3, police considered only Adam's convenience in arrangements for Julia to collect her things despite the fact that it was Adam's abuse that had necessitated her leaving. Julia felt that Adam was able to "manipulate" the police.

> ***Julia, interview 1****: I still feel like the police looked at it, that it was all too hard, or that I was making it up . . . the police wouldn't be the first place that I look now. I've lost a fair amount of faith in the police, and as horrible as it sounds, and not that I would, but you can understand why people take the law into their own hands when you're made to feel that you're making it up.*

Julia and Adam separated 5 months ago after a 3-year relationship. Julia is in her early 30s, and she has a child with Adam called Billy. After Billy was born, Adam became very controlling; his favorite saying was "You just need to shut your mouth and do as you're told." Sometimes he would scream in Julia's face and stand on her foot so she couldn't move; sometimes he would hit her. He broke her glasses (she can't see without them), and she often had bruises. Out of embarrassment, she said she had become "a bit of a recluse"; she didn't go far from home and did all her shopping online. Julia and Billy are now living with Julia's mother. Julia finished high school, then did a diploma and had a job for a few years, but since having her child, she hasn't had paid employment. She is trying to sort out her social security entitlements, including child support payments. Julia supervises contact between Billy and Adam once a week at a public place like a park or shopping center. She is breastfeeding Billy, so she can't be far away, but she would like a legal order about this so she can have some certainty.

The physical abuse stopped when she left Adam, but he still contacts her all the time. On one day alone, she received 48 phone calls with "abusive" voice and text messages. Although she was worried about the "backlash" from Adam, she took her phone to the police station and showed an officer the messages. He said that Adam sounded "angry and frustrated" and told her to go and get a protection order from the court but warned that getting a protection order would "blur the lines" around child contact arrangements. Confused, upset, and feeling "like an idiot" and that the police thought she was trying to "get attention," Julia rang the police administration line. The operator suggested she try a different station. She then contacted another police station and told them about Adam's behavior, and this time also about his cannabis habit. She says police got interested then and decided to search Adam's house; they recommended she get a protection order before they did this. With the evidence of the abusive text messages and help from an IPV support service, Julia has obtained a temporary protection order and is waiting for that to be served on Adam. She has also applied for legal aid to try to get a lawyer to help her with family law issues. Police told her Adam has been charged with drug offenses.

> ***Julia, interview 2:*** *Initially the police were really quite good. They took photographs of the damage. Then they told me . . . that he would be charged for the assault. Then when I rang them to find out what was going on, I was notified that because the only third-party witness was [our child Billy] and Adam was saying that I did it to myself and no one could verify the truth, they weren't going to pursue the criminal charges.*

I catch up with Julia 10 months after our first interview. She says Adam consented to a final 2-year protection order. Julia's support worker recommended that she and Adam should do a parenting class together as this might work in their favor and help them come to an agreement about caring for their child through mediation and avoid a family court case. The classes went well, and 7 weeks ago, Julia and Adam decided they would try to live together again so they could co-parent. They went to court together and withdrew the protection order; however, with their first disagreement Adam became violent and hit Julia in the face as she was holding Billy, leaving a clear handprint on her face. Julia went to the police station immediately, but it was closed for a public holiday. She rang the police, and the operator asked if there was somewhere safe she could go. She went to her mother's place and waited for the police to attend. Some 7 hours later, the police attended to take a statement and photographs of her injuries. Julia feels that the closed police station and 7-hour wait don't "give you a lot of incentive." Initially the police officer said Adam would be charged with assault, but this did not happen. Julia says that the police seemed to believe Adam's claim that Julia's injuries were self-inflicted, which Julia found shocking. One police officer was supportive of Julia, acknowledging, "It's pretty difficult for you to get your hand in that direction." This time, a police prosecutor represented Julia to obtain a new protection order. Initially police told Julia their child, Billy, would be protected on the order too. Now the police have told her she will have to make a separate application for Billy to be included on the order. This would mean going back to court. Julia is now receiving social security and living with Billy in private rental accommodations. She hopes to get some kind of court order that allows only supervised contact between Adam and Billy in a contact center at some stage.

> ***Julia, interview 3:*** *I ended up having to pay for a removalist to go in and pack everything and move it all. Because the police told me that I would have maybe an hour if I was lucky, to grab whatever I could. They had to sort out a time that was convenient for Adam to be home from work and things like that. I just felt that they weren't really considering the fact that I am a single mum with a 2-year-old. . . . I just feel like Adam was able to manipulate the police really well in this whole situation.*

When I catch up with Julia 7 months later, she still has a protection order in place. It prohibits Adam from coming within 500 meters of her, contacting her in abusive ways, or trying to find out where she lives. The order required that the police attend Adam's house with her so she can reclaim her possessions; however, as Julia's comment shows, she feels the police were not accommodating of her situation. Adam still constantly sends text messages, calls her on the phone, and leaves abusive voicemails. He still blames her for breaking up the family and running away. She feels "angry" with the police for "not doing anything" and no longer bothers to report these incidents. She facilitates contact once a week between Billy and Adam at a play center where there is supervision. She has become increasingly worried about pursuing orders through the family court. She is concerned about the family court's assumption that there should be shared care. She thinks Billy would not be safe with Adam, and the family courts might not realize that. Julia says, "I'm happy that finally the police actually acknowledged the abuse and did something, but a lot of the process I wasn't really happy with. They lied to me a lot."

WOMEN WITH CHILDREN

Julia's story outlines the particular issues women face when they have children with the abuser. Under Australia's constitutional arrangements, Australian police who are the first responders to IPV are state-based police, while child custody issues are dealt with through the national family courts and national police (Dragiewicz, 2015, p. 128). This arrangement adds another level of complication for state police when there are children in the relationship. At the second interview, many study women (n = 37) had concurrent family law orders and protection orders in place. Police often identified inconsistencies between the conditions of protection orders and family court orders as the explanation for a refusal to act. However, even when custody orders were not in place, several women reported that state police were reluctant to become involved because of concerns that they may interfere with future child custody cases or cut off fathers from their children.

Indeed, in cases where the woman had children with the abuser but did not have a family law order, women sometimes stated that police were particularly reluctant to become involved, even when children are fully breastfed. For example, Felicity had separated from her partner, Jason; she had a protection order and an informal agreement with Jason that he could have contact with their fully breastfed baby for 2 hours a day on weekends. When Jason was very late to return the baby from a contact visit, she called the police on the emergency line. She tells me:

> The police said, "There's nothing we can do. There's no parenting orders." I said, "He's a 5-month-old baby that's being breastfed." The policeman said, "Well, can he buy him formula?" . . . [then] he said, "Why can't you just go round and pick the child up from [Jason's home]?" I said "because last time he threatened to shoot me."

Eventually Felicity was able to talk to more a senior officer and confirm that the child was allergic to dairy, did not yet eat solid food, and so may have been at risk of not being fed. It was this information, not the IPV, that demonstrated a risk of harm to the child and was the catalyst for police intervention.

Similarly, Rosa's (CALD) partner failed to return their breastfed baby to her after an informal contact visit. She became anxious and called the police, who said: "It's not like he stole the child. The child is OK with [the] father." Rosa did not understand how the police could respond in this way; she felt this would never happen in her home country. She called the police several more times, and finally a police officer advised her to go to the family courts and apply for a recovery order, a family court order allowing the federal police to recover the child and return him to Rosa (Harland, Cooper, Rathus, & Alexander, 2015, p. 296). Rosa did not see her child for a month and a half, by which time she was no longer able to breastfeed the child.

Evie related a similar story. She experienced significant physical and emotional violence from her partner, Simon, but decided to leave when he threatened to kill her. She put their baby in a carry cot and proceeded to walk out of the house. Jason snatched the carry cot from her hands, and Evie called the police. When they arrived, police asked Simon to return the child; he refused, and the police told Evie they couldn't intervene because there was no family court order. The police advised Evie to leave the house and get a recovery order.

Evie later obtained a recovery order, and the federal police returned the child to her, but this took 3 days. She found the wait terrifying.

The federal custody law trumps state law protection orders if there is any inconsistency. In cases where women had both a protection order and a family court order, inconsistencies were common, creating particular issues for women. Ingrid (CALD) observed that "the fact that there are also family court orders that allow him access to the child is a concern to the police also." Sandra was particularly frustrated with this aspect of the police response, but had some ideas for change:

> When the family court order comes into place, the police are powerless. . . . Police seem to pass the buck now there's a family court order in place. I see that the family court order needs to put conditions in that order relating to domestic violence and make it a combined one order. It will make police be able to do their job.

Doya's Experience

Doya's story highlights a number of the issues identified by study women with children who engaged with police. As an undocumented migrant woman, with limited English language skills, no access to independent finances, and no contacts in Australia, Doya was at high risk of serious IPV, and indeed she reported being strangled.[2] She faced significant barriers to seeking help (Allimant & Ostapiej-Piatkowski, 2011). Doya's central concern, after leaving her abusive partner, Bob, was the police approach to reconnecting her with her preschool-aged child and baby.

Even in a case like Doya's, where the children were very young, had spent most of their life in their mother's care, and one of the children was still breastfed, police refused to intervene. Doya's case was particularly complicated because her children were born in Australia, to an Australian father, and therefore had Australian citizenship, whereas Doya was in Australia illegally. Nevertheless, similar to many other cases in this study, police appeared to prioritize the father's relationship with the children, despite his abuse and any consideration about what might have been less disruptive and safer for the children. By the time of interview 3, Doya reported that Bob was violent at contact handovers but police refused to act.

> ***Doya, interview 1:*** *You know, I went to hospital that day, then after 2 days, I try and get my kids back from Bob, but he says no, he's not agree. Then even police said, "You can't have your kids, you will not take your kids from their father." I was, like, wondering, what? This person is trying to kill me, why he has got my kids?*

Doya is very distressed and cries often during our interview. She hasn't seen her baby and toddler for several months. Aged in her 30s and tertiary educated, Doya was born overseas and speaks English as a second language. She met her Australian partner, Bob, while they were working overseas. They moved to Australia together around 2 years ago, and their two children were born in Australia. Doya originally came to Australia on a tourist visa, but this ran out a while ago and she has been living illegally in Australia since then. Since they arrived in Australia, Bob has physically abused Doya and detained her and the children in the house they shared. Doya has no independent income and no family in Australia. Bob is tertiary educated and employed but has a drug habit and is most violent when he is coming down off the drugs. During the relationship, Doya felt that she had to "tiptoe around Bob so as not to make him angry." When he was angry, he would yell at her, calling her a "slut," "whore," and "bad mother." He would kick and punch her and sometimes put his hand over her mouth and squeeze her neck. She always had bruises on her body. Although Doya was scared he would kill her, she was also scared to contact the police because she feared deportation. In addition, Bob had told her that if she left, she would never see her children again. Two months ago, Bob tried to kill her. She ended up in hospital with serious injuries.

At the hospital, the police came to talk to Doya, and she told them she was worried about her children, especially because one was still breastfed. The police then visited Bob at home, but he wouldn't open the door. The police returned to the hospital and helped Doya to get a protection order, but they told her that she couldn't take the children away from their father.

After the police visited the hospital, CPS assessed the children as safe with their father. Bob's mother has moved in to help him care for them, and she has let Doya speak to them on the phone a few times. A support service has provided Doya with some financial aid and arranged for her to stay in a shelter. The support service has also helped her apply to the immigration department for a bridging visa, but she is worried she will be deported to her home country without her children. She feels desperate.

> ***Doya, interview 2:*** *The police maybe, you know, they don't believe me . . . that's why police not charging him, I don't know.*

Nine months later, when I speak to Doya at the second interview, she is still staying in a shelter. She is now on a bridging visa awaiting a decision about her residency in Australia. She lives on a special benefit from social security, and for the first time since arriving in Australia she has her own bank account. She has a 1-year protection order, although she is not sure what the conditions are. She has a legal aid lawyer who has arranged for interim family law orders about the children. When they went to court, Bob had many statements from his family against Doya saying she was crazy. She says, "It hurts my heart." Despite these statements, Bob consented to an order that specified the children should live with Doya and spend time with their father on the weekends. The child handovers happen at a contact center. Doya has to go back to the family court in a couple of months to find out what will happen in the longer term. She says Bob is no longer her "controller," and she thinks the protection order is helpful in keeping her safe. She recently spoke to police about criminal charges, and she is shocked that Bob will not be charged with criminal offenses in relation to the assault that resulted in her hospitalization and their separation. She wonders if the police don't believe her.

> ***Doya, interview 3:*** *Yes, because he's just fighting—calls names, you know, whatever he wants, just come in here to my house. I said, "Get out." But he's not listening to me, just do what he wants. I called police three times . . . . So then police said, "We can't—you have to talk with your lawyer." I said, "Can you go with me or pick up my kids with me, to his house?" They said, they can't do anything, you know, because you have a parenting arrangement.*

Ten months after our second interview Doya is now living in private rental accommodations with her children. She was granted a permanent resident visa in Australia. She found the immigration process very difficult and had to have meetings with people from the immigration department and write several statements, but she had good support from a local agency. She receives social security and has applied for child support from Bob. Doya and Bob have a new parenting arrangement of "50-50 equal time"; because she doesn't have a car, Bob picks up and drops off the children at Doya's house. This was arranged by consent, with Doya represented by a lawyer from legal aid. Doya finds child handovers very stressful. Bob pushes her, calls her names, snatches the kids from her, and is always late. Her first protection order expired, but because of Bob's behavior, she was able to get a new protection order. She has called the police several times over the past few weeks, but even with the new protection order, the police say they can't do anything because there is a parenting order in place. Doya says, "He's still using drugs, he has bad friends, maybe, you know, he can kill me, I don't know. I'm very scared of him."

GOOD-PRACTICE IPV POLICING

At her first interview, Lahleh (CALD) emphasized that the police found her credible and prioritized her safety: "The police were nice. They believed me. They kept my ex-husband busy, talked to him, and police helped me to put my stuff in the taxi and then they didn't let him to touch [the child]. . . . They really changed my life. They gave us a new life." Lahleh's comment shows police can play a very positive role in the transformation of women's lives. Most of the 59 women who interacted with police during the study period reported inconsistent experiences with police, but only around half of them ($n = 27$) were able to identify at least one positive experience. When asked what made an experience positive, the most common response was that police officers were kind, understanding, or compassionate and treated the woman with respect. For example, Hong (CALD) said, "Most of them, they're all right, they're trying to comfort you and find out what's going on, trying to protect you, try to—in their duty, try to do their best to help you." Although Frieda's experience was mixed, she had a positive experience of one male police officer who attended: "He just sort of listened and sort of understood . . . I guess he was just empathic and he just believed me." For Frieda, as for a number of women in the study, feeling like police officers believed her story, that she was credible, was a positive aspect of police interaction.

Study women also highlighted police assistance in obtaining a protection order as a common example of positive police behavior, even though this is expected of police in certain circumstances (Jeffries, Bond, & Field, 2013). Many of the women pointed to other positive police actions that are part of standard police operations. These included explaining a woman's options to her, taking her statement, and investigating the incident of reported violence as a potential criminal matter—including taking photos of property damage and injuries, arrest and removal of the abuser, charging the abuser, or taking the woman to safety.

Other positive practical actions the women identified, that went beyond the basic requirements of standard police operations, included police assistance and supervision when a woman packed up her belongings after leaving, staying with her until she felt safe, and following up to make sure she was not in danger days and even months after the initial police attendance. For example, Monica said, "It depends what police officer came. There was one police officer that came that was really quite good, and he'd stay quite a while . . . and make sure I was OK. He'd usually come around the next day to see if everything was still OK." Sandra said that, overall, her involvement with police has been "excellent." In her second interview she reported that "the police have been working very closely with me in a sense. They've been ringing me . . . 6 weeks would go by—Sandra, are you all right? We haven't heard from you. We haven't seen you. So they were very—quite concerned." Similarly, at her third interview and 2 years after she had separated from her partner, Skye reported that a police officer still does half-year check-ins to "make sure nothing is going on."

Having to engage with different police all the time was an issue for many women. Anna said that "it doesn't matter how many times I ring up, I feel like I'm annoying the police because obviously I'm calling and it's always speaking to a different officer." Some women became deeply engaged with particular police officers over time and developed personal relationships with individual police officers and police stations. For some this built their sense of safety. Melissa (ATSI) said:

> I actually formed a bond with one police officer. . . . He was a good bloke, because he followed through, and it was like, you know, because he's seen the history. I traveled to [his] police station . . . and he wasn't even in my area . . . and I traveled over to [the new station he was moved to] because he just followed through. I trusted him.

Fiona recommended there should be "one point or two points of contact . . . at your local police station. Not talking to 10 different people . . . you get transferred to someone else and they don't know your background and your story."

Some women had other strategies to achieve safety. Fiona, Kim, and Susan repartnered with police officers or security guards during the period of study and said this made them feel safer. Fiona said her security officer partner was "very protective" and "strong," and she felt confident to go out in public when he was with her. Vera had chosen to rent a house across the road from a police station, and that made her feel safe.

CONCLUSION

Consistently, study women pointed to three issues: police failing to recognize nonphysical forms of IPV, a sense that the police were aligning with the abuser, and police failing to intervene where there were children in the relationship. For some women, despite repeated calls over time, there was little or no improvement in police response. Segrave, Wilson, and Fitz-Gibbon (2018, p. 105), in their interviews with police in Victoria, Australia, reported similar concerns, found that "on the whole, deserving victims of IPV existed for [police] officers only on a purely hypothetical plane, drowned out for the most part by a steady procession of imposters, liars and timewasters, presenting what were regarded as highly suspect claims to victim status." The concerns expressed by women in this study, and in the work of Segrave and colleagues (2018), point to the need for significant and sustained cultural change in policing. The limited understanding of IPV exhibited by some police as described by the interviewees may be explained to some extent by the fact that the crimes generally are focused on a single incident rather than ongoing coercive control. Stark (2012b, p. 206; see also Segrave et al., 2018, p. 110) suggests that this focus may contribute to flawed approaches to policing IPV. In the Australian context, the different state and federal regimes for protection orders and custody matters are being used as a justification for failure to intervene. While this is an ongoing problem in Australia, an improved understanding of coercive control may help police to better understand how children can be part of the abuser's coercive control strategy. Improved understanding of IPV and coercive control may also help to address credibility concerns because police will be able to see a more holistic picture of the abuse (AIJA, 2020, [3.1.8]).

There is evidence that appropriate training can make a difference, improving police empathy for victims and their understanding of victims and the need for intervention to ensure safety (Dowling et al., 2018, p. 15). Some studies have identified promising results from IPV specialty units in improving victim experience of police, increasing the formal sanctioning of abusers, and reducing DFV (Exum, Hartman, Friday, & Lord, 2014, pp. 1003, 1024; Klein, 2009).

Researchers have drawn attention to the role of women's police stations in South American countries, including Brazil and Argentina, in reducing femicide (Carrington, Guala, Puyol, & Sozzo, 2020). Some of the distinguishing features of women's police stations include that they are designed to attend to the needs of women who have experienced gendered crimes. Police collaborate in multidisciplinary teams that include lawyers, social workers, and psychologists, acting as a gateway to provide women with integrated services and aiming to "break the cycle" of IPV (Carrington et al., 2020, p. 60). Women police staff the front counters, the stations look different than traditional police stations, and the role of police officers tends to be very broad (Carrington et al., 2020, pp. 48–49). The stations are designed to be welcoming, usually painted in bright colors, with televisions in the waiting areas and children's play areas. When women attend, they may be given emergency provisions such as food, clothes, and other support. One of the key roles of women's police stations is to work with the woman and her family, including abusers, to prevent IPV and revictimization, and they do not prioritize the criminal justice process (Carrington et al., 2020, p. 52). Co-location of support services in a police station may not work for all who have experienced IPV. For example, the complex and tense relationship between police and ATSI people in Australia and African Americans in the United States means people from these groups are less likely to call the police for support (Alexander, 2010; Nancarrow, 2019); co-location may result in excluding some people from support if this is the only option.[3] However, aspects of the women's police station model may be able to be integrated into current policing approaches and help to reduce IPV and revictimization for some.

NOTES

1. Depending on the facts and circumstances of the particular case, the family court may order that the parties to child-related proceedings take part in an assessment conducted by a family consultant. This will result in the production of a family report (AIJA, 2020, [10.4]; Field, Jeffries, Rathus, & Lynch, 2016).
2. Nonfatal strangulation is identified as a high-risk behavior for future death and serious injury (J. Campbell et al., 2003).
3. In at least one Australian town a domestic violence services is co-located with a police station. A review of the service found that it was meeting the needs of clients but that ATSI people were reluctant to use the service (Seuffert, Mundy, & McLaine, 2018, pp. 42–44).

7

Lawyers and Legal Representation

INTRODUCTION

While women in the study who had access to lawyers had reasonably positive experiences with them, many raised significant issues about lawyers and legal representation. Many of the issues they raised about legal representation compounded their experience of intimate partner violence (IPV). The lack of access to state-funded legal aid was one concern. A second concern was the very high cost and ensuing debt associated with retaining a private lawyer. Often proceedings were initiated and prolonged by the abuser as an aspect of coercive control, and the heightened legal costs associated with this behavior were experienced as a form of secondary abuse, limiting the financial security and options for women and their children after separation. Pressure to settle cases unfairly or unsafely was a common theme that women connected to legal representation; this came as a consequence of both a lack of and the cost of legal representation.

Most women (n = 56) in the study had some contact with a lawyer during the period of the interviews. Women accessed public and private legal advice and information services via telephone and in person. Most women accessed a mixture of legal services, including legal aid–funded lawyers (either via private practice or state-employed lawyers), community legal centers (CLCs), and privately paid lawyers (Table 7.1). As in

Women, Intimate Partner Violence, and the Law. Heather Douglas, Oxford University Press (2021). © Oxford University Press.
DOI: 10.1093/oso/9780190071783.003.0007

Table 7.1 Models of Lawyers in the IPV Context in Australia

Model	Description
Lawyer	Broadly divided into two categories: solicitors and barristers. Solicitors generally have an ongoing relationship with their client and do all of their preparation prior to court. Barristers are associated with advocacy in court. However, in family law and protection order matters, solicitors often do both the preparation and the court work (Littrich & Murray, 2019, pp. 134–138). Women in the study did not usually make a distinction, usually referring to their "lawyer."
Lawyers in Private Practice	Generally operate for profit, although sometimes they act for clients who are provided with a grant of legal aid. Sometimes they provide some services for reduced cost or for free (pro bono).
Legal Aid	State-funded legal service that helps financially disadvantaged people. Legal aid employs lawyers but also provides grants to lawyers in private practice to run cases for eligible people. Some legal aid lawyers are specialists in IPV (Legal Aid Queensland, 2018).
Community Legal Center (CLC)	CLCs are independent, nonprofit, community-based organizations that provide free legal services. Some CLCs, or lawyers working in them, are specialists in IPV.
Duty Lawyers	Work in the courts and are funded by legal aid. Duty lawyers can provide legal advice and represent a person in court. They do not usually have an ongoing relationship with the client. Some duty lawyers specialize in IPV.

other studies (e.g., Trinder et al., 2014, p. 21), many of the women experienced periods of partial or no legal representation. For example, they may have been represented for their family law matter but not for their protection order matter.

The fluctuating nature of this situation makes a binary description—as either represented or unrepresented—vague and inaccurate. For many women, CLCs provided an important safety net; women often connected with CLCs between receiving grants of legal aid and to obtain referrals or advice and information. Women not only found it difficult to remember the kind of legal support they had for each legal problem, but there also were discrepancies in the stage of the legal proceedings for which they had legal support. Sometimes women were legally represented at court hearings, but on many occasions they only had legal support to prepare for hearings. Some had only obtained general information or legal advice about how to proceed. Because the women were mainly recruited to the study by specialist domestic violence support services, CLCs, and private lawyers, it is perhaps not surprising that so many of them had some contact with a lawyer.

Numerous studies have explored the relationship between women, their lawyers, and IPV. Studies have found that women had a negative experience with their lawyers when their lawyers lacked understanding of the dynamics of IPV or prioritized physical violence (James & Ross, 2016; Jordan & Phillips, 2013; Laing, 2013); had insufficient IPV training (Neilson & Renou, 2015; Roberts, Chamberlain, & Delfabbro, 2015; Saxton, Olszowy, MacGregor, MacQuarrie, & Wathen, 2018); or provided insufficient information (Saxton et al., 2018). Some studies have found that women felt they were encouraged by their lawyers not to mention IPV in litigation (Feresin, Folla, Lapierre, & Romito, 2018; Laing, 2013) or that their lawyer colluded with the abuser or the abuser's lawyer (DeKeseredy, Dragiewicz, & Schwartz, 2017, p. 129; Saunders, Faller, & Tolman, 2016). These concerns were raised infrequently by women potentially because they largely engaged with lawyers who were experienced in working with victims of IPV. In many cases, women had been referred to their privately funded lawyers by a specialist IPV support service that usually maintained a referral list of trusted and tested private lawyers. Several women had obtained legal advice and information from a specialist IPV CLC. Furthermore, IPV-related legal work is now a significant aspect of the work of state-funded legal aid services (Legal Aid Queensland, 2018, p. 28), and most legal aid lawyers who had contact with the women would have had at least some training in IPV.

Previous studies have identified common features that make for a positive experience with lawyers in the context of IPV. For example, several studies have found that women have a positive experience when lawyers are empathetic and provide emotional support (Laing, 2017, p. 1327; Renner & Hartley, 2018; Saxton et al., 2018) and when they understand the dynamics of IPV (Jordan & Phillips, 2013; Lea & Callaghan, 2016). Numerous women identified empathy and emotional support when talking about their positive experiences with lawyers. Kirsten said her privately funded lawyer was "amazing. . . . If I hadn't had her support there's no way, absolutely no way I would have done it." Yvonne said:

> I was just totally trusting [of the privately funded lawyer]. She did a really good job. I didn't like being in the same room with [the abuser], but [the lawyer] was sort of saying stuff to me like, "I'm in the middle of you two guys." She'd just sort of talk me through the whole thing. So it made it better. . . . Right from day one I could see that [the lawyer] was very aware of a lot of things that a lot of lawyers wouldn't be, although I really haven't had much experience with lawyers, but very humane.

Despite the women's generally positive experience with their own lawyers, five key themes emerged from the women's stories in relation to their engagements with lawyers. First, many women reported on difficulties in getting access to and retaining state-funded legal aid, and on its restrictions and limitations when they did. Second, those women who paid privately for legal advice and representation often faced mounting debts at the time of interviews 2 and 3, causing significant anxiety. Third, some women found their stress and debt were augmented significantly by abuse of legal processes resulting from the abuser's specious extensions to litigation and, in some cases, the unethical behavior of the abuser's lawyer. Fourth, numerous women reported that their circumstances in relation to legal representation and potential costs contributed to their decisions to settle on inappropriate orders relating to safety, children, and property or in their decision to withdraw from litigation. Finally, women identified a range of strategies and compromises they employed to access legal support but also identified stress and challenges they faced when they were only partially represented or unrepresented.

ACCESSING AND RETAINING STATE-FUNDED LEGAL AID

As in other countries, legal aid is difficult to access in Australia, especially for civil matters like protection orders and family law (Kaye, 2019b, p. 143; Kelly, Sharp, & Klein, 2014, p. 115). In Queensland, strict tests are enforced to determine eligibility (Legal Aid Queensland, 2019a). Broadly, these include a means test that takes into account income and assets. Alongside this, a merits test is utilized that considers the likelihood of success of the legal action, a consideration of whether a prudent self-funded litigant would risk their financial resources on the legal action, and generally the appropriateness of spending public funds on the case. The path to access legal aid includes completing complex forms, providing various support documents, and then, if rejected, facing the prospect of appealing that decision.

Many women in the study expressed frustration with the high threshold for legal aid support, and in many cases they were not clear about why they had been refused. For example, Hannah stated, "Legal aid kept saying I wasn't entitled because I've got a business that owes me $80,000 [USD55,000], and that's considered an asset. How is that an asset? It's not in my hand. . . . It won't ever be." Hannah ultimately borrowed money from her father to help pay for a private lawyer in her family law custody and her civil protection order matters. She was eventually able to get some legal aid support when her custody matter went to trial. However, despite a legal aid grant paying for some of her lawyer's fees, at the time of interview 1, she owed a significant sum to her lawyers and to her father, which she was slowly paying off.

At interview 1, Colleen explained that she had some part-time work: "I earn . . . under $20,000 [USD13,000], and you're just trying to find work and . . . even with all that and no money and being chucked out of the house and having somebody be violent against you, I didn't pass muster for [legal aid] funding. I wonder who does?" Colleen was not able to get legal aid for her protection order, but she had help with her preparation from volunteer lawyers at a CLC.

For family law custody matters, several women—including Evie and Anna—expressed frustration that they would only be able to receive legal aid once their ex-partner applied for custody. Anna's child, Manuel, was living with her, and her ex-partner, Nathan (the child's father), had not had contact with Manuel for some time. Anna was fearful Nathan could remove Manuel at any time. At interview 1, Anna said she had inquired about getting some support from legal aid, but she was advised she would not be eligible until Nathan either took the child or made an application through the family courts to see the child. Anna reported similar concerns at interview 2, during which I referred her to a CLC. At interview 3, Anna reported that the CLC was helping her, describing the CLC lawyer as a "lifesaver . . . because literally everyone was pushing me away. I had no help, I had no money. [L]egal aid wouldn't help me, no one would help me. I couldn't even go for a loan to get money to pay for a lawyer . . . he was all lawyered up."

Some of the women in the study were able to secure legal aid, but it was difficult to retain. Some adjusted their employment to ensure they continued to fall below the means test. This was Ingrid's (CALD) experience. At the time of interview 1, she had legal aid for a protection order and had purposefully reduced her working hours so she could maintain it. Ultimately, she was not able to retain legal aid for her family court matter, even with her lowered income, so she relied on assistance from a CLC. Alex had a similar story, choosing not to upgrade her employment—despite her professional skills—so that she would not lose legal aid. Inevitably, some women who were refused legal aid turned to seek legal help from private lawyers.

THE HIGH COST AND RESULTING DEBT ASSOCIATED WITH PRIVATE LAWYERS

Lawyers' Fees

Many of the women pointed to the very high costs associated with retaining a privately funded lawyer. This issue has been identified in previous research (Jordan & Phillips, 2013; Neilson & Renou, 2015; Ragusa,

2012; Roberts et al., 2015; Shepard & Hagemeister, 2013). In a study by Slote and colleagues (2005, p. 1380) of human rights violations in Massachusetts family courts, more than half of the participants interviewed reported that they suffered financial hardships related to their family court ordeal. A recent review of Australia's family law system found that family law judgments have regularly identified disproportionate legal costs in family law proceedings, describing costs as "obscene," "eye watering," and "extraordinary [and] grossly disproportionate to the subject matter of the litigation" (Australian Law Reform Commission, 2019, p. 332). Debts resulting from legal fees were a significant issue for many of the women in the study.

Bianca had been separated from her husband, Tom, for almost a year at the time of interview 1. She had engaged a private lawyer to help her obtain a protection order as well as family law custody and property orders. Bianca worked full-time in a professional capacity, earning $87,000 (USD58,000) per year; however, when I met her at the first interview, she had already spent about $85,000 (USD57,000 on legal fees, almost a whole year's salary. She mentions that financial situation was complex:

> I've paid for my barrister. . . . So I've paid him off and I've also—I've got no money left but my mum's going to lend me $4,000 [USD2,900] and I've got about—I managed to get one of my credit cards extended by another $7,000 [USD5,000]. I'm hoping that will cover it. If it doesn't, [the lawyer] has said I can pay her off. . . . I've still got a lot of debt anyway. I've actually put in an application to access my [superannuation] early on compassionate grounds for medical reasons because I've got the chronic PTSD and my psychiatrist has written a letter to say "yeah, she needs ongoing help" and we've estimated how much that will cost.

Over the period of the interviews, Bianca's debt spiraled. At the root of her high debt problems were her legal fees. Bianca elaborated on her financial distress in her second interview, she emphasized the moving expenses she incurred as a result of separation and discussed how she had reached the maximum limit on all credit cards due to the combined cost of legal fees and separation.

At interview 3, her financial circumstances were precarious, and again she emphasized the other "costs" she had incurred as a result of separation. Specifically, she pointed out she had used her work leave to stay home with the children after her separation to make sure they had some security. Further, she drew on her superannuation funds, which are supposed to support her in retirement, and amassed significant credit card debts. This impacted her credit rating and ability to move on even if she was able to move past the debts.

Bianca's story was not uncommon. Kim had large legal debts at the time of interview 1. After finalizing a custody matter, she had recently repartnered. She told me:

> I had $62,000 [USD43,000] [debt] and I'm down—I think I'm down to probably close to $40,000 [USD27,000]. . . . I've tried to withdraw money from my [superannuation], but because I'm not on a [social security] payment, they won't let me withdraw any money for hardship or compassionate grounds because I'm partnered. Some other services have recently told me that I should separate from my partner so that I can gain access to government services. That's not fair.

When I met Kim again at interview 3, she was working and managing to continue to pay down her debts. By then she owed $16,000 (USD11,000). Her lawyer informed told her that if she could find $10,000 (USD6,700) to pay him, he would "wipe" the rest of her debt, but Kim did not see this as a possibility unless she was permitted to withdraw money from her superannuation, an option that had already been refused to her.

Being in her late 60s, the issue for Jennifer was ensuring she had enough money to live on for the remainder of her retirement. In the period before her protection order application was heard in court, Jennifer received many letters from her ex-partner's solicitor "demanding" she get a solicitor. Despite her resistance, by the time of interview 2 Jennifer had appointed a private lawyer to assist her with her protection order, and by the time of interview 3, she had spent around $15,000 (USD10,000). Worried about the costs she was amassing, Jennifer said, "I have other debts that I've paid out. I've got enough money to live on, now, in my retirement, but the way the money's going I won't have. . . . He's ruining me. It's a slow, sure death but he is taking me on."

The women's stories demonstrated that the various strategies commonly used to pay down debts—including taking out bank loans, extra credit cards, accessing superannuation, dipping into retirement savings, and borrowing from family members—often served to entrench women's debt and financial precarity. Hannah stated:

> Each time I went to court for a mention or a hearing, it'd be $2,000 or $3,000 [USD1,000 or USD2,000]. . . . I've had to fork out so much money in legal fees for both the [protection order] and the family trial. The family trial was due to happen [soon], and Dad put in $18,000 [USD12,000] into the trust fund for the lawyer, for the family trial.

Women's legal debts also had implications for their housing security. Fiona drew down her equity in the family home to pay her legal debts. At interview 1, Fiona explained she had owned unencumbered property with her ex-partner when they separated and had not been eligible for legal aid. She now had $15,000 (USD10,000])in legal debt and described her financial situation as "cooked." At the time of interview 2, Fiona's property settlement was finalized, and after paying off the legal debts ($25,000 [USD17,000]), she was left with $20,000 (USD13,500). This was not enough for a deposit to buy a house.

Similarly, at interview 1, Susan said she was in a good financial position because she had previously invested in both a property to live in and an investment property. She had sold the investment property to fund the family law custody trial. At the time of interview 2, Susan had spent more than $100,000 (USD67,000) on legal fees over a 2-year period and was considering mortgaging her family home to pay the lawyer's fees for the continuing family law custody matter. By the time of interview 3, Susan's custody matter was still unresolved and further hearings were planned. She had moved in with her parents and was renting out her house so she could pay her legal fees.

Secondary Financial Costs

While the particularly high financial debts women faced were largely a result of lawyers' fees, the other significant financial costs associated with engaging with the legal system contributed to women's financial issues even when they had legal aid. Sandra explained in her first interview:

> It cost me a lot of money—even though I've had legal aid representation, it's still cost me a lot of money. . . . Well, you've got photocopying phone logs and there's a lot there. I mean I had a great stationery company in the local community in the end where they'd run me a tab just so I could have money for food. . . . You need to get . . . your evidence. You need to then print stuff off the computer as well to try and read up on stuff. You also need supporting documents for this sort of thing.

Other costs identified by the women included parking fees and court filing fees. At interview 3, Kirsten reflected that although her legal fees were relatively low, there were various other costs associated with separation and legal engagement, including time taken off work, changing locks, and the ill health that comes with the whole process. As Kirsten stated, "I think you've got to quantify that in terms of cost as well." Colleen was disappointed with her lawyer. She retained a lawyer to help with her family law property settlement and was keen to protect the artwork she had been making over many years. In the end the lawyer's fees were extremely high and her lawyer demanded some of Colleen's favorite pieces as payment. Colleen said her lawyer turned into a "vampire and went straight for all the valuable things I was trying to protect. You know what? I felt sick in the guts. . . . Fuck the lawyers right off because I can't trust them. No, but God bless the lawyers if they are genuinely coming from the right place. But that whole cutthroat thing where . . . 'this has got to serve me.' It is too surprising."

From a purely financial perspective, in some cases, the costs do not seem worthwhile. However, for some women the financial costs were worth it precisely because the litigation took so long. Susan commenced litigation in the family courts when her son was only a few months old. By the time of interview 3, which took place 4 years after commencing proceedings in the family courts, Susan explained that the length of the proceedings and thus the costs were worth it because they bought time:

> I've spent nearly $200,000 [USD135,000]. . . . I have to think of it as a good investment. It's bought me time. . . . My whole thing was I didn't want [child] to spend too much time with his father when he was so young and vulnerable. . . . I had all my own money for a long time. I had to sell a property; I've sold all my shares. Just in the last 2 months I've gotten a $15,000 [USD10,000] loan from Mum and Dad, but that's the first time I've had to borrow money.

Leah (CALD) said at interview 2 that she has "lost" about $25,000 to $30,000 (USD17,000 to 20,000) on legal fees. Leah explained that she continued to pursue the property settlement despite the ever-increasing fees as a matter of principle and personal self-worth:

> I wanted to do that because—it's not for the money, I know I won't be getting much. But I wanted to show him that I'm not worthless. Like he can't—he should not think that [anybody] is worthless, and nobody doesn't know anything, and he is the king. He feels that he has the control and can do whatever he wants.

Hilary's Experience

Hilary retained a private lawyer to assist her with family law property matters. She described her experience of mounting debts over the period of the interviews and difficulties in paying them off, and how her ex-partner used his legal representation in various ways to continue his abuse. He delayed instructing his lawyers and constantly sacked and rehired different lawyers, prolonging litigation and increasing Hilary's stress and costs.

> ***Hilary, interview 1:*** *My brother is a lawyer who works up here. He then was saying, well, Hilary, that's domestic violence. He gave me numbers, including . . . I was ringing going, well, I need some advice, I don't know, I need to find out more about this.*

I meet Hilary in a tiny room at a service where she has received some support in the past. Hilary and Bruce, both in their early 40s, were married for more than 15 years and separated about 6 months ago. Hilary has a bachelor's degree and part-time employment working with children, while Bruce did an apprenticeship and always had work while they were together. They have several school-aged children. Hilary is getting some child support from Bruce and some social security money. She mentioned that since separating she has been seeing a psychologist regularly because she suffers from anxiety.

Hilary has recently instructed a private lawyer to help her with the property settlement because she did not think Bruce would agree to anything. She said, "It's going to be expensive but we're just going to have to go to the courts." However, she wanted to avoid getting court orders about the children:

> I don't want some magistrate deciding what is . . . in their best interests. I've heard the horror stories from my counselor about newborn babies being given to their fathers. . . . I stayed with Bruce for as long as I did because he used to say things to me like that. . . . "You'll have to give me the children if we separate, you realize that, don't you?"

Hilary says Bruce is a perfectionist who liked to control things from the beginning. She recalled pressure to work in paid employment, even very shortly after having each baby. Bruce frequently used to tell her she was fat and had a mental illness. Toward the end of the relationship she became extremely anxious.

Hilary recounted the first time she experienced real fear of Bruce, when she was pregnant with their first child. He "came storming into the room with two knives, was threatening to hurt himself, lifted the mattress up and tipped me off the bed, put his fist through the wall . . . and I felt really scared, obviously." On another occasion Bruce became angry with her, grabbed her, and kicked her in the hip. She had a large bruise on her hip and bruises on her arms. One of the children's childcare workers noticed and told her about available support, but Hilary stated that at that stage "it just went over my head."

On a later occasion, Bruce hit Hilary hard with a piece of electrical cord, again bruising her. Bruce said he did this to "discipline" her. After this incident, Hilary moved to her father's place, taking the children with her. She rang lots of services to try to get some help, but no one rang her back. After a few days she moved back in with Bruce. He continued to be verbally abusive, but it became clear that he was controlling the finances as well. They had a joint account, and she realized he was no longer contributing to it. He had set up a separate account. It was difficult for her to pay all the daily costs of living. She decided she had to leave and went to get advice from social security. When she was told she would be able to get only $130 (USD90) each week, she decided she could not afford to leave—she wouldn't even be able to pay rent.

Things came to a head when Bruce became angry and again punched a hole through a wall of the house. It was Bruce who called the police on this occasion, the first time they were ever called to the house. When the police arrived, Hilary told them about the previous incidents of physical violence, and they recommended Hilary obtain a protection order. Police removed Bruce from the house. Hilary called her brother, a lawyer, and he helped her get a temporary protection order the next day. The order required Bruce to stay out of the house, but he could use the garden shed where he kept his tools. When Bruce was served with the temporary protection order, Hilary said "he was very, very, very, very, very angry, and it pretty much has been a nightmare ever since." At the time, Bruce constantly called the police. When they arrived at court a few weeks ago to finalize the protection order, Hilary was served with a copy of his application for a protection order against her.[1] Both applications were adjourned, and over the intervening weeks the police were called many times. Eventually, Bruce was charged with breaching the temporary protection order, and he received a fine.

In one of the court hearings related to the temporary protection order, Hilary had attempted to vary one of the conditions to ensure that Bruce stayed out of the house because he kept coming inside. She felt that the judge blamed her for refusing to accommodate Bruce's needs. Bruce didn't want the children listed as protected on the final protection order. Ultimately, Hilary got the final protection order conditions she wanted, with the children named as protected. However, Hilary allowed Bruce access to the shed in the backyard, and in exchange Bruce withdrew his application for a protection order.

> ***Hilary interview 2:*** *I probably will have a debt, because the appearance in the city where the lawyer was there for 4 hours, that bill's yet to come to me. This one, where we were there 3.5 hours, is yet to come to me . . . with all the domestic violence stuff— yeah, it'd easily be somewhere between $10,000 and $20,000 [USD7,000 to 13,000] easily. The amount of court appearances . . .*

Since we last met 10 months earlier, Hilary had removed everything from the shed and had a new protection order in place with a condition that Bruce is not permitted to come to the house at all. She said this is "just wonderful, because it's really helped me feel safe and secure." Bruce hasn't seen the children for nearly a year. With these precautions in place, Hilary was focused on the family courts and sorting out orders around the children and property.

The family court had ordered a family report, and Hilary, Bruce, and the children had some interviews with the report writer.[2] Hilary was still seeing a counselor, who helped her prepare for the interview with the report writer. Bruce told the report writer that Hilary is "controlling and coercive" and that "the law enforcement, and legal system is biased toward women, and he feels that he hasn't been . . . able to get his point across as far as his view of what's gone on." Hilary felt very self-conscious during the interview with the report writer and stated that she wanted the child handovers to happen at a contact center; the report ultimately suggested the local police station or MacDonald's.

Hilary had also applied for a property settlement in the family court. Both she and Bruce had instructed private lawyers. They had 4 hours of family court shuttle mediation, after which he offered to settle the property at 55% to 45% in Hilary's favor.[3] However, the lawyers told Hilary she should get 70%. At that stage, Bruce had sacked several of his lawyers. Hilary stated that in relation to the most recent court date, "He did what he always does, which is see the lawyers late and apply and put all this paperwork in really late. The night before going to court, I was wading through these documents, trying to have some idea of what I thought, and it was really hard." Bruce had also contacted the law firm where Hilary's lawyer works on numerous occasions demanding to talk to her lawyer and harassing the reception staff.

Hilary was not eligible for legal aid because she has equity in the family home. Instead, she had borrowed some money from her mother to pay for the upcoming legal fees. Hilary said it would be impossible for her to cope emotionally without a lawyer. Even though she and Bruce had then been separated for more than 18 months, she felt that her physical reaction to him had worsened, making it impossible to be in a courtroom unrepresented. She feels very security conscious and plans to get security on her house upgraded, including fixing the fence and putting security screens on the windows.

> ***Hilary, interview 3:*** *Bruce has been trying to control me and control everything through his lawyers. When we go to court, he's trying to control everything—he's still getting at me through his lawyers. I think that that's just so wrong that they can do that without the correct information. It's hard because I know that Bruce is just telling them what he wants them to write, but it's almost like, you know, it's continued domestic violence.*

I meet Hilary again 7 months after the second interview. Hilary mentions she has had a few new sets of orders from the family court since we last met. The initial family report recommended that Bruce should have weekly contact with the children in a contact center and that both parents attend a parenting program. Bruce had been having contact with the children in a contact center and Hilary says she has completed a parenting course. Bruce made a surprise application the night before the previous week's court hearing to see the children overnight on weekends at his brother's house. In response, the judge ordered that that another family report be produced. Hilary understood that this would be much more in depth than the previous one. Additionally, property settlement has not progressed because Bruce has still not produced any financial information, even though he is required to do so.[4]

Hilary is still instructing the same private lawyers. She states: "If I know I'm going to see him and he's going to be in the building, in the room kind of thing, that's when I don't cope as well." Her lawyer's bills have continued to grow; she mentions that she has had three or four bills from her lawyer of about $2,000 to $3,000 (USD1,300 to USD2,000) each. She had a debt of about $20,000 (USD13,000) in legal costs at the time of the third interview and was only managing to pay off the interest. Bruce continued to harass Hilary's lawyer and others who work at the law firm, telephoning them constantly and sometimes attending their office in person. She believes Bruce is using his lawyers, and even changing his lawyers, as a form of continuing domestic violence. From Hilary's perspective, nothing has progressed.

ABUSE OF LEGAL PROCESSES

Systems Abuse

Hilary experienced legal systems abuse as a part of her ex-partner's coercive and controlling behavior. The link between legal systems abuse and increased debt was identified by numerous women. Specifically, the manufacture of countless court appearances by the abuser is recognized as a form of systems abuse and coercive control (Kaspiew, Carson, Coulson, Dunston, & Moore, 2015). It adds to the already "daunting and traumatic" nature of the court process, leading to emotional and financial trauma (attorney interviewed in Slote et al., 2005, p. 1388). Many of the women pointed to similar strategies their ex-partners used to prolong, repeat, and renew litigation in their continuing efforts to control the women's lives.

At the time of interview 2, Ingrid had a protection order in place for another 2 months but did not plan to apply for a new one. She was concerned it would lead to new applications from her ex-partner: "Even my lawyer [said] he's just going to be excited to do more paperwork." At interview 3, Ingrid said that her ex-partner used the courts as his hunting ground:

> It was really like a hunting thing. Like . . . I got the [protection order] so he took the [protection order] against me. Then I wanted to go to [home country] so he said no. Then he did the thing in that court and bringing all these people along that I didn't even know and it was really like a manhunt kind of. I mean, it was a literal hunt in between as well with the stalking.

Reflecting on 10 years of involvement with legal processes associated with her experience of IPV, at interview 3 Sandra said that for her ex-partner "his purpose is to bully me. The courtroom is his playground."

For those women who had to pay lawyers' bills, this misuse of the legal system operated to heighten economic abuse, often trapping women in poverty and debt. Some women, like Hilary, clearly identified that their ex-partner was using court proceedings as part of an ongoing strategy of coercive control and financial abuse.

Jane's ex-partner also used the legal system to continue his abuse. Jane and Richard had been in a relationship for 20 years and had two teenage children. Richard had earned a good salary throughout the relationship, while Jane had earned less and cared for the children. Jane retained private lawyers to assist her with her property settlement. Before our first interview, she emailed me saying her ex-partner, Richard, was "able to *continue* to abuse me through the legal system, such as delaying things and increasing my legal fees . . . the lawyers didn't seem to have any real way of protecting me from this legal abuse without it costing ME more money." Ultimately, her legal fees were approximately $100,000 (USD69,000) and resulted in a significantly diminished property settlement, limiting her housing options. At interview 1, she identified how Richard's behavior contributed to her fees: "He wouldn't answer, he'd go overseas, he would be uncontactable. He didn't have a lawyer—he had a lawyer, he didn't have a lawyer, he had the lawyer again." She said he "used the legal system to punish me by racking up my legal fees and the legal system allowed it. There was no mechanism in the law to stop him from doing this . . . there should be a trigger in place that stops the 'misbehaving person' from doing this." Her frustration with the "legal system's failure" to acknowledge Richard's bad behavior continued into interview 3. From her perspective, the legal fees were a form of "financial abuse indirectly perpetrated by Richard."

Gillian also identified the connection between legal systems abuse and legal fees. When I met Gillian at her first interview, she told me her ex-partner, Kyle, used the courts as a "weapon." She received social security as her principal income and was able to get legal aid for her child custody matter. Orders were ultimately made that the children should live with Gillian and that they spend time with Kyle. After the custody matter was finalized, however, Kyle made a further application in the family court for property, even though there was no property to divide. Gillian was still receiving social security benefits, but she was refused legal aid and had to fund a private solicitor to defend the property matter. At interview 2, she reported that the family court had dismissed the property application in recognition that there was nothing to divide. However, she was not confident to represent herself, and as a result she was $10,000 (USD7,000) in debt to her privately funded lawyer. Her debts were the result of Kyle's frivolous application. She had borrowed money from her grandparents and mother to pay some of the legal costs and was still paying off the debts to her lawyer and family at the time of interview 2. During the third interview, Gillian reflected that the specious property application "was more of a power and control thing. He never intended on me walking completely away and just cutting ties. He always thought he'd have that control and how dare you think you can walk away . . . it took 3 years."

Increasingly, the dangers lawyers face in practicing in the domestic violence context have been recognized. Some lawyers have been killed by their client's ex-partners (Laird, 2018), and others have experienced stalking (*R v. Conde*, 2015). Some of the women in the study, like Hilary, identified that their ex-partner attempted to exercise control through stalking and harassing their lawyers. Alex's lawyers were also harassed, as she reported at interview 1:

> My lawyers have had dreams, because [ex-partner] threatened to kill them. He's threatened to nail them to the fucking cross and do all these sorts of things. All the evidence is out there. He's abused them. He's accused them. He's reporting them to all their [professional] bodies.

Alex further reported in interview 2 that her ex-partner had decided to subpoena her parents and lawyers, perhaps in a further attempt at exercising coercive control and increasing the financial burden of the proceedings.

Unethical Behavior of Ex-Partners' Lawyers

While women in the study rarely had negative things to say about their own legal representatives, in several cases women identified that their ex-partner's lawyer behaved unethically or inappropriately toward them. Several legally represented women said that their partner's lawyer had tried to contact them directly rather than via their legal representative. Such behavior is unethical (Littrich & Murray, 2019) but also can be experienced as an extension of the abuse via the proxy of the abuser's lawyer.

Some of the women's complaints related to lawyers' extremely adversarial approach to the litigation. For example, Lisa explained that when her ex-partner had legal representation

> it was horrible. His solicitor was hitting me left, right and center with just nastiness. Even in the court, we were there in front of . . . the judge's . . . [associate] "here's the statement, here's the paperwork." The judge goes out of the room and [the judge's associate] stays. His solicitor turned to me and he was just being so rude and nasty. I turned to [the judge's associate] and said, "Can you hear the way he's speaking to me?" She goes, "yes, actually, I can. . . . He was just ripping me, ripping me.

Ingrid reported at interview 2 that she had been to the family court to get an order so that she could travel back to her home country with her daughter to visit extended family. Her ex-partner wanted to put a stop on the child's passport, and he retained a lawyer to run his case. Ingrid recalled that his lawyer

> was terrible, to be honest. He was really weird . . . his lawyer talked for like an hour of his case—[he said] I was lying, of all the things I'm apparently doing to [the child] and that I would be a flight risk and all kinds of stuff. But he kept always referring to me as "my friend" and I'm like I'm not a lawyer and certainly not your friend, but just the way he did that it was really unnerving.

Some women believed that their ex-partner's lawyer was actively facilitating his extension of spurious litigation. At interview 1, Susan said: "[His lawyer is] very young, obviously very inexperienced. Almost like she was jumping on the bandwagon egging on the fight. She's not interested in conflict resolution." Jennifer at interview 3 also had little respect for her ex-partner's lawyer. saying: "They all stick together. The lawyers are in it for money. There is no honor. Even when they see that these people [the abusers] are not normal people, they do it for the money."

Like the US legal system, the Australian legal system is adversarial. Lawyers must be loyal to their clients and try to promote the best outcome for their clients. This may involve using delaying tactics, bluffing in settlements, and filing strategically motivated claims (Markovits, 2010, pp. 1–4). How far lawyers can ethically and lawfully go is not always clear. Sandefur (2015, p. 911) has identified that lawyers' relational expertise, for example, knowing what a certain judge will accept, can be very important. While stressful, many of the "abusive' lawyers" behaviors women identified may have been neither unlawful nor strictly unethical.

THE PRESSURE TO SETTLE OR TO WITHDRAW FROM LITIGATION

Many of the women in the study talked about the relationship between legal representation and the pressure they experienced to settle for what they perceived as unfair outcomes. Jane decided to settle property in mediation. Her lawyers pointed out the inequity of her ex-partner's offer but informed her that she would have to pay another $100,000 (USD67,000) in legal fees to continue to trial, and she could not afford such costs. Similarly, Vera (CALD), at interview 2, explained that she had already paid about $20,000 (USD14,000) in legal costs, and these would be taken out of her share of the property settlement. She said she settled the property because "I'm worried, I [will] need a lawyer again, all the costs, I don't have money." Some women pointed to their lack of legal representation as underpinning their decision to settle. For example, Ingrid (CALD) said in interview 1 that she decided to settle her family law custody matter because she was not able to access legal aid.

Several women reported that lack of funds to retain a lawyer or their ineligibility for legal aid resulted in their effectively giving up their legal rights. For example, at interview 2, Fiona explained that property had been stolen by her former partner from the family home, including house fittings, appliances, and even the toilet, reducing the value of the family property pool. To follow up on the losses through further property proceedings in the family court and to dispute her ex-partner's claims would have required more funds that Fiona did not have.

Family court orders about child contact were also potentially expensive to enforce. Both Leah (CALD) and Shelley would have liked to enforce their family court orders, but due to the financial implications of such action, they decided not to.

At interview 1, Jacinta explained that she had explored the idea of getting legal representation for a protection order hearing. She had already applied for a protection order, and her partner had applied for an order against her:

> I went in for a legal aid appointment. They basically said because I earn $1,150 [USD800] a week, because I work my arse off every night just to pay the rent, the car payments and feed my two children because I don't get maintenance, that I have to pay $600 [USD400] to have a lawyer turn up with me to this court. I can't afford $600, I don't have $600. Then they explained to me that if it goes to a hearing, I really need several [thousand dollars], because even though you can represent yourself, you've got to do affidavits and subpoenas and whatever, and you really, really need to have legal advice. I couldn't afford it, and I was so stressed out and tired from the job that I do . . . to go and sit in court and wait for 4 hours. I couldn't do it, so I said he's going to stand there and say that it's not true. I'm going to stand there and say it's not true. The judge is going to go OK off to a hearing on whatever date, and you need solicitors, get legal representation, which I can't afford to have. I said, so what do I do? I said, is there any way to just drop it? They said yes you can ask for . . . an undertaking.[5]

Jacinta went to court and accepted a 12-month undertaking. At interview 3, the undertaking was no longer in place, and Jacinta's ex-partner had recommenced his stalking and harassment. She had spoken to police, who recommended a protection order, but Jacinta did not plan to pursue this because "he's just going to lie, he's going to do what he did last time and [make up] his bullshit and I'm not spending three, four, five grand on representation taking it through the court."

Cost orders in the protection order courts are generally limited to cases where the application is malicious, deliberately false, frivolous, or vexatious; such orders are rarely made (Alexander, 2018).[6] Nevertheless, the threat of cost orders was a powerful incentive for women to settle, and a disincentive in some cases for women to pursue their rights. Vera (CALD), Celina (CALD), and Trisha (CALD) all experienced this pressure and fear of being ordered to pay their ex-partner's costs. In Celina's case, she accepted an undertaking from her ex-partner instead of going through with her protection order application on this basis.

Trisha's Experience

Trisha stated in interview 3 that her fear of costs was a disincentive for applying for spousal maintenance. Trisha was not happy with the conduct of her lawyer, who had been assigned to her at the court and was funded by legal aid. Trisha identified the pressure she experienced from the whole system, including her own lawyer, to settle the custody arrangements for her child in way that she thought was not safe.

> ***Trisha, interview 1:*** *I'm not quite so sure about [this] because I have signed something, because last time we were at court and we were discussing the agreement, the family report recommendations. In the future, if we ever come to court, will I be given enough chance for me to think it over, to take—to think things through and not decide on the spot, because I'm so concerned that the next time around, I will be pressured to make a decision right in there.*

Trisha is nervous and soft-spoken when I meet her at a local agency that has been offering her some support. We use a telephone interpreter, although for the most part, Trisha is keen to speak in English as much as possible. Trisha, in her early 20s, was born in Asia and met Australian-born Jarrod, in his late 40s, on a dating website. Trisha finished high school in her home country and then worked in a factory before meeting Jarrod and moving to Australia to marry him. Jarrod, who worked as a tradesman, sponsored Trisha on a prospective marriage visa. Trisha moved in with Jarrod, his mother, and his teenage daughters from a previous relationship. They were together for nearly 3 years before separating about 6 months prior to interview 1. Trisha's permanent residency in Australia was already confirmed before the trouble really started in their relationship.[7] They have a preschool-aged son together.

After meeting online, Jarrod visited Trisha in her home country on a couple of occasions. She didn't have much money, and she said it was her first time "dealing with a foreigner or a white person, so I was slightly apprehensive . . . I am not able to speak much English." Things went well, and she agreed to marry Jarrod. After arriving in Australia, she attended English lessons and helped with housework. Trisha soon realized that Jarrod and his mother shared a joint bank account, and Trisha was excluded from information about household finances. She also saw text messages to Jarrod from his daughter calling her "pan face" and alleging she smelled of and ate chicken feet.[8] When Trisha returned home one day, all her things were broken and some of her clothes were burned. She believed Jarrod's daughter broke everything, but it might have been Jarrod. Jarrod had told her she should go back to her home country. At this point Trisha disclosed that she was pregnant. This seemed to confuse Jarrod, who could not determine whether his loyalty should be to his daughter or to Trisha.

Trisha and Jarrod lived in Jarrod's car for a few days before she agreed she would return to her home country—which she did for 6 weeks. However, Jarrod constantly contacted her there, saying he was lonely, so she returned. After she returned, things were OK for a little while until the baby was born. After that, Jarrod was always angry if Trisha asked to go to her church. He constantly abused her emotionally and sometimes yelled at her. He withheld money from Trisha and refused her access to a telephone. About 6 months ago he smashed her laptop, which was her only way of communicating with family overseas. He then grabbed her around the neck, pushed her onto the floor, and put his foot on her chest. Trisha was scared and asked her friend to call the police. When Trisha showed the police the broken laptop and the mark on her neck, they assisted her to move out with her son and to obtain a protection order.

Trisha talked to a lawyer but was concerned that the lawyer might not have understood everything. Trisha wanted Jarrod to have contact with their son at a contact center, and Jarrod wanted contact at his house. Trisha subsequently agreed that Jarrod could see their son at Jarrod's house, but she doubted the safety of this arrangement. She felt pressured to agree by her lawyer, whom she believes is funded through legal aid.

> ***Trisha, interview 2:*** *I'm a bit scared and confused because if I push the property settlement . . . he gets angry with me and he will harm me because I left him and, you know, because of the domestic violence. I spoke to my lawyer a while ago. I am asking about my . . . mediation last July or June. He said, "I'm not working [for] you anymore because [you are] not paying," when [will] the government . . . pay him? If the government will pay him, he'll work with me.*

The second interview takes place 10 months after the first, and we again meet at the support service to talk. We have an interpreter again, but this time Trisha mainly speaks in English. Trisha is quite distressed when she tells me her family court order was made by consent. Trisha was represented by legal aid. The order states that Trisha and Jarrod have "equal shared parental responsibility" for their son, who must spend three nights each week with Jarrod and four nights with Trisha.[9] Jarrod's extended family is not allowed to be present when the child is exchanged. Trisha cries during the interview, stating that she felt like she was pressured to agree to this arrangement in the mediation. She recalls that her lawyer said, "Why don't we just come to an agreement." She is worried for her son's safety when he is with his father.

Trisha is renting a room in a friend's house but is listed as priority for social housing. At the time of the interview, she is receiving social security and is learning to drive. She states:

> I find it hard to move on. I still thinking, you know, I have a broken family. For example, I was traveling in the train, or maybe I was in

> the building while I'm studying, sometimes I feel: Shall I jump off the building, shall I jump off the train station? But I try to fight it.

The legal aid lawyer told Trisha that she needed to apply for a property settlement, but she is worried for her safety if she pursues that. She is also worried that Jarrod will take her son away. There was supposed to be a mediation soon after the first interview about schooling, but her lawyer has not been paid by legal aid, and he is refusing to assist her further.

Trisha has a protection order in place, and she thinks it is helpful in keeping her safe. She keeps a record of all her interactions with Jarrod just in case, and only meets Jarrod in places where there are cameras and he cannot harm her. The protection order expires next year, and she hopes to get another one when it that happens.

Because of my concern for Trisha's well-being, at the end of the interview I ask if she would be OK with talking to one of the counselors at the service. She says she is willing to do that.

> ***Trisha, interview 3:*** *Unless the third party has a private lawyer, to do what they want . . . the lawyer, they can do what they ask to them. Unlike the legal aid, they're not going to fight for you, because you don't pay them.*

Trisha did not want to engage an interpreter for this interview. It has been 10 months since we last met, and she mentions that she passed her driving test last week. She also has a secondhand car that she bought on eBay. She is still in the same accommodations, and the same arrangements are in place for her son. Jarrod has organized their divorce. Trisha is feeling a bit better about things, meeting friends and studying. When I ask her about new relationships, she says that someone really likes her, but she is not ready. Jarrod has stopped working in a job where he has to declare his income, so she is no longer receiving any child support. She is finding it hard to make ends meet financially and is reliant on social security payments. Her lawyer suggested it might be possible for her to apply for spousal maintenance but warned her that if she lost, she may have to pay Jarrod's legal costs. She asks me, "How can I do this if I'm not going to win to the court? How can I pay him and how can I pay his lawyer, [when] I don't have a job yet?"

Her protection order has expired, but she is no longer planning to get another one. Additionally, she has noticed that one of Jarrod's daughters has been following her in her car. To protect herself, Trisha has learned how to use the camera on the back of her car and has plans to take some photos to the police if this happens again. She sees a counselor regularly. Sometimes she gets "flashback[s]—I feel I'm hurt again, I'm hurt."

When I ask Trisha to think back on her experiences and what could have made it better, she singles out her experience with her lawyer: "So that's my disappointment, the government lawyer, they not really fighting. . . . They're not really doing their job."

STRATEGIES AND ALTERNATIVES

As mentioned at the beginning of this chapter, most of the study women had legal advice or assistance at some point in their journey through the legal system, accessing a mixture of legal services through legal aid, CLCs (including volunteer lawyers), and privately paid lawyers, with some periods when they did not have any legal representation. Women talked about the various ways they managed this fluctuating situation.

Some women in the study had a steady income or equity in a major asset (almost always the family home), and these factors often resulted in ineligibility for legal aid. For these women, full legal representation costs were unaffordable without mortgaging the family home or taking on debt. Researchers have referred to this group as the "missing middle" when it comes to accessing legal services (Petrie, 2018; Saxton et al., 2018). In Australia, as in other countries, including the United Kingdom, United States, and Canada, it is possible to retain a lawyer to do some, but not all, of the legal tasks associated with a legal case (Castles, 2016). This approach is referred to as "unbundling" legal services and is considered a kind of halfway point between full and no legal service. There is very little empirical evidence about the effectiveness of unbundling, although some American studies suggest that those with full legal representation do better than those who have only partial support (Greiner, Pattanayak, & Hennessy, 2013), and it is likely to depend on the level and kind of legal support the person had access to (Steinberg, 2011). Unbundling was one way that some of the women were able to access legal assistance. Most women who accessed unbundled services did so because they did not qualify for legal aid, they did not have enough funds to pay for a private lawyer, or they wanted to protect their equity in the family home.

For example, at interview 1, Maddy mentioned that she had applied for legal aid, but by the time of interview 2, she knew it was refused. She paid a private solicitor to assist her with her protection order application. She went to the court dates by herself because it was too expensive to instruct the lawyer to appear on her behalf. Ultimately, she was successful in obtaining the protection order. She explained:

> Instead of having to pay per hour and things like that, I paid per service. So, they would usually get a retainer of about . . . $4,000 [USD2,700] in order to do anything, but . . . I didn't really need her for a lot. I just needed her to help me tick all the boxes and do all of that sort of thing.

Martha said she had instructed a private lawyer, but she prepared everything in draft form and then her solicitor "settle[d] the documents." The solicitor told her this would cost about $10,000 (USD6,800). She has already spent $20,000 (USD13,000) on legal fees for her protection order application and property mediation—debts that will ultimately be paid from her property settlement. Chi (CALD) had some legal aid for her family law matter but still had to prepare documents: "I have to prepare everything for the lawyer . . . I really found it hard because—my English not good and then I need to write everything in [my language] and then I need to translate and then to the lawyer."

Some women searched for lawyers who offered flexible payment arrangements (George & Harris, 2014; Jordan & Phillips, 2013). For example, Frieda eventually found a private lawyer who didn't require a big upfront fee. Colleen moved between being unrepresented and represented by privately funded lawyers. She explained in interview 1 that she would "keep dropping into the legal system. I'd try and scrape together six grand and then I'd go and see a lawyer. Then the lawyer would say . . 'you've got to put five grand in the pot to start.' . . . I did that twice but then I had no more money."

Many of the women talked about the difficult study and reading they had to do when they were unrepresented. Bianca took this to the next level, studying for a law degree "just to have access to all the legal databases, information, and lecturer expertise." She pointed out that deferred university debt was more manageable than legal fees, and she was not eligible for legal aid.

In some cases, women reported that despite the hard work involved, there were sometimes advantages in being formally unrepresented. Lack of formal representation allowed women to manage their case in a way that a lawyer may advise against or ethically not be able to recommend. These experiences challenge the conception of law and justice (Smart, 1989, p. 164). For example, Faith says she did a lot of her own preparation, and she found reading the law frustrating and repetitive work. At interview 2, Faith commented on her property settlement experience and the advantage of being unrepresented and thus able to run unusual arguments: "I said I need about 10 years to refinance [her home loan]. Every solicitor I saw said, 'You'll never get that.' I said everything I've read has said at the end of the day it always comes down to the judge. They said, 'You will never ever get it. There's no point trying because you will not get it.' I just got it!"

At interview 1, Lisa, had received help from a community legal service in relation to preparation for a protection order and family court matters, although she had "done most of it" despite not having any legal background. Lisa reported at interview 2 that while the CLC lawyers recommended she settle rather than go to trial over the child custody arrangements, she "stuck to her guns" and went to trial. She did manage to get the arrangement she was hoping for but found the court experience "horrible," "intimidating," and "frightening," and she consistently doubted herself and her decision. Ultimately, Lisa was grateful she had help and support from the CLC lawyers to assist with background preparation.

Felicity quoted the judge in her custody case, who found that lack of representation put both her and her ex-partner at "extreme disadvantage with regard to the court's need not only to understand each case, but in fact to ensure the trial was fair." Felicity's partner was ordered to have supervised contact with their child, the outcome Felicity was hoping for.

Pari (CALD) had accessed a mixture of legal aid duty lawyer assistance, legal advice from a CLC on the telephone, and internet research to get advice and information about civil protection orders and family law matters. Pari commented in her first interview that in her home country she would have to have a lawyer, whereas in Australia

> I represent myself every time . . . so it's a privilege here that we can fight our case alone. In [home country] it's not like that, you need to have a lawyer. I think like if I have that confidence and if I have that knowledge, I've got that help from legal aid and from internet, I'm confident enough to fight my case.

Pari had mostly represented herself in the protection order courts and had successfully obtained a protection order. She was university educated and said at interview 2: "I did my research. That's your education, it helps you." When she found out her home country was not a signatory to the Hague Convention, she had returned her child to her home country to live with her parents to avoid the Australian family law system.[10] This was an approach lawyers were unlikely to recommend. In Pari's view she sacrificed the day-to-day contact with her child in exchange for his safety.

Despite recently migrating to Australia, Pari spoke English as a first language. For women with limited English, being unrepresented was a major disadvantage. During interview 2, Lahleh (CALD) mentioned that she wanted to change the contact center where her ex-partner has supervised access because it had no public transport. With help from a support service she had been using taxis, but this was unsustainable. Though Lahleh's ex-partner was employed and had his own car, he contested the change. He was also legally represented. When I attended court with Lahleh, she brought a plastic bag full of documents in no particular order. She could not read the documents, and when the judge asked for information, she sifted through the bag trying to locate what she wanted. Although I was able to help her find the relevant documents, Lahleh was extremely stressed. The judge reserved his judgment, and I did not see Lahleh again.

CONCLUSION

The comments from the women in the study show how restricting legal aid can lead women to give up rights that might have been enforced by the courts (Kelly et al., 2014, pp. 115–116). Legal aid rationing may lead women to settle matters in order to retain legal aid, compromising their security and that of their children.[11] Furthermore, where women give up or reduce paid work or change careers to reduce income to comply with income restrictions and maintain legal aid, this may have implications for women's (and children's) longer- term financial well-being. Women's stories point to the need for an expansion of legal aid to support women interacting with the legal system after IPV. Current legal aid arrangements contribute to the financial hardship and stress faced by women leaving relationships that involve IPV and are experienced as a form of secondary victimization (Herman, 2005).

In the absence of legal aid, many women turned to private lawyers. Again, they often felt pressured to settle matters to minimize their costs, often losing rights to property and compromising their safety.[12] In many cases in which private lawyers were involved, women carried high levels of personal debt into their postseparation lives. In some cases, these debts contributed to a devastating cycle of poverty, including credit card debt, reduced superannuation for later life, and lost annual and long service leave. This debt inevitably impacted women's health, their housing, and their ability to cope financially with the high costs associated with raising children.

Even in those cases where women were able to repay legal costs and debts, the sources of repayment were almost always their extended families and their equity in the family home. In some cases, the property pool was reduced so significantly by legal costs that women will never be able to buy into the property market. Some women, like Trisha, moved from private housing within the relationship to being on the social security housing list after separation.

The women's stories also show how abusive ex-partners often contributed to women's legal debts. Abusive ex-partners, and sometimes the abuser's lawyer, used delaying tactics such as adjournments, refused to disclose financial information, served documents late or not at all, and made multiple applications (sometimes doomed to fail) that women had to prepare for and respond to. This form of coercive control through abuse of legal system processes also operated as a form of economic abuse where it contributed to women's high debts and loss of equity (S. Miller, 2018, p. 165; Toews & Bermea, 2017). Judges have a role to play in limiting legal systems abuse (see Chapter 8), and this could contribute to reducing legal costs and debt. In some cases, however, where lawyers facilitate their clients' legal systems abuse, both directly through their cruel treatment of women in the courtroom and through unnecessarily prolonging legal cases, their behavior could be treated as professional misconduct. Notably, some survey research conducted in the United States has suggested that, compared with other specialties, family law "had the highest percentage of unethically adversarial lawyers" (A. Schneider & Mills, 2006, p. 617). Certainly, greater focus on training lawyers about coercive control and IPV and their ethical responsibilities seems needed (Burman, 2003).

Ineligibility for legal aid led some women to try alternative approaches to finding legal help to avoid acquiring crippling debt, including enrolling in law degrees, unbundling legal services, engaging with CLCs, and receiving pro bono legal support. These approaches rarely resulted in "full" legal representation, with women usually needing to do significant background work in reading and preparing legal documents with limited support. When women were not "fully" represented, it was usually their representation in court that was most compromised. Being without a lawyer in the courtroom, although not always unsuccessful in terms of results for women, was particularly stressful, and women usually had little or no support when confronted by their abuser in the courts. This was especially an issue for CALD women who did not have a good command of English.

The poor mental and physical health and reduced financial circumstances women face after leaving IPV are well documented (Fehlberg & Millward, 2014; Hess & Del Rosario, 2018; Loxton, Schofield, & Hussain, 2006). For many women the mental, physical, and financial stresses of engaging with law will be exacerbated where their access to legal support and representation is costly, unstable, or unattainable. Inappropriate legal support and representation can facilitate both the secondary abuse women experience through engaging with law and the "weaponization" of the legal system, enabling abusers to continue their coercive control through legal systems abuse.

NOTES

1. When both parties make an application against each other or have a protection order against each other, these are referred to as *cross* or *mutual applications* or *orders* (Douglas & Fitzgerald, 2013; Durfee & Goodmark, 2019).
2. Depending on the facts and circumstances of the particular case, the family court may order that the parties to child-related proceedings take part in an assessment conducted by a family consultant. This will result in the production of a family report (Australasian Institute of Judicial Administration [AIJA], 2020, [10.4]; Field, Jeffries, Rathus, & Lynch, 2016).
3. *Shuttle mediation* refers to mediation that takes place between parties who are not in the same room. The mediator "shuttles" between them (Harland, Cooper, Rathus, & Alexander, 2015, p. 94).
4. For further discussion of financial disclosure requirements, see Harland et al., 2015, pp. 130, 439.
5. An undertaking is an informal promise made by a person to the court. A breach of such an undertaking has no formal implications (AIJA, 2020, [7.11]).
6. Note that in Australia if one party is ordered to pay the other party's costs this order will be made once the litigation is finalized (Littrich & Murray, 2019, p. 229).
7. A permanent resident is a noncitizen who holds an Australian permanent visa or is usually resident in Australia and holds a permanent visa. It is similar to lawful

permanent resident status in the United States and permanent resident status in the United Kingdom (Borges Jelenic, 2020).

8. *Pan face* is a racist insult referring to her face as being flat, as if it had been hit with a pan.
9. Equal shared parental responsibility confers joint responsibility on the parents for long-term decisions relating to their children, including everyday needs such as clothing and food and longer-term decisions such as those regarding schooling and medical treatment (Harland et al., 2015, p. 118).
10. The Hague Convention on the Civil Aspects of International Child Abduction entered into force in 1983, with both Australia and the United States among the signatories. It applies to children under 16 years of age and aims to provide an expeditious way of returning a child who is abducted internationally from one member country to another (Harland et al., 2015, pp. 604–605; Malhotra, 2014).
11. Research conducted in the United States and in Australia has shown that lawyers make a difference to the claims made in protection order applications (Durfee, 2015; Fitzgerald & Douglas, 2019).
12. This experience is reflected in other Australian research, which has shown that a party who has experienced violence is at a disadvantage in the family law property settlement (Fehlberg & Millward, 2014).

8

Judges in the Protection Orders and Family Law Systems

INTRODUCTION

Although some of the women in the study ultimately got the order they had sought from the beginning of their engagement with legal processes, it was often years after their case began and much damage—including emotional trauma and financial cost—had been done. Ultimately, many of the women felt their court orders compromised their safety or the safety of their children (Elizabeth, 2019). The behavior of the judge and the way judges managed legal processes often left women feeling they were reliving the violence and abuse all over again (Gutowski & Goodman, 2020; Laing, 2017, p. 1321). Over time, some women reported that their interaction with judges improved. Sometimes this was because the judge, after several appearances, finally seemed to recognize the pattern of abuse, eventually accepting the woman's account. At other times this was because women's financial circumstances changed and they were able to obtain legal representation, which often enhanced their experience of court proceedings (see Chapter 7).

When the women discussed their interactions with judges, they usually talked about protection orders and family law proceedings. Women appeared before judges in these matters on multiple occasions throughout the period of the study (see Table 8.1), and some reported they had been to court so often they could not remember the number of times they had

Women, Intimate Partner Violence, and the Law. Heather Douglas, Oxford University Press (2021). © Oxford University Press.
DOI: 10.1093/oso/9780190071783.003.0008

Table 8.1 Engagement With Protection Order and Family Law Systems During Study Period

Interview	**1**		**2**		**3**	
	Past 12 Months		**Between Interviews 1 and 2**		**Between Interviews 2 and 3**	
	n	%	*n*	%	*n*	%
Total number of women interviewed	65	—	59	—	54	—
Has a protection order (temporary or final)	54	83	34	58	21	39
Appeared before a judge about protection order	55	85	16	27	8	15
Has a family law custody/property order (interim or final)	23	35	27	46	22	41
Appeared before a judge about custody or property arrangements	31	48	27	46	14	26

attended or exactly why. Most women reported, at best, inconsistent treatment by judges both within and between the protection order and family court systems, which they found frustrating and confusing (see Burgess-Proctor, 2012, p. 82). Fifty-five of the study women said they had attended a court about a protection order in the year preceding the first interview, and 31 had attended a court about child custody or property matters on at least one occasion.

As observed in previous chapters, in Australia, national legislation governs family law decisions about property allocation and child living arrangements, while state-based statutes and courts regulate protection orders (Dragiewicz, 2015, p. 128).[1] Canada similarly takes a national versus state approach (Ursel, Tutty, & leMaistre, 2008). By contrast, in the United States, state law covers both child custody arrangements and protection orders (Lemon, 2018), and in England and Wales, a patchwork of national laws cover these issues (Hunter, 2019).

Importantly, in Australia, women who apply for a protection order may see many different judges throughout the course of their hearings and may have contact with a different judge every time the matter is returned to court. This system often makes it difficult for a judge in a protection order case to develop an appreciation of the pattern of abuse engaged in by the perpetrator or to understand the pattern of abuse and identify the coercive and controlling nature of the abuser's behavior (Lynch & Laing, 2013, p. 12).

The inconsistency also provides an opportunity for legal systems abuse, with abusers often successfully applying for multiple adjournments. Many judges develop reputations for being, variously, responsive to allegations of IPV, suspicious about them, or neutral and open-minded. It is possible for parties who are aware of these reputations to "forum shop" and adjourn matters until the "right" judge is on the case. Potentially this provides an advantage to parties who are legally represented, or parties who have some familiarity with the court—as some serial abusers have. Although some protection order courts in Australia have introduced specialist domestic violence courts and specialist judges, most cases are not heard before a specialist judge or by a specialist court (Bond, Holder, Jeffries, & Fleming, 2017).

In contrast, in the family courts, cases are allocated to a specific judge who usually has carriage of the matter until it is finalized (Australian Law Reform Commission [ALRC], 2019, pp. 55–56). However, even though parties usually have the same family court judge throughout the process, a knowledgeable lawyer can still forum shop to get the "right judge" at the outset. For example, Bianca told me:

> You see, [ex-partner's] solicitor for the parenting matter actually filed in [a town outside of Brisbane] because he knew that [judge] would be sitting and that we would get on his list. . . . That's the thing with the law that I've discovered is it's not just about whether you know the law and what the legislation means and how it's interpreted and what the common law says about things, it's tactical. It's about . . . which judge—and you just don't know that unless you're in the legal field. How do you know which judge is going to view this particular thing this way and where to file? That sort of stuff makes self-represented

litigants at a real disadvantage. . . . It's more that you just don't know who's who in the zoo.

Bianca's comments are a reminder of a well-known saying in legal circles: "A good lawyer knows the law. A great lawyer knows the judge" (Ewick & Silbey, 1992, p. 746).

Four interrelated themes emerged from women's experiences of judges. First, many judges failed to understand the dynamics of IPV and coercive control (Stark, 2007), often prioritizing physical violence and minimizing other forms of abuse. Second, judges sometimes appeared to align with the abuser, discounting the woman's experience of abuse. This view was underpinned by judicial officers' lack of preparation for hearings, rubber-stamping witness subpoenas, and failing to stop irrelevant witness examination. These approaches often facilitated abusers' misuse of the legal system. Third, women reported that judges, especially in the family courts, prioritized fathers' rights to contact with children over safety. Finally, women's stories also demonstrated resistance to their abuser's control over them through the courts, and their efforts to ensure the safety of their children regardless of court orders. These four themes are addressed in turn.

Understanding the Dynamics of IPV

Research has consistently highlighted judges' lack of understanding of the dynamics of IPV and their regular discounting or minimizing of forms of nonphysical abuse (Agnew-Brune, Moracco, Person, & Bowling, 2017, pp. 1929–1930; DeKeseredy & Dragiewicz, 2014, p. 236; Laing, 2017, p. 1324; Ptacek, 1999). This was the experience of many of the women in the study. Many appeared before more than one judge in relation to their protection order cases. For some, this compounded judges' failures to appreciate the ongoing coercive and controlling dynamic of the relationship and the continuation of this dynamic after separation. Sandra reflected that when there is a different judge each time, they don't get to see the pattern of abusive behavior: "So they're not aware of each individual case, when it keeps occurring." Similarly, Gillian explained:

> It wasn't so much problem judges it was the problem of having different ones along the way. So that made it exceptionally hard because [the judge] hasn't got a clue what's going on . . . so then of course it would just get put back to another mention and, oh, we'll deal with it again in 6 weeks and . . . I think three or four different judges, it made it very difficult.

Judicial comments often ignored past physical abuse (Jeffries, Field, Menih, & Rathus, 2016, p. 1362) and minimized nonphysical abuse, especially text messages and stalking-type behaviors. In Ingrid's (CALD) case, after a 2-hour hearing the judge refused her application for a protection order. Ingrid explained he "threw out the sexual violence" that had occurred during the relationship, noting that it was difficult to prove and, because the parties had separated, it wouldn't happen again. Excluding the previous sexual violence ignores the high risk of future harm to Ingrid that is associated with it (J. Campbell et al., 2003). Although Ingrid had evidence of hundreds of text messages, the judge determined that they were not "directly abusive or threatening." The text messages from her abuser were numerous and could have been interpreted as stalking and a red flag for future risk (Mechanic, Weaver, & Resick, 2000).

Even where evidence of physical violence was available, this was not necessarily enough to ensure that a woman's claims were taken seriously. Gillian had tried unsuccessfully to get a protection order. While she continued to fear IPV, the judge determined that the serious physical abuse that underpinned her fear had occurred too long ago, even though she had been physically harmed only a few months previously. Frieda attended court to apply for a protection order and heard the judge refer to her application and say to a police officer: "Oh, is this another pushing and shoving case?" Frieda had been physically assaulted, and the police ultimately prosecuted her abuser for assault.

Some judges assumed that because the couple had separated or that the abuse had not continued while a temporary protection order was in place, there was no longer any danger for the woman. For example, Carol's abusive ex-partner, Rod, regularly traveled between Australia and overseas. Whenever he was in Australia, he stalked Carol. He constantly sent her flowers and text messages, up to 12 a day, and visited her workplace. On one occasion he sent a photo of a dead child lying on a beach. Carol interpreted this as a veiled threat. In an email, which she sent me after interview 1, Carol said, "I have changed my home phone number, my mobile number and email address countless times, and he always manages to find me." Rod was difficult to locate, and the police had trouble serving him with the protection order application. As a result, Carol's application had been adjourned on many occasions. Each time she attended court she had no idea whether Rod would be there or what would happen. At interview 2, Carol reported on a recent protection order hearing where the judge was "was horrible, shocking . . . abrupt." The judge refused to extend her protection order, failing to see Rod's behavior as coercive and controlling. Carol believed Rod carefully avoided service of the application specifically to avoid any final order being made so he could continue his abuse.

Rosa (CALD) believed that several of the judges discounted her fears because she was separated from the abuser, and they believed that the risk of future violence had dissipated:

> I didn't get the [protection] order because the relationship had been over for [some months] and the violent incidents were a long time ago by the time I got to court. Also we had a family court agreement for the child transfer to happen regularly and in front of the police station, so the [judge] thought that having that sorted out meant that I wasn't in danger.

Yet for Rosa the threat of violence after separation was ongoing. She found the child handovers, recognized as a risky time for further abuse (DeKeseredy, Dragiewicz, & Schwartz, 2017, pp. 115–140), intimidating. Judges often failed to accept that women frequently experience continuing coercive control and intimidation after separation, and therefore women's ongoing fear of future abuse is rational (DeKeseredy et al., 2017; Macdonald, 2016, p. 837). In some cases, judges interpreted the IPV as a relationship issue. In Jacinta's protection order hearing, the judge said, "If you just don't get on anymore, then just don't talk to each other." The comment suggests mutual violence but also that separation, and not talking to him, will necessarily end the violence.

Aligning With Abusers

Judges' dismissal of women's stories, failure to carefully manage court procedures, and lack of preparation can facilitate abuse, allowing perpetrators to use legal processes to continue their abuse and extend their control.

Dismissing and Silencing Women

Bianca attended court to finalize her protection order application. She thought it would be straightforward because the police had applied for the order on her behalf and had recommended that the children should be protected under the order. Her partner, Tom, had already been charged with kidnapping and assaulting her. The judge in the first mention of the protection order matter had a different view: "He said to Tom, 'Oh, this is ridiculous mate, you don't have to agree to this.' He actually used the word mate. . . . That didn't give me a very good feeling." Bianca's comment underlines the importance of choice of language used by judges (Hunter, 2008, p. 87). In Janet's protection order hearing, the judge said, "I am sick of women like you coming into here, putting [protection orders] on guys, and then hooking back up with them." Janet had never applied for a protection order, and this was a big step for her. She could not believe she was "abused" in this way and felt "guilty" leaving that court.

Hilary similarly felt she was "blamed" for applying for a variation of her protection order. Hilary had a protection order with a condition that required her ex-partner, Bruce, to stay out of the house but allowed him access to a shed in the yard. She had consented to this condition believing that Bruce would be less angry as a result. Despite the order, Bruce came into the house, sometimes leaving telltale signs, such as dates highlighted on the calendar and food taken from the refrigerator. Because Hilary found this behavior intimidating, she decided to apply for a variation to the order so that he could not use the shed:

> [Judge] said to me, "Well, I don't know what you want, you've got an order, what more do you want?" I'm going, "Oh my god, it's in the application." I was just thrown and she—the way she was talking was very much like I'd done the wrong thing . . . I'd done the wrong thing by asking for another variation on the order. She said, when it got to the bit about the fact that he'd been in the house when it clearly says he's not to enter the property at all, [the judge] said to me, "Well, what did you expect him to do if he needed to go to the toilet?"

The message implicit in Bruce's behavior of entering the house is that he is still watching Hilary and can enter her space whenever he wants to. He is the one still in control, and her space for action is limited depending on his whim (Sharp-Jeffs, Kelly, & Klein, 2018). Hilary found that the police took her concerns seriously, but "it was the judges who maybe didn't so much, and helped to make it hard."

Frieda attended court to finalize a 12-month protection order. Because the police had applied for the order, the police prosecutor spoke for Frieda in the courtroom. Frieda had never met the police prosecutor, who had limited knowledge of her case. When Frieda's ex-partner, Drako, asked the judge to reduce the 12-month period for the protection order, Frieda said, "I don't agree." Immediately the judge said, "You're not allowed to talk." Frieda took up the story:

> I just came out and said like, "This is a joke. Why are we in this court that's a joke? . . . Why is this in a court where judges can say whatever they like and there doesn't seem to be any clear process?" . . . I just had this sense of, like, this is going to be really hard. These judges

> don't believe me. But it just gave me this sense of, like, I don't know what sort of process this is but this is some sort of crazy not proper court. . . . That was the sense I got out of it. . . . In a separate sense where you just feel like it operates more to its own rules. . . . It felt like unaccountable.

These comments illustrate the silencing and discrediting that women experience in the legal system, a phenomenon that has been widely recognized (Epstein & Goodman, 2019, p. 403; Goodmark, 2005, pp. 742–745; Person, Moracco, Agnew-Brune, & Bowling, 2018, pp. 1486–1487; Smart, 1989, p. 11).

Failure to Manage Proceedings

Women provided many examples of judicial failure to manage legal processes, allowing abusive men to take control of proceedings, and by extension continue their abuse and efforts to control them. One way this can occur is through abusers being given more time to speak than is necessary (Slote et al., 2005, p. 1385). For example, Jennifer said:

> The [judge] was as weak as they come. In court, as I was giving evidence, [abuser] was sitting behind—you know that bar that divides the public area from the court proceeding, he was sitting on a bench there. As I was giving evidence he was waving his arms in the air going, "Ssh, ssh, ssh," belittling everything I said. I could hear him and I wouldn't look at him. The judge said to him he would be removed from court, but he didn't remove him from court.

Several women reported that many of their friends and relatives had been subpoenaed by the perpetrator to give evidence in the perpetrator's case, even though their testimony would not assist the perpetrator's claims. Where this occurred, interviewees saw it as a form of continued harassment by the abuser. Despite their wide powers to manage their courts (AIJA, 2020, [3.1.11]), this type of behavior was not recognized by the judge as abuse.

Lack of Preparation

Most interviewees attending protection order hearings or the family courts for the first time found that judges had rarely read the material on file at the commencement of the case. The civil nature of both the protection order and the family court systems is based on a premise that equal players will come together to negotiate and consent to mutually suitable orders. This expectation is at odds with a context where one party is trying to continue to abuse and control the other. Although the expectation of settlement may explain, in part, a lack of judicial preparation in advance of court matters, this approach can play into the hands of the abuser. Long court lists no doubt also contribute to the lack of preparation, but an unprepared judge may not understand the abuse history and may, as a result, allow adjournments and other system abuses (Hunter, 2008, p. 123; Laing, 2017, p. 1329).

Lack of preparation by judicial officers can place extra stresses on a woman who has experienced abuse, especially if she is unrepresented. Yet again she may have to explain herself, retell her allegations, and revisit her experiences of abuse. Carol said: "I said my piece because you have to every single time. Surely they have got some record, some history. Then there are different [judges]. . . . I don't believe they read the background before they come in. . . . I don't trust the judge's decision." Faith said that the judge did not read her lengthy statement in support of her protection order application. She found this "disappointing" and wondered about the point of submitting it in advance. Shelley expressed similar frustrations about her experience in the family courts: "I don't think the judges actually read what costs you thousands and thousands of dollars to get generated by your solicitors. . . . I had an image of a judge, a judicial system and how it works. I have no respect for a man that, it is quite obvious to me, has not even read the documents that cost me thousands of dollars to get to him."

Lisa's Experience

Lisa's story illustrates how inconsistency between judges and judicial alignment with abusers allowed her ex-husband to continue his IPV through the courts. Lisa felt she and her child were "dismissed" and "not heard" by the courts. She facilitated her son's family court ordered contact with her abusive ex-husband even though there was evidence that it was unsafe. Lisa struggled to comprehend how her ex-partner's history of abuse and the continued evidence of his dangerous lifestyle did not affect family court decisions about contact arrangements. She was frustrated that it took 3 years for the family courts to make the orders that she had suggested at the outset.

> ***Lisa, interview 1:*** *At the beginning [the judge] was very dismissive toward me and very stern with me and very matter of fact . . . family reports and all the other stuff, I've done everything that the court has ordered me to do and he's refused.*[2]

Lisa met Sean at work, and they were initially friends before moving in together. Lisa already had children from another relationship who she cared for. Sean didn't want Lisa to work; he wanted her to stay home and "play wife." She says, "I thought I had finally found Mr. Perfect." She resigned from work but felt increasingly isolated, Sean did not allow her to have contact with her friends. When she complained that he was allowed to contact his friends, "he always turned it so I was being paranoid or I was being jealous."

About a year into the relationship, Lisa became pregnant. Lisa knew Sean had had a drug habit in the past, but he started to use the drug ice again and became angry when he was coming down. One night, when she was about 6 months pregnant, he smashed his phone and flung his heavy leather biker jacket at her stomach. She began to hemorrhage and was rushed to hospital. Despite this incident, the child, Noah, was born safely a few months later.

After the birth the family moved to a small town with fewer than 2,000 people, 4 hours' drive from the nearest major town but close to Sean's work. Lisa says, "Now you are talking isolated." Lisa was mostly at the house with the children, without a car, phone, or money. She had to spend her government child allowance on groceries. Sean monitored her Facebook, rarely assisted with the children, and routinely called her lazy. One evening he grabbed her by the shoulders and pushed her into a wall, badly dislocating her shoulder. She had surgery to repair her shoulder, and the hospital staff referred Sean and Lisa to counseling. Lisa blamed herself, thinking maybe she was experiencing postnatal depression. On another occasion, Sean picked her up and pushed her into a door frame. She recalls a time when she was taking painkillers and Sean wanted sex. She said normally, the sex was "partially submissive, partially OK, I don't know. But, yeah, for the first time ever I had said 'no,' and that started a huge fight." She left after that incident and set up a place with her kids. Later, Sean convinced her to come back. She said: "I wanted the family thing."

Things soon escalated again, and so Lisa moved out about a year before our first interview. At the time, she applied for a protection order, but Sean implored her to drop it, which she did. Also around the same time, Sean applied to the family courts for 50 percent of time with Noah. Currently, Sean sees Noah every second weekend, and the handover takes place at the childcare center. Lisa says Noah often comes home from these visits with "bruises" and "gashes," and she has "just treated him, healed him" and sent him back. Sean has a lawyer; Lisa does not and has been refused legal aid. There is an independent children's lawyer who is supposed to look after Noah's interests, but Lisa says he is never prepared.[3] Sean and Lisa have had several appearances in the family court, and a family report has been prepared, which recommends Sean and Lisa undergo drug testing. Lisa feels that the family court judge is "dismissive" of her.

During the 2 months leading up to the interview, the windows in Lisa's house and car were smashed with rocks, her house was broken into, and the house security camera was stolen. She suspects Sean but can't prove it. He pulls up outside her house sometimes and posts threats to harm her on Facebook. She reported these incidents to the police, who recommended she apply for a protection order.[4] Last month she applied for a protection order, but before the matter was to be heard in court, Sean lodged a protection order application against her.[5] She says that so far "nothing has come of it. That's where the system fails."

Lisa is currently living in social housing with her children and is studying for a diploma. She says, "My house is set up with security doors.

I've got another dog now . . . he scares people. . . . I'm not living in fear, but I have fears."

Between the times of the first and second interviews, Lisa sent me a news report about her partner being caught up in a raid at his house where the police recovered weapons, ammunition, methamphetamine, and steroids. Despite the seriousness of the news report, her email seemed relaxed and casual; she said: "Don't know if this is relevant, but thought I'd share this with you. It was at Sean's house, I don't believe Noah was there at the time, but it gives you an idea of what goes on at Sean's house."

> ***Lisa, interview 2:*** *[The judge] wasn't happy with me. Like the judge said, "He seems sorry for what he's done and he's not going to do it again." I couldn't even fathom that. It was like, are you serious? . . . Again, different judge, so the third different judge on the [protection order application]—he was like—he's saying here that "he's not going to do this stuff to you anymore and he seems like a nice gentleman and a man of his word" and all this sort of stuff. I'm just standing there looking at him like, shaking my head.*

Nine months have passed since our first interview. Lisa says both their protection order applications were heard in court recently. Both Lisa and Sean filed statements in support, and neither of them had a lawyer representing them for this process. Lisa had some help from a community legal service lawyer writing the statements for the protection order and the family court matter. She says she would have been "buggered" without this help and "would have lost her kid." Lisa finds the court appearances "intimidating, frightening."

The protection order proceedings have been protracted. The first judge in the protection order matter was very "dismissive," saying Lisa's allegations of abuse were "all in the past," and the matter was adjourned so they could file statements. At the second mention, Lisa received a copy of Sean's statement, in the court, when they were both in front of the judge. Sean's statement claimed she "was a prostitute for 10 years, that she was a drug addict, racist, apparently sexually abused him." She read these things for the first time in front of the judge. She says it is "horrible that he could get in there and say all that just horribly untrue stuff and I can't defend it." However, the second judge "sort of ripped into him," and so Sean sought another adjournment to get legal advice. Eventually the third judge, despite describing Sean as a "nice gentleman and a man of his word," gave Lisa a 12-month protection order and dismissed Sean's application. Lisa is waiting to receive a copy of the order.

For the family law matters, Lisa's advice from the community legal center was to negotiate and be flexible with Sean so they could settle custody. Sean was represented by a lawyer, and an independent children's lawyer was still involved. Ultimately, after several court mentions, two sessions of mediation, and two family reports, Lisa got the orders she wanted. She says, "I stuck to my guns and said he could have every second fortnight. . . . Pretty much what I'd said I'd wanted, you can take him every second weekend."

I ask Lisa about her experience of the judges in the family court. She says, "Dismissive," and "like, at first it was like, oh, she's a nasty woman, she's trying to keep him away from his child. Then it's, oh, she's a nasty woman who's trying to take all his money." She says it has taken 3 years of "battling" to get an order for child custody arrangements that she asked for from the beginning, including a regular payment from Sean for Noah's medical expenses.[6] She says, "Part of me is like, yay, it's all over and it's done with. The other part of me is really frustrated that he got away with all the stuff that he did. . . . I'm just getting myself healthy, taking care of myself mentally and now physically and concentrating on the children, children, children."

> ***Lisa, interview 3:*** *I think the [IPV] and the family court need to be connected. The fact that he could be smashing cars and having the police siege with [police] teams going through [his] house. Yet being in court 2 weeks later and be granted a shared custody of our son. They're making me out to be evil because—hey—I admitted I smoked [cannabis] once. I had been honest all the way through and he's lied. . . . Their word is just accepted.*

Lisa and I meet 9 months after the second interview. She tells me, "It took however many years . . . to get what I said at the start—he'd have him every second weekend—and 3 years later and that's exactly what he's agreed to. So we wasted 3 years of courts and everybody's time." She says, "No one's listening, do you know what I mean?"

Lisa says that the child support money is coming through every month, and Sean is having contact with their child every second weekend. The handovers are "pleasant." The protection order ran out recently. She says she feels lucky that child protection services didn't get involved with her case. She tells me, "We have moments where . . . he'll get angry for 2 weeks or 3 weeks and there'll be nasty emails and no phone contact. So, it still sort of flicks in and out," but she does not plan to renew the protection order. She still has that "looking over the shoulder feeling."

Prioritizing Fathers' Rights to Contact With Children Over Safety

Lisa's experiences were not uncommon among the women in the study. Lisa found that some judges implied she was doing the wrong thing by challenging Sean's "right" to have contact with their child, regardless of evidence that he was engaging in risky behaviors. Despite her belief that her child was at risk on contact visits, Lisa thought she would have risked more dangerous orders if she denied contact. She was fearful that child protection services might get involved in her case if she challenged contact altogether. In similar contexts, many of the women felt pressured to settle matters or risk a worse outcome from a trial (Jeffries et al., 2016; Laing, 2017).

Of the 43 women who had children with the perpetrator, close to half ($n = 28$) of them were engaged with the family law system during the study period in relation to issues about their children. Six women had children who were 14 years or older and were not subject to family law orders.[7] Notably, some women reported they had endured years of abuse so that when they separated, they could avoid the family courts.[8] Nine women had children with the perpetrator, who were under 14 years but were not engaged with the family courts, and nine women had children in state care at some point during the study or in the 12 months preceding interview 1 (see Chapter 4). One woman, Shelley, was involved in both the family courts and the child protection system.

Women who did engage with the family courts had orders for some form of contact with the father regardless of the type of violence alleged, suggesting that courts prioritize the father's rights to contact with children in spite of the violence. This phenomenon has been identified by other researchers (Dragiewicz, 2015, p. 139; DeKeseredy et al., 2017, pp. 29, 166; Manjoo, 2015, p. 25; Rathus, Jeffries, Menih, & Field, 2019).

A number of women (n = 11) reported that they attended the family courts in the preceding year (or less) at all of the three interviews. Their experiences demonstrate a failure by some judges to understand how past IPV underlies the continuing interaction between parents after separation. Judges often exhorted women to give their ex-partners more "chances," idealizing the idea of the family (Naughton, O'Donnell, Greenwood, & Muldoon, 2015, p. 353; Saunders, Faller, & Tolman, 2016). Many judges misunderstood the long journey to separation that had preceded the women's court appearances, and the fact that women had already given their ex-partners many chances in the past (see Chapter 9). Such attitudes show a failure to comprehend how these extra chances might afford further opportunities to the abuser to continue his abuse through the courts and beyond. Faith's custody matter was adjourned on many occasions by her ex-partner, Ryan. He kept seeking, and getting, more chances to fulfill various court directions. At interview 1, Faith told me she wanted contact to take place at a contact center; Ryan wanted to see the children, with his parents supervising:

> [The judge] said, "OK, so the parents, I'll order to go at the parents' house and they need to put an affidavit in," and I stood up then and I said, "I think they've already had a chance to do that and they didn't, they didn't supervise." He said ". . . we need to give the family a chance."

Kim suggested that judges start from the position of blaming women so they can give yet another chance to abusers, and this causes long delays. At the third interview, she said:

> If one partner is a perpetrator of [IPV] . . . the judge has to be able to deal with that. Not just forget that and just continually drag the woman through so that the woman—this is the woman's fault. The woman's a game player. The woman's this, the woman is . . . Instead of looking at the hard facts of what's actually happened, instead of just saying, well—it was always, give him 100 chances and give me none. It feels like—well, it feels like you're drowning when you're in that situation. It feels like you can't get to the top where the air is.

Extra unwarranted chances contribute to delay. Of the 23 women who were interviewed a third time, and had family court orders about children, 14 women said their engagement with the family law courts was still ongoing, and only 9 thought they had "final" orders. Twelve of the women had been involved with the family courts for 3 years or more (see Table 8.2).

From the beginning of their engagement with the family courts Lisa, Shelley, and Kim sought orders that specified the children should live with them and have contact with the father. In the end, after 3 years for Lisa and after 5 or 6 years for Shelly and Kim, and many hearings, the orders they sought from the beginning were finally made. The delays in Shelley's case were devastating for her relationship with her children. After several years in the family court, with the children living with her abuser, she was

Table 8.2 STATUS OF ENGAGEMENT WITH THE FAMILY LAW SYSTEM AT INTERVIEW 3 (CUSTODY)

Number of Years Engaged	Number of Women Involved in Ongoing Proceedings	Number of Women With Final Orders
1 to 2	6	5
3 to 4	6	2
5 to 6	2	2

estranged from the older two and was trying to rebuild her relationship with the youngest one. She said, "In the end of the day I think we took too long to get to where we were. If [the judge] had done more earlier . . . but kids [were] in a toxic environment for 12 months."

Kim experienced years of IPV and after leaving with her child then had to navigate an ongoing family court matter for 6 years. At interview 3 she reported that she had achieved the outcome she sought from the outset. Kim's comments at interview 3 underscore her frustration with the family court processes and the toll it took on her:

> What I've had to go through, people shouldn't have to go through this. . . . I'm really angry with the family court. . . . I have sole custody. I'm happy that that eventually happened. . . . But that should have happened in the beginning. There needed to be some psychological testing done of both of us, or something to show that he was the perpetrator. They never—the family court never accepted any information to do with [IPV]. They just dismissed every bit of it. It wasn't till the very end when Her Honor saw it and actually took it into account that she actually did anything. But it kept us in court for 6 years.

Felicity's Experience

Felicity has had contact with at least three judges in her journey through the courts, two in relation to protection order applications, and one in the family court matter. Her story highlights how multiple judges have dismissed physical, emotional, and religious abuse against Felicity and placed pressure on her to settle for unsupervised contact between her child and her violent ex-partner. By the time of interview 3, Felicity's custody case had been in the family courts for 3 years and was still not finalized.

> ***Felicity, interview 1:*** *[The judge said,] "He's telling me here today that he still loves you. . . . Why don't you two go outside and sort this out because this man has clearly changed. He's saying that he wants to resolve this." I think this is a matter for the family law court to decide.*

I meet Felicity at her workplace, and we spend nearly 2 hours talking about her experiences with the legal system. Felicity describes her ex-partner, Jason, as "tall, masculine and intelligent." Early on in their relationship, Felicity felt that they had a lot in common: Both were in their 40s, had children with previous partners, were tertiary-educated professionals with good jobs, and were practicing Christians. They separated, after a 2-year relationship, just over a year before our first interview. Thinking back, she says, "Even how we met was quite deceitful." They met at a hotel when they were socializing with separate groups of people. Jason began talking to Felicity, he asked for her number, but she refused—several times. Jason then offered to give her his number so that she could call him. Felicity agreed and started putting his number in her phone. It was difficult to hear, and she was slow. He said, "Look I'll do it for you." He took her phone, put his number in, and dialed: "So . . . he had my number, which I didn't even realize until the next day when he texted me."

They were married within a year. Worryingly, Jason told Felicity's parents and sister they were not welcome at the wedding or later in their home. As the relationship progressed, her girlfriends were also excluded. He would say, "You shouldn't be on the phone talking to your girlfriends. I'm home. This is our time together."

Felicity recalls being assaulted by Jason on their wedding night. He yelled at her, pushed her, and ripped her necklace from her neck. A few months after their wedding, Jason became very angry when she announced she was pregnant. He waved a knife at her, but she says, "I knew he wasn't going to slash me open. It was just his way of putting me in my place." Every 6 weeks Jason would have an explosion. On one occasion "he got all the drawers out . . . and threw them out on the lawn, had smashed my makeup." Jason had access to guns. When he threatened to shoot her, Felicity left and she called the police. She said the police did not mention getting a protection order: "They didn't offer me a single thing. Trust me, you could tell I was preggie. . . . I was enormous. They didn't even say, look, we need to do a child at risk. There was nothing." Later, Jason promised to seek help, and they reconciled after a few weeks apart. Felicity gave birth to a baby boy, Henry, but the home environment became increasingly oppressive, with outbursts of anger, yelling, and throwing things. On one occasion Jason said, "I'm going to put a $2.50 bullet through your brain and that's overcapitalizing on you." Given Jason had access to a gun through his work, Felicity was scared by this threat. She locked herself and the child in a room in the house, then left the next morning when Jason went to work. She shows me some of the 800 text messages from the weeks after she left, many with religious references pointing to her lack of faith and claiming that her behavior was disappointing God.[9]

With the help of a lawyer, Felicity applied for a protection order but was later served with Jason's application for a protection order. On the day of the planned hearing, Jason withdrew his application, and after a 1-day hearing the judge issued a protection order in favor of Felicity. Felicity paid $10,000 (USD6,100) in lawyer's fees.[10] After this, Felicity allowed Jason contact with baby Henry in "2-hour snippets" on the weekends. Handovers were very stressful. Jason behaved in an intimidating way and said things like "Happy you destroyed the family?" The police said they couldn't do anything about the child handovers unless there was a parenting plan. On one occasion, Jason refused to return Henry, and Felicity contacted the police. Initially police suggested that Felicity should collect the child from Jason's house. Felicity reminded them about the history of violence and explained Henry was breastfed. Then the police assisted her because the child was in danger of not being fed—not because of a risk of violence.

The protection order expired 3 months prior to our first interview, and Felicity had already applied to renew it because she believed that it had ensured Jason did not contact her. This time she represented herself. Jason told the judge he loved his wife and that the protection order affected his work. By the time Felicity applied for the new protection order, the physical violence occurred some time ago. Felicity says the judge believed Jason, refused to renew the order, and suggested they "go and sort it out." Since then, she says, "The emails [have] just kept coming and coming and being demanding and spiteful." Jason applied to the family courts for shared care of Henry. Felicity and Jason tried shuttle mediation, but this was unsuccessful so now Felicity is preparing for a family court hearing.[11]

Felicity is living in privately rented accommodations, has changed jobs, and now works part-time in order to juggle work and childcare. Henry has been diagnosed with a disability.

> ***Felicity, interview 2:*** *Every time we've appeared before [the judge,] he hasn't even read the file, and he said that. I said to him, "Well it's in the file," and he goes "Well I haven't read the file." He goes, "Do you know how many cases I have?" I said, "No but I said I assume that's why I sent it in." He said, "Well, no, because we assume that you two are going to be able to resolve this."*

Twelve months have passed since out first interview, and Felicity says she feels she is "living the roller-coaster ride in the family court." Jason applied for unsupervised contact with Henry, whom he has hasn't seen for months, mainly because he has been working interstate. There have been three appearances at the family court, and there is a hearing scheduled for next month. Felicity is frustrated because the judge never reads the file in advance of the court process. When she expressed her frustration to the judge, he said, "We assume that you two are going to resolve this." The judge put significant pressure on Felicity and Jason to settle, saying, "Well, why can't you guys just try and resolve this issue?" and "You've got to give me something." Throughout, Felicity maintained that she was happy to settle with the recommendation of the family report for Jason to have supervised contact—a position that did not satisfy Jason.

Felicity says that currently Jason is allowed to have contact with Henry for 2 hours a week under supervision. Felicity feels that the family court judge, the same one for all the appearances to date, is "quite hard" on her, but so far the interim orders have required Jason's contact to be supervised. Felicity and Jason must share the costs of a contact center.[12] Felicity says Jason breaches the contact agreement all the time by turning up early or late so he can see her, and "there's no consequence."

Since the last time we met, Felicity and Jason have attended court on several occasions to meet with registrars and file documents. Felicity gets all her paperwork in on time, but she says Jason is never ready, and this leads to new dates being set. She says, "It's all to have contact with me," and tells me, "I still don't feel as though the whole process has supported me."

At the time of the second interview, a new family report is being written, and Felicity says she is stressed about the future trial. Both Felicity and Jason are still unrepresented, but Felicity is getting some advice from a lawyer to prepare her affidavits. Felicity still doesn't have a protection order, and Jason continues to email her all the time. His emails are long and "waffle on"; they accuse her of all sorts of bad behavior but always include something about Henry. Because of the mention of the child, she feels the police won't do anything.

> ***Felicity, interview 3:*** *The judge said: "If these long emails are introduced to represent family violence, I don't see it—they are not threats, they are not intimidation . . . they are simply the father seeking to see his [child]."*

I meet Felicity 7 months after our second interview, and she and Jason have eventually had their hearing in the family court, with both of them represented themselves. The second family report was prepared and presented to the court. Felicity says it was very positive about her and highlighted that Jason does not understand how to deal with Henry's disability. The judge decided to make an interim order. In doing so, he quoted from a number of the lengthy messages Jason has sent to Felicity. Jason's messages are implicitly abusive. For example, he refers to the "string of male role models" that have visited. Felicity interprets this as an accusation of bringing multiple men into her home. Jason suggests she has a lack of empathy and urges her to follow "God's will" and love one another. Felicity understands this is emotional abuse and an attack on her religious observation. Amid these comments are references to Henry. However, the judge found that, despite their profusion, the comments did not support Felicity's claims of continued IPV.

Despite all of the text messages, the family court judge did not find there had been a pattern of violence that he should take into account. Rather, his order states that the parties should "not denigrate each other" in the presence of the child.[13] The judge noted, that he was perplexed that the father referred to his natural right to be a father . The judge also expressed his frustration that Felcity expeted him to 'trawl' through all the documents. The judge made interim orders that the child continue to live with the mother, with the father continuing to have supervised contact at a contact center at a minimum of 2 hours per week. The judge stated his concerns about allowing unsupervised contact with the child were not about IPV but rather about the father's lack of understanding of his child's disability. Before making final orders, the judge wanted to ensure the father had a chance to develop an understanding of Henry's disability and the necessary skills to respond to it. Felicity expects to return to the family court again within a year.

Keeping Children Safe

For women who had children with their abuser, the safety of their children was central to their decision-making. Citing their children's safety, many women resisted the orders made by the court or were determined not to engage in family court processes at all or took alterative legal approaches. Four women reported they had withheld their children from contact and breached family court orders in an effort to keep the children safe from abuse. In all four of these cases, unsupervised contact was ordered to the father, and in all four cases IPV had been recognized by the family courts. Three of these women also had a protection order in place.

Evie's ex-partner, Simon, had served long sentences for a variety of offenses, including attempted murder and assault, and was not allowed to get a job working with children. His abuse of Evie included gradually isolating her from her friends and family "one by one," endless insults, and cutting her off from money. She was fearful of his rages. The first time Evie and her daughter left Simon, she managed to get legal aid, and the court ordered the child to live with Evie. However, the court also ordered that Simon could see the child every second day unsupervised at his house. Evie asked: "He can't be around children but yet he can be unsupervised . . . around his daughter. What's the difference?" Evie had asked the judge to use a contact center and offered to pay, but the judge "refused to listen." Evie says it was a "horrible time" in her life, and she experienced high levels of abuse at both drop-off and pickup. Evie decided to move back in with Simon because it was better than trying to manage the contact arrangement. She had moved out again a few months before the one and only interview we had. By this time she had obtained a protection order and was living at a secret address, and Simon had not had any contact with their daughter.

Anna has family court orders but has also stopped contact with the child's father, Nathan, because he was constantly breaching the family court orders or turning up under the influence of drugs. She feels like she receives conflicting advice. The family court tells her Nathan should see their child unsupervised, while the child protection and police services praise her for acting protectively when she refuses to allow contact between her child and his father. The price of refusing court-ordered contact can be high. It is possible to be criminally prosecuted for contravention of family court orders, although a defense is available if a person can show that he or she reasonably believed this behavior was necessary to protect another person.[14] At interview 2, Yvonne explained she had stopped the children's court-ordered contact with their father because "the whole point for me has always been the safety of the children." When I spoke to Yvonne again at interview 3, the children's father, Emir, had initiated an application in the family court for the children to live with him. The first time the case was heard in the court, Yvonne's lawyer tried to explain why Yvonne had stopped contact. But Yvonne says: "[The judge] said, 'Sit down, don't say a word, your client has breached the orders, how dare you?' . . . About a year and a half had lapsed since [my son] had seen his father, but I believed I had mitigating circumstances." Contravention charges did go ahead but were dismissed. The initial family court orders have been reinstated, with the youngest child now seeing his father regularly pending a further hearing. Yvonne thinks Emir's aim was "to basically get me in jail or some kind of punishment." Yvonne still thinks Emir's contact with their son is unsafe but facilitates it as best she can.

Nine women who had young children in their care decided to avoid the family courts. They all reported that there had been no application made to the family courts by their children's father. In general, this group of women had carefully considered their options and taken a different path. In two cases women had sent children to live with their extended family in their country of origin. Both Euni (CALD) and Pari (CALD) pointed out that because their home countries were not signatories to the Hague Convention, there was no risk their partners could apply to the Australian family courts to seek return of the child.[15] Pari's ex-husband had seriously injured her on many occasions during the relationship, and he often threatened that if she left, he would take away their child. Pari did some research and decided to send her son back to her home country "because they say that if you stay here, no matter what, you both will have dual custody and equal parenting responsibilities and all that stuff." Pari says her son is growing up safely with her extended family, and she visits every summer.

Chi returned to her home country with her child, but her ex-partner took action under the Hague Convention to have the child returned to Australia. Chi returned to Australia with her preschool-aged child; at the airport, they were met by police, who helped Chi and her child find a shelter to live in. They lived there for several months, and she obtained a protection order because of her ex-partner's continued abuse after her return. The family courts have ordered that she should have sole responsibility for the child, and in light of the danger the perpetrator poses, he is allowed only a couple of hours of supervised contact at a contact center each week. Chi would prefer to return to her home country with her child, where she has support, but she is not allowed to leave. At the time of interview 3, she was waiting for a hearing date at the family court to get final orders.

In seven other cases, the children were living with their mothers in Australia and their ex-partners had not initiated any applications in the family courts. Three of these women had protection orders in place. Francis's protection order included a condition that her ex-partner, Mark, should not contact the children unless there was a family court order in place. At the time of the third interview he had not seen their children for more than a year. Francis would have liked some certainty through a family court order for when her oldest started school, but her lawyer told her not to make an application because it would be "opening up a can of worms."

Two women separated while pregnant with their abuser and did not identify the abuser on the birth certificate as the child's father. Martha made this decision. She thought it meant that she could not claim child support but also that she did not have to allow child contact to the father. By the time of the third interview, her ex-partner had not challenged the decision to exclude him from the birth certificate, nor had he sought contact. Martha said:

> I also don't see anything good of having a relationship with [the father]. I think that's true for anyone who's experienced domestic violence from their partner. That's why I don't understand why the courts keep on going, "Oh, look, if you bash their mother, he's still allowed to have a relationship with the child."

Julia is avoiding the family courts. During their relationship, Julia's ex-partner, Adam, regularly threatened that he would "get full custody" of their child, and this was her "biggest fear". She has a protection order but does not trust the family courts: "I am a bit concerned that I am going to come across a biased opinion of, you know, the father's entitled to 50 per cent and they're not actually going to take into account the risk to the child."

IMAGINING BETTER JUDGING

When judges fail to understand the dynamics of IPV and coercive control, when they do not prepare for hearings or maintain control of the court, and when they commit to facilitating the abuser's ongoing relationship with his children regardless of the level of abuse, there is a risk that the safety of women and children is sacrificed. These failures also open up the opportunities for perpetrators to use the legal system to continue the abuse, allowing legal processes to be a vehicle for further traumatization (S. Miller, 2018, p. 107; Toews & Bermea, 2017). These failures may also drive women away from seeking formal justice, which may further compromise their safety and the safety of their children.

Women survivors of violence place great importance on feeling that the court is a safe place. In many studies, including this one, women emphasize the judge's tone, empathy, and language, along with denunciation of the perpetrator's violence, as important to them (Bell, Perez, Goodman, & Dutton, 2011; Ptacek, 1999; Roberts, Chamberlain, & Delfabbro, 2015). When judges get this right, it helps avoid and reduce retraumatization. At her first interview, Doya (CALD) said the judge in her protection order hearing made the court very private, asking a lawyer not involved in her case to leave. He then gave a "strong" and "clear" message to the perpetrator, stating all the conditions of the order and threatening jail if the order were breached. Skye similarly praised the judge's compassion in her protection order hearing:

> She just was like, "No, it's OK, I'm helping you, this is going to protect you . . ." She listened. She was very respectful, especially because it was still very fresh to me and I was very scared going in there. But I felt more relaxed after she granted me the temporary protection order. [She spoke] with compassion, with understanding.

Leah (CALD) said that the two judges she appeared before were "understanding . . . not in a hurry," and she remembered one of them asked her how safe she felt. Colleen said the judges in the protection order courts were "respectful," they had read the material, and she was able to sit away from the perpetrator.

Women highlighted the importance of judicial understanding of the dynamics of coercive control; judges needed to recognize that legal systems abuse was part of this dynamic. Shelley reported: "The system allowed him—I think he manipulated it skillfully . . . it's like as if they knew how to mess this system up, to drag this system out or something." Similarly, Jane said: "I am just wondering if judges understand that the legal system protects those who choose to fight unfairly."

In some cases, women believed judges understood the dynamics of IPV and responded appropriately. Ingrid said the family court judge "took the case seriously and described the perpetrator as vexatious and saw through his tactics." Radha mentioned a positive interaction about a protection order. She explained that after obtaining a temporary protection order, her abuser pressured her to withdraw her application. She attended court with him, with the intention to withdraw. However, while the judge agreed to remove some of the conditions of the order so the couple could be in contact without breaching the order, he left the order in place with a condition that her abuser be on good behavior. Radha explained:

> I told [the judge] that I just want to give him a last chance because he has been begging and he is promising me that he will prove that he has changed and he won't do the same mistakes again. But the judge said that he will remove the other conditions, like not approaching me and the premises of 100 meters, but not the domestic violence one . . . thankfully that the judge understood what's going on, and what might happen, that he didn't change the orders.

One of the women, Jennifer, had a negative experience with the protection order courts, describing them as "an old men's club. They all stick together." The reality is the proportion of women judges in the protection order and family courts is getting close to 50 percent in Queensland (Douglas & Bartlett, 2016), the state where this study took place. There are many good reasons for ensuring gender equality in the makeup of the judiciary, but this development, by itself, will not necessarily change the experience for women (Sommerlad, 2013). Appropriate induction courses and regular refresher training may go some way toward helping judges understand and appreciate the dynamics of family violence (Breger, 2017, p. 191; George & Harris, 2014, p. 184). Jennifer also emphasized the role of training: "I suppose it comes down to . . . educating the judiciary, and changing the law. I mean, they go hand in hand really, but essentially the judges and the magistrates." Intimate partner violence accounts for an ever-increasing share of the workload of the courts, underscoring the need for continuous judicial training and support. Up to 70 percent of parents involved in family law proceedings have children who have been exposed to IPV (Kaspiew, Carson, Coulson, Dunstan, & Moore, 2015, pp. 41–42). Insufficient resources and judicial "burnout" have been recognized in both the protection order courts and family courts (ALRC, 2019, p. 32; Hunter, Burton, & Trinder, 2020).

High caseloads, lack of training, and focus on settlement in protection order and family law systems can play into the hands of abusers. Some abusers exploit the judge's lack of awareness of IPV and the history of a matter, and engage in systems abuse by delaying the closure of matters and returning the woman to court through serial adjournments. Constant delays and repeat court appearances operate as a form of secondary abuse, increasing trauma and undermining the victim's safety. As Spencer (2016, p. 226) observes, delay is a case-management issue that has a number of significant and damaging effects in IPV cases. Delay allows the perpetrator to continue offending; allows time for the complainant to be pressured by the perpetrator or the extended family to withdraw proceedings, thus allowing the perpetrator to avoid accountability; and undermines victim well-being due to the protracted stress of ongoing proceedings (p. 226).

Inherently connected to delay is preparation. Many women emphasized the importance of judicial preparation. Carol believes "judges should have the history of you before you walk in so you don't have to say the same thing over and over again. You can say what's recently happened and why you still want this order, and why you want another order." Sandra had a similar suggestion:

> What would probably be really interesting for some judges is to listen to some of the [previous] transcripts of the case before they take it on. . . . Because that's going to give you pretty much an update. . . . They wouldn't be coming back all the time.

Improvements may come with more connected legal systems (ALRC, 2019; Australian Law Reform Commission and New South Wales Law Reform Commission, 2010). Fragmented legal systems, including the disconnect between the family law and protection order systems, provide opportunities for systems abuses and require women to retell their stories in different forms and for different purposes over and over again, deepening their trauma (Herman, 2005). But even within a fragmented system judges can do better. Knowledge and training about coercive control, awareness of the possibility of systems abuse, preparation, and a focus on safety are all key to better judging.

Although it is possible to imagine better judging, there is still a long way to go to ensure that women's experiences of abuse are heard, believed, and understood by judicial officers. The women's knowledge of their own experience of the abuse often appeared to be "disqualified" (Smart, 1989, p. 13). Over the period of the study, some judges eventually understood the women's story of abuse, but this often took many years, causing significant stress in, and damage to, women's and children's lives. Women questioned the processes and the judges they encountered, sometimes finding them both unclear, inconsistent, biased toward their abusers, and unaccountable—in Frieda's words, not "proper." Such perceptions are at odds with a system that prides itself on rule-of-law principles of accountability, justice, openness, and impartiality. From the perspectives of many of the women in the study, the legal system fails to abide by its own rules, continuing to reinforce women's entrapment in abusive relationships (Ptacek, 1999, p. 176) and in some cases driving them away from seeking legal redress.

NOTES

1. Note also that I have used the title *judge* to describe decision makers generally. This refers both to the lower level magistrates' courts where civil IPV protection orders are dealt with under the Domestic and Family Violence Protection Act 2012 (Qld) and to the family courts (both family circuit courts and family courts) where custody and property matters are dealt with under the Family Law Act 1975 (Cth).

Although there is scope under Australian family law to order an injunction for the personal protection of a child or a parent involved in family law proceedings (see Family Law Act 1975 (Cth) s 68B, inquiries have suggested that local police are reluctant to enforce them (ALRC, 2019, p. 119).

2. Depending on the facts and circumstances of the particular case, the family court may order that the parties to child-related proceedings take part in an assessment conducted by a family consultant. This will result in the production of a family report (AIJA, 2020, [10.4]; Field, Jeffries, Rathus, & Lynch, 2016).
3. Independent children's lawyers are appointed to represent the interests of children who are the subject of a dispute between their parents or guardians (Kaye, 2019a, p. 101).
4. Notably, the police did not suggest that she could make a statement and pursue criminal charges; for example, stalking could be charged in these circumstances (McMahon, McGorrery & Burton, 2019).
5. Mutual orders, sometimes called cross orders, are reasonably common in Australia, and there has been significant criticism of their use (Douglas & Fitzgerald, 2013; Wangmann, 2012).
6. Child support is dealt with administratively in Australia (Douglas & Nagesh, 2019).
7. Depending on a child's maturity and level of understanding, his or her views may be taken into account; see Family Law Act 1975 (Cth) s 60CC(3)(a) (see also Parkinson & Cashmore, 2009).
8. This was Fiona's experience; see Chapter 3.
9. This may be understood as religious or spiritual abuse (Bent-Goodley & Fowler, 2006).
10. This is significantly more than the legal aid solicitor fees, which are less than $2,000 for similar work (Legal Aid Queensland, 2019b).
11. *Shuttle mediation* refers to mediation that takes place between parties who are not in the same room. The mediator "shuttles" between them (Harland, Cooper, Rathus, & Alexander, 2015, p. 94).
12. Contact centers provide a safe place for supervision of periods of contact; fees are often associated with using them (Harland et al., 2015, p. 102).
13. This condition is not uncommon in family court orders because it avoids the attribution of blame (Harland et al., 2015, p. 388). Implicitly, however, it suggests both parties are to blame, i.e., that there is mutual abuse.
14. Family Law Act 1975 (Cth) pt VII div 13A. Notably, parents have been penalized for refusing to facilitate contact pursuant to family court orders see *Saldo & Tindall* [2013] FamCA 951 (December 5, 2013).
15. The Hague Convention on the Civil Aspects of International Child Abduction entered into force in 1983, with both Australia and the United States among the signatories. It applies to children under 16 years of age and aims to provide an expeditious way of returning a child who is abducted internationally from one member country to another (Harland et al., 2015, pp. 604–605; Malhotra, 2014).

9

The Process and Conditionality of Separation

INTRODUCTION

The role of the legal system, and its various actors, both in discouraging or supporting women in separating from their abusive partner and in stigmatizing them for their decisions to stay or return, provides another common thread between the study women's narratives. Some women reported on the inflexibility of law and legal actors, including police, lawyers, and judges, in dealing with the flux and change in their relationship status. Women often described separation as "a process" rather than a fixed moment, and their comments highlighted the conditionality of separation.

The requirement for and definition of separation vary between different legal responses. Divorce, for example, requires that the parties have been separated for 12 months, although they may continue to live together under the same roof (Harland, Cooper, Rathus, & Alexander, 2015, pp. 48, 72–73). Access to orders about children and property assume that parents are legally separated (Goodmark, 2012, pp. 88–96), although people need not be legally separated in order to be the subject of a domestic violence–related criminal charge. In Australia, it is possible for a woman who has been abused to obtain a protection order from the courts even though she remains in an intimate relationship with her abusive partner.[1] Separation may have implications for visas. Women may seem less credible in relation

Women, Intimate Partner Violence, and the Law. Heather Douglas, Oxford University Press (2021). © Oxford University Press.
DOI: 10.1093/oso/9780190071783.003.0009

to their claims about intimate partner violence (IPV) if they stay and may miss out on more secure visas as a result (Borges Jelenic, 2020). For the most part, legal responses to IPV can operate even when women stay with their violent partner, or at least continue living in the same dwelling. As previous chapters have highlighted, however, the expectations from many legal actors, including child protection workers, police, lawyers, and judges, is that women who are abused should leave their abuser. The underlying expectation is that women will be safer if they leave (Goodmark, 2012, p. 81). Legal documents assume that separation is a binary concept, a box that can be ticked, when the reality may be much more uncertain and fluid. This chapter explores the role and impact of law, through its processes, through justice actors, and through law's misuse by abusive partners, in women's decisions and experiences around staying, leaving, and returning to their abusers.

Similar to other research, many women who participated in this study reported that separation, and interacting with the legal system, marked a period of heightened danger and failed to deliver on the promise of safety for them and their children. Based on the women's stories, four aspects of the relationship between the law and separation are explored. The chapter considers women's dynamic experiences of leaving in the shadow of static legal understandings of separation and the dangers women face when they engage with legal systems and processes. Drawing on the experiences of two women, two areas of law where separation underpins the legal response are highlighted: the migration and visa system, and the family law system. The chapter concludes with some recommendations for change.

THE DYNAMIC EXPERIENCE OF SEPARATION

Choice and Lamke (1997) posit that women examine two questions in deciding whether to leave an abusive relationship: Will I be better off? And can I do it? Answers are informed by an exploration of available resources and potential barriers, and a woman's answers change depending on when she asks herself these questions (Choice & Lamke, 1997, p. 310). Hamby

(2014, esp. Chap. 5) has suggested a strengths-based approach to understanding leaving and staying, identifying that women who have been abused weigh the risks of leaving. These include not just physical, financial, social, and personal risks but also legal risks, including court orders that might endanger them or their children or reduce their emotional or financial well-being. The two approaches can be read together to understand women's decisions to stay or leave (Amanour-Boadu et al., 2012). Though many women single out an incident or factor as the catalyst for their choice to leave, there are usually complex narratives underpinning their decisions (Baker, 1997, p. 63; Mullender et al., 2002; Semaan, Jasinski, & Bubriski-McKenzie, 2013) and the path to separation for most women is "non-linear" (S. Miller, 2018, p. 51), with women usually leaving and returning multiple times (D. Anderson & Saunders, 2003, p. 164; Dobash & Dobash, 1979, pp. 144–150; Goodmark, 2012, p. 81; Ptacek, 1999, p. 121).

Most of the study women had left their partner more than once and returned for a complex range of reasons before leaving again and again. Their reasons for staying and returning often included a mix of social and financial pressures and desires, emotional ties, loneliness, a wish for their children to have a father or be a family, fear and safety concerns, and the man's promises to change or that things would be different. Hope of improvement in the relationship often drove women to stay, return, and ultimately, in some cases, to leave (Ahmed, 2017, p. 46). For example, Pari (CALD), who endured a cycle of abuse for many years, told me at the first interview: "When he apologizes and then always [I] think of like having those air castles and dream and that everything is going to be all right one day, he going to be changed, I have to be calm, I have to give him love and all that thing, . . . so that was my hope."

Many of the women pointed to the importance of extended family, social workers, priests and elders from their place of worship, doctors, teachers, ambulance workers, and individuals at other agencies in undermining or supporting them in their attempts to leave and remain separated from an abusive partner (Hamby, 2014, Chap. 8; S. Miller, 2018, Chap. 5). Legal processes, responses, and support also contributed to women's decisions about whether and when to leave and return.

Most of the study women were separated from their abusive partner at the first interview:

$n = 14$ (22%) of the 65 women had separated in the past 12 months
$n = 18$ (28%) had separated in the past 12 months to 2 years
$n = 12$ (19%) had separated in the past 2 to 4 years
$n = 16$ (25%) had been separated for more than 4 years

At the first interview, five of the women said they were still in the relationship with the partner who had abused them. However, these figures oversimplify the picture and risk reinforcing the notion that separation is a clear and static concept. Some of the women who said they were separated from their partners continued throughout the interviews, at least sometimes, to live with them (Faith, Carol, Terri); cook and clean for them (Vera); have sex with them (Melissa, Dara, Lyn, Jacinta); and share finances (Mira, Carol, Jacinta). They continued with these activities for diverse reasons, including fear of what would happen if they resisted, because alternative options for housing and financial support were limited or they considered that staying was better for the children. Some continued to "love" their partner and sometimes hoped to ultimately reunite with him (Hamby, 2014, pp. 88–89; Henderson, Bartholomew, & Dutton, 1997; Seuffert, 1999). Most of the women who had children with their partner navigated ongoing parenting with them.

At the second and third interviews, some study women reported they had recommenced their relationship with their abusive partner or were contemplating doing so. Other women reported being in a relationship with their abusive partner in the first interview but had separated by the time of the second or third interview. Some women were not sure about the status of their relationship. Cassie and Chi, whose partners were, respectively, in jail and on the run from authorities throughout all three interviews, were unsure whether the relationship would continue in the future, and their views about this fluctuated over the course of the interviews.

Many of the study women pointed to a specific incident that steeled them in their resolve to separate, often despite years of similar forms of abuse. However, despite pointing to a single event as the catalyst, the underlying reasons were always complicated and layered. The incident women identified as underpinning their separation was often an episode of serious abuse or one that took place in front of the children. On occasion, women pointed to the discovery of sexual infidelity of the abuser as the catalyst for leaving; other women said they just "got tired" of the abuse.

Roseanna, an Aboriginal woman said: "Every time the kids would come home, I always had a black eye or my lip was busted, or there was a bruise on me somewhere. I got tired of it." On the day she left, her abuser held a knife at her throat and she told him, "'Do it because I've had enough. I said, I'd rather be dead than live with you.' . . . I made myself strong." He lowered the knife, and she left in a taxi with the children and never returned. She remained separated at the time of the third interview.

Fifteen women identified a specific event of serious violence or a threat that they marked out as crucial to their decision to leave; these included a partner's threat to kill them or to commit suicide, or being strangled or raped. Kim experienced 10 years of abuse, including physical, verbal, and financial abuse, and was isolated from friends and family. She says she ultimately "left for good" with her child and an emergency bag because she was assaulted while she slept, making her fear for her life:

Kim: In that first year that [daughter] was born, he held me by my throat up against a brick wall and he pushed me into the brick wall. I did leave, I left, but I came back. . . . Then the next time . . . I left for good. . . . It was like this continual roller coaster of being awful, being abusive, being hurtful; and then saying sorry, saying it won't happen, and I'll go to the doctors and all of this.

Interviewer: What drove you to leave him [that last time]?

Kim: He hit me while I was asleep . . . 4:30 in the morning and I thought I had been stabbed . . . I was feeling my nightclothes for blood. . . .

> *I had an emergency bag packed. . . . Because I knew I was going to have to leave . . . I thought I would die. I thought he would kill me, because a couple of nights before that, he told me he had plans for me. If I wasn't going to be compliant, he had a plan. The way he said it, it was like I was going to die.*

Some of the study women (*n* = 11) highlighted an incident of violence against their child or in front of their child as the catalyst for separation (Semaan, Jasinski, & Bubriski-McKenzie, 2013). For example, Francis and Mark were together for nearly 25 years, and Francis had endured serious levels of violence and control for years. She could instantly recall the date 12 months before her first interview with me that she had separated permanently from Mark. At the time of the separation, Francis and Mark were living apart because of his bail conditions associated with child pornography offenses. They had not yet decided to separate and had agreed they would attend marriage counseling to try make the relationship work. Francis had taken the children for a holiday, and Mark had arrived at the holiday apartment in contravention of his bail conditions. Francis asked him to leave. He became angry and threatened to throw her off a second-floor balcony. Their preteenaged son intervened, kicking and punching Mark and yelling, "Let Mum go, let Mum go!" Mark eventually calmed down, but the next day Francis said her son was feeling sick "because he stood up to his father and stress and all that." She recalls her daughter's feet were covered in blisters because she had run away in fear. The following day Francis had an appointment with her doctor, and she decided to tell the doctor "everything." Her doctor told she had a "duty of care" to leave and referred Francis to a shelter. Francis moved in to shelter accommodations with the children and started her complex legal journey. At the time of interview 3, she remained separated from Mark but was dealing with an ongoing family law property matter and was in the process of trying to get a protection order renewed. She says it was "tough," and she still had many panic attacks. She continues to be supported by a counseling and IPV support agency.

Some women ($n = 5$) identified proof of infidelity as the critical incident that led to their final separation from the abuser. They found evidence that their partner was seeing a sex-worker (Valeria [CALD]); was gay and dating men (Radha [CALD]); was accessing a dating app (Martha); or was having an affair (Skye, Faith). The women described their discovery as a "crunch point," "going too far," and "unforgivable" and as making them feel "broken." Faith, in her story outlined in this chapter, identified her discovery that her partner had sex with another woman in Faith's bed as the moment that "solidified" the separation.

LEAVING IS DANGEROUS AND GOING TO LAW CAN EXACERBATE THE DANGER

Research has shown that separation, or expressing the intention to separate, is one of the most dangerous times for women, and it is recognized as a risk factor for future serious harm and death (J. Campbell et al., 2003; H. Johnson & Hotton, 2003; Mahoney 1991, p. 6; Rezey, 2020). The effect of leaving is unpredictable. It can trigger violence or control in relationships that were previously without any form of abuse (Bruton & Tyson, 2018, p. 340; DeKeseredy, Dragiewicz, & Schwartz, 2017, p. 115). Women who have experienced control during their relationship are much more likely to be subjected to stalking and violence after separation (Ornstein & Rickne, 2013). In circumstances where the relationship has been controlling, separation may simply lead to changes in the tactics used to exert control (Crossman, Hardesty & Raffaelli, 2016, p. 467; Laing, 2017, p. 1315; Sharp-Jeffs, Kelly, & Klein, 2018, p. 182). Dobash & Dobash (2015, p. 39) found that separation may result in abusive men simply "changing the project from attempting to keep her within the relationship to destroying her for leaving it." The commencement and maintenance of legal proceedings may be part of the project of maintaining control (Gutowski and Goodman, 2020; Kurz, 1996; S. Miller, 2018, p. 107). Although abused women usually commence legal proceedings hoping to improve their safety and promote closure of the relationship, often this also triggers postseparation violence

(Ellis, 2017; Gutowski & Goodman, 2020; Kurz, 1996). In Australia, as in the United States and the United Kingdom, the fragmented nature of legal responses and the varied aspirations and definitions embedded in different legal responses can also contribute to women's danger (Agnew-Brune, Moracco, Person, & Bowling, 2017; Jeffs, Kelly, & Klein, 2018; Stubbs & Wangmann, 2015, p. 114).

Many of the study women experienced separation as a period of heightened uncertainty and danger, and the legal responses they engaged generally offered insufficient protection and support. In many cases, the disconnection between various legal responses exacerbated their sense of uncertainty and danger. Sometimes women's turn to law resulted in retributive legal actions and violent responses; for one of the women, the consequences were fatal.

Monica separated from her ex-partner, Ken, early on in their relationship because of drinking and fighting, but they got back together when she discovered she was pregnant. The relationship became progressively more violent over the years. She explained: "He was sort of a bit clever about what he used to do. He used to kick me and strangle me, but he wouldn't punch me in the face, where it could be seen. He'd punch me in the back of the head." He broke furniture and her precious things, like her grandmother's tea set. Monica left and returned many times. She had regular interactions with police and thinks she had around eight protection orders over the 10 years of their relationship. She sometimes rang support services, which offered shelter accommodations, but she had horses, dogs, and fish to care for and was worried about what Ken would do to them if she left them. He killed her fish once, and her dog had "disappeared" once in the past. She recalled the moment she finally decided to leave for good was when Ken was kicking her and at the same time telling her son "this is how you treat women." She thought, "This has got to stop now." She left and applied for a protection order; this time she added others, including the children and a close friend, as protected individuals under the order. Police efforts to serve Ken enraged him, and he texted Monica many times. Ultimately, he killed one of the protected people on the order, her close friend, the day police tried to serve him. When I met Monica,

Ken had been charged and was on remand. Throughout the interviews, I followed Ken's efforts to get the charge downgraded, sometimes meeting Monica at the court. She was greatly relieved, at interview 3, that he had been ultimately sentenced to life imprisonment for murder.

Anna and Melissa, whose stories are told next, also identified the riskiness of separation and going to law.

Anna's Experience

For Anna, the direct physical abuse she experienced mostly ended when she decided to separate from her violent partner, Nathan. However, at each of the three interviews, she continued to report her constant fear of Nathan and her uncertainty about how the legal system would respond to her circumstances. Despite Nathan's serious violence toward her in the past and the high risk of her situation, Anna tried to ensure that Nathan continued to have contact with their child, Manuel. She didn't believe this was safe, but she worried about what the courts would do if she tried to block contact. She tried to do her best to ensure there were conditions in place to guarantee safety in contact arrangements. At the same time, she lived in constant fear that child protection authorities would remove Manuel into state care because she exposed her child to Nathan's violence. Anna struggled financially throughout the period of the interviews, but she feared Nathan's response if she sought child support from him. She was eligible to apply for victim's assistance but found it difficult to apply because she had to keep moving and had mislaid the forms.[2] At the time of interview 3, nearly 7 years after separating, her legal situation is far from clear and she still does not feel safe.

> ***Anna, interview 1 :*** *Just trying to get people to hear me and actually say, you know, you can't keep letting him off. He might not be doing anything physically to me now, but emotionally, psychologically, it's impacting mine and my son's life. . . . It just feels like no one's listening, no one wants to help. This legal system, these papers and the law stuff,*

and there's nowhere I can turn. I've had legal aid tell me over the phone I won't get funded.

I am meeting Anna at a support service she has been working with for several years. She cries often during our interview but says: "I just want to get my story out there because it sucks to be failed by the system." She is in her 20s and met her partner, Nathan, when they were both 16; both of them had already left school. She says she used to be a party girl and, in the past, took a mixture of prescription drugs, cannabis, and Ecstasy. Anna describes a difficult childhood; she was in and out of the hospital for mental and physical ill health and, by the time she was 12 years old she was seeing a mental health worker regularly. Nathan was a drifter who earned a sporadic income "hustling," shifting stolen goods, and selling drugs. He was a drug user, starting initially with cannabis but by the end of their relationship, 5 years later, he was using ice and heroin; there were stolen goods in the house, and drug dealers from other states were staying with them while they sold their gear. Nathan became affiliated with a gang and was involved in fights that included guns.[3] He was charged with several offenses and got a court probation order at one stage. In the midst of this situation, Anna and Nathan had a child together.

Anna says the abuse really started when she became pregnant with her child, Manuel.[4] She mentions "emotional abuse" and tells me, "He would accuse me of cheating or talking to other guys. There would be a few times where he'd get drunk and if I was being smart to him, apparently, he'd just start on me. He's choked me in front of people, he's hit me in front of people." Child protection authorities visited while she was pregnant, and Anna says she was "pretty much scared that when I went into labor that they would come up to the hospital." To guard against having Manuel removed into state care, she moved in with her mother, and she did "all the parenting and antenatal classes." After Manuel was born, she moved back in with Nathan. Anna says the last "really serious" incident was when Nathan came home one night after a "bender" and strangled and bashed her until she blacked out. She woke up the next day in the hospital with bruises and fractured bones. After being released from hospital, she returned to him, and the violence continued.

Eventually, worried about the future of their child, Anna separated from Nathan 4 years ago "for good." Their child was still preschool-aged. Anna lived with her mother for nearly a year and got a protection order with the help of a support service. Nathan has breached it several times "by being abusive, threatening me, stalking me," and she has reported him to police. She believes he has been charged several times and fined, but the police refused to provide her with information. She says:

> I've had to change my number so many times. My appearance. These last 4 years I've changed my hair, I've lost weight, put on weight, changed my routine of going places. . . . I've blocked all his friends and family. I've changed my number for the 50 millionth time because of the harassment. I've had to change everything. I've had to change my locks just to be sure. I sleep with a knife under my bed.

She is hoping to get a 5-year protection order when she has to renew her current protection order soon.

At one stage Anna lodged a parenting plan with the family court.[5] It stated that Manuel should live with Anna, and Nathan could have contact every second weekend. Nathan's family was supposed to manage the handover. Nathan kept breaching the order, usually not turning up at all or abusing her when he did. She stopped contact last year. She feels her "family law order overruled [her] protection order." Anna and Nathan had mediation at the family court 2 months before our first interview, and Anna "offered" supervised contact as long as Nathan had regular drug testing.[6] Part of the new parenting plan that Anna proposed included transition toward unsupervised contact if the drug tests were clear. Nathan's legal representative convinced him to accept the conditions. Nathan didn't manage to turn up for the three scheduled contact visits and hasn't seen Manuel since mediation. Anna tells me: "I'm trying to do everything by the book because I don't want to get in trouble." She says: "It's hard to get people to hear you and understand you, and the legal system will only help him because he doesn't get to see Manuel . . . but that's not my fault."

Recently she has received death threats from Nathan via his mother, and she has told the police. Both Anna and her child struggle with mental health issues, including anxiety and depression and live in constant fear of Nathan. They live in state housing, and the housing department has been very responsive to their needs, moving them around regularly so no one knows where they live. Anna relies on social security payments and has an exemption from collecting child support from Nathan because she knows that would incite more violence.[7] She says: "I'm scared that he's going to use that I'm an unfit mum. I've told so many lawyers, so many people, I will fight to my last breath. I'm trying to protect my child."

> ***Anna, interview 2:*** *He's abused the system and that's my problem. Like after all this time I'm like can I see a judge? . . . Can I just see somebody? Can I do court? Like what can I do: because I don't feel safe, and I was just denied that the whole time.*

Nearly a year has passed when Anna and I catch up for a second interview. The parenting plan was in place for 1 year and was supposed to be reviewed. However, Nathan did not have a contact visit with their son for more than a year, and the plan lapsed. She asked legal aid what she should do, but they won't help her because Nathan hasn't made any application. The legal aid lawyer warned Anna against initiating an application because that would be "opening up Pandora's box."

There is a new temporary protection order in place; both Anna's mother and Manuel are protected under the order. Nathan has breached the protection order a number of times: He has become abusive toward her and their son when they have come across each other at shopping malls, he has made threats, and he has been driving past her mother's house. She believes he is trying to find out where she lives. Anna has reported these breaches to the police. She says, "The more breaches you put in, the more paper trail there is." Nathan now has nine charges of breaching the protection order; he has also been charged with more substantive criminal charges such as making death threats to her, threatening to shoot her, and various weapons charges. These will be heard in court next month along with Anna's application for finalization of a 5-year protection order. She is applying for the protection order with assistance from a support service. Despite her high-risk situation, the police have not been willing to assist. One police officer told her: "Well, he's not physically harming you."

Since we last met, someone reported Anna to child protection services, and she was investigated. The child protection workers recommended a parenting course, which she has completed, but she says child protection is still in the background. She is still finding it difficult to get someone to hear her story. She tells me:

> When it's quiet, you don't know what's going on because you don't know who he's got watching you or keeping tabs on you. You don't know who he's been associating with. . . . I'm known as his kid's mum, so they're going to come through me to get to him.

Every time she sees the legal aid lawyers she feels "belittled . . . blamed, that it was my fault that he was doing all this stuff." I tell Anna I will try to find an appropriate legal referral for her for the next court matter.

> ***Anna, interview 3:*** *Because they don't do anything, they're like—the police prosecutors or your solicitors or the judges or the police will say "Oh, we'll get him, he's looking at jail time." He's . . . reoffended so many times. Yet when they do pick him up he gets charged, he gets a court date, he doesn't go to court, and he gets a warrant, doesn't go to court again, he gets another warrant. He's a floater; by the time he does go back to court, he gets a fine and gets to walk out.*

For the third interview, 8 months after the second one, Anna and I talk on the telephone. She has been back to court about the protection order a few times since we last met. Each time it is adjourned and the temporary protection order extended because Nathan never comes to court. After interview 2, I referred Anna to a community legal center (CLC), and now she has a CLC lawyer. Last week she went with her lawyer to court, and Nathan did not turn up. There was a different judge, who said he wasn't comfortable providing a 5-year order without Nathan being present. There are several active warrants for Nathan's arrest, but police haven't been able to find him to bring him to court. Anna calls the police all the time but feels like she annoys them. Her lawyer has told her they will deal with child custody issues once they have the protection order sorted out. She plans to apply for victim's assistance, but recently had to move again and lost the forms. She tells me:

> [It] was hard, because it was either you stay and you're going to die or you leave and you're going to die. So I'd rather left and risked it, but that was, that was challenging. It was scary. . . . There needs to be a bigger voice and mine's only a little one at the moment, but I tell you, I'm just fighting a battle every day and triggers, and having to deal with triggers and mentally and just having flashbacks of stuff. That's disturbing.

Melissa's Experience

Melissa had experienced years of physical violence from her partner, Ben. She had separated from Ben on many occasions throughout their 20-year relationship. Often she returned to him because it was "easier," she was lonely and missed intimacy, or wanted respite from the children. Melissa struggled to get support from the police, and protection orders were often useless in keeping her and the children safe. Ben was frequently able to evade police. Even if he was located and charged, the justice response, from Melissa's perspective, was overly lenient. Melissa faced financial instability after separation, but her efforts to collect child support led to further assaults, and her access to victim's compensation was unnecessarily complex. Although she was optimistic by the third interview and had a strong sense that the relationship was ended, at that time there was an active warrant for Ben's arrest because of a recent and serious assault on Melissa.

> ***Melissa interview 1:*** *But then we got back together again. Yeah, it was just easier. You know, I had a nice house; I had all the bells and whistles. I thought I only have to put up for 4 days every 10 days, you know, I can do this. When you're in that, its crisis management.*

I first meet and speak with Melissa at her workplace. She offers me a cup of tea and wants to launch into telling her story straightaway. She laughs at many points during the interview. Melissa is an Aboriginal woman. She met her non-Aboriginal partner, Ben, nearly 20 years ago and says they have "come in and out of their relationship." They have sometimes separated for 2 years at a time and then reunited. They have several children together, all of whom are school-aged. Both in their 40s, Melissa has a diploma and Ben has a trade and has often earned a good wage.

Ben has been violent toward Melissa since before they even moved in together. Over the course of their relationship, he has been in jail for assaulting Melissa on a few occasions. Sometimes he went on drug binges and then wanted sex; now and then Melissa refused him, leading to "fights." "We'd fight over money, we'd fight over anything . . . he'd be hitting me, spitting on me, calling me names, forcing sex upon me. I had scans on my brain and things like that but it was ongoing for years I can't exactly pinpoint things."

Melissa left with the children and stayed with her mother or friends when things got bad, and then came back. She tells me, "I felt financially stable with him, because he was a high-income earner . . . I think I had that little rebellion streak. I wanted a bad boy, and I got my bad boy and now I'm paying for it." She says Ben was a "good dad" and she didn't want to be lonely.

The police were often called by neighbors, and sometimes police would get a protection order for her. Mostly the police would just take her statement and ask her what she was doing staying with him. Melissa says she didn't expect police to feel sorry for her but would like "a bit of compassion."

She is frustrated that there is "too much leniency" in the legal system. She points out that her protection orders have usually required that Ben have "no contact" with her, yet he has "seen the kids and flogged the shit out of" her while these conditions have been in place and nothing much has happened:

> [A protection order] is just thought of, as Ben said, "a piece of paper" . . . it's really a smack on the wrist. I think it needs to get a bit more serious. You can't assault Joe Blow on the road . . . it's worse to assault your partner and if you're just going to get a fine or slap on the wrist, I think that it needs to be more harsher penalties, really.

Ben has been successfully prosecuted for breaches of the protection orders but has usually received fines, which he is never able to pay.

Around 8 months before our first interview, while Ben was in jail for a short time for some fraud-related offenses, Melissa moved away with the children. She says, "I'll always have a connection to him," but the relationship is finished. "I just don't want to revisit that anymore. He's not what I want and I'm not getting any younger." She has a parenting plan registered with the family court giving her daily care of the children and alternate weekend contact to Ben. The police have ensured there is a temporary protection order in place, but the finalization hearing for the protection order keeps getting adjourned because lately the police can't find Ben to give him the details.

> ***Melissa interview 2:*** *Then I slept with him, but I knew I didn't want to be with him and I told him that. I think it was just intimacy that I was looking for.*

It is 9 months since I first spoke with Melissa. She says she has been intimate with Ben a few times since we last spoke, but she knows now that she doesn't want to be with him. She has told him the relationship is over. Just a week before we meet for the second interview, Ben came to the house at night, and she woke up with him standing at the end of the bed. He left when she threatened to call the police. Melissa telephoned the police the next day and asked them to make a record of Ben's intrusion, but they refused to do that. Police said she would either have to come to the police station or they would send a car around. She didn't want the kids to see the police at home, so she went to police station. When the police officer asked if she was fearful, she said, "I think the fear has gone away." The police noted the incident and told Melissa her house would be "red-flagged." She says:

> I think [protection orders] work to a certain degree. It depends on the perpetrator really because, if you're mad, you're under the influence of drugs, you're doing whatever, a piece of paper's not going to stop you. That's exactly—Peter wrote that to me in jail: "It's just a piece of paper; I'll get out one day." But if Peter's going to do something, he's going to do it. If I could close doors, Peter's the type of person, he'll kick the door in. . . . Nothing's a deterrent for him; he just doesn't care. So if he's got a fine, it's, "Oh, I'll slap it on the bill."

Melissa has been getting support for herself and her kids from a local agency. One of her children has been diagnosed with post-traumatic stress disorder (PTSD) as a result of the IPV. Saying this makes her cry. She recalls one of Ben's threats, made several years ago, in front of her primary school–aged children. He said, "'I am going to put your mother in a box,' and he cut my throat and it was bleeding. Not thick blood. Enough to scare . . . just enough to . . . say I'm in control here." Melissa's daughter has cleaned up a lot of blood over the years. Referring to Ben, Melissa says, "He doesn't control me anymore, but I do think about getting a break from these kids. I work full time . . . but he's a bad partner, besides the kids seeing violence, and that's obviously unacceptable." She says, "We've been separated properly really for 3—well, 2.5—years, except for the rendezvous." Melissa's last protection order expired more than a month ago, but she is thinking of getting another one.

> ***Melissa interview 3:*** *I just don't want any of his drama. . . . I don't fear him, anymore, like I did in the past. He's got no control on my life, anymore. It makes me angry more than anything else.*

Another 9 months have passed since Melissa and I talked at interview 2. We talk over the phone this time. She is in a new job, working full-time. She suggested I meet her at her house, but we would have had to meet late in the evening, and she has moved to a new suburb that I am not familiar with. She says she's disappointed that I couldn't come over. As we start the conversation, she tells me that there is currently a warrant out for Ben's arrest. Given the experience Melissa relayed at our second interview, I imagine Ben turning up midinterview drunk or stoned, and so I am glad that we agreed to talk on the phone.

Three months prior to the third interview, Melissa discovered that the child support agency took some money out of Ben's account. She was worried about Ben's reaction and went to the police, who helped her apply for a temporary protection order. The next night she was at a football game watching one of the children play. She relays what happened next:

> The next minute, I've seen him come from nowhere, to the football field. Then I have just continued to walk to my car, to get my phone . . . then Ben has come from nowhere and just started punching into me, at the football field, in front of everyone. I was screaming. . . . A split mouth, split gum, black eye, and just bruises on my cheekbone.

Police and ambulance attended and took witness statements. Ben was charged with a serious assault. He was supposed to go to court 2 months ago, but he didn't show up, which is why there is a warrant out for his arrest. Melissa thinks he will probably go to jail, and so he's on the run.

Melissa says she is very happy in her new job, telling me her life is "awesome" at the moment. Ben still has a child support debt, but she doesn't expect to see that money and, given what happened when child support money was taken out of his account recently, she doesn't want to push it.

She currently has a protection order, which also names the children as protected.

She applied for some victim compensation more than a year ago, in relation to a tooth she lost after one of Ben's assaults. She contacted the compensation agency recently because she wanted to add a claim for the latest assault. She said filling in the form was difficult as she struggled to remember dates and times: "I've had that much violence from this person. Just to pinpoint and isolate one particular time, I can't even remember that." The agency staff said they would have to wait until the most recent assault claim is finalized in the court before they could process the application. They also told her the new assault would be considered as part of the original claim because it is part of a "series" of offenses; thus, they have stopped processing her claim while they await the outcome of the most recent assault case. She is "disappointed" about the delays and could do with some money.

Melissa tells me she feels confident the relationship is over:

> I just look back and I think, I can't believe . . . that I stayed there for so long and let this person control me. When you're in it, you're just so scared. . . . I gave it a good go and I stayed there for a long time. Now that I'm out of it, I thought . . . there's no way. I'd rather be single though, now, and I don't need a man in my life to feel whole. I'm busy with my children and seeing them succeed and be successful. . . . I just don't have time for the negativity, anymore. I just don't like drama in my life. . . . I feel like I've grown, I'm a completely different person. I like the person who I am.

THE IMMIGRATION SYSTEM AND SEPARATION

Many women on a sponsored visa face an uncertain future if they leave an abusive partner (Maher & Segrave, 2018, pp. 509–511). In Australia and the United States, spousal visas require that the sponsoring citizen and the sponsored noncitizen have a "genuine" relationship for 2 years to attain permanent residency (Borges Jelenic, 2019, p. 2). Although there is an exception to this 2-year requirement in some circumstances where there is IPV, women cannot rely on the exception being exercised in their favor. Furthermore, not all sponsored women have access to the IPV exception under Australian migration law. For example, women who are sponsored under their sponsor's work visa do not have access to this exception (Segrave, 2017, p. 9). As observed in Chapter 3, as part of their tactics of coercive control, some abusive sponsors use threats of withdrawal of sponsorship, deportation, and the woman's separation from her children (Ghafournia & Easteal, 2018, p. 4; Maher & Segrave, 2018, pp. 509–511; Segrave, 2017, pp. 23–26; Vaughan et al., 2015, pp. 19, 24–25). Many sponsored women are also socially isolated, and if they leave their partner, they may have no access to financial support or public health services (Shabbar, 2012, pp. 158–159; Vaughan et al., 2015, p. 24). Migration legislation operates as another pressure on women to stay with a violent partner.

Some study women arrived in Australia sponsored under their abusive partner's work visa and the IPV exception did not apply to their visa.[8] This was Rosa's experience. By the time of interview 3, Rosa was placing herself at risk searching Facebook to find a new Australian sponsor so she could stay in Australia with her child. Tabora had similar issues. At interview 1, she was concerned that Paulo would be deported to their home country and Tabora and the children would be deported also. She was very worried that her abusive partner "has no fear" in their home country and that she and the children would be even more unsafe there. Tabora was uncontactable at the time of interview 3. Doya was an undocumented migrant woman, and her lack of a visa had kept her trapped with her abuser for months.

Shuang's Experience

Throughout the time of the interviews, Shuang's relationship with Mac was in an almost constant state of flux. Her love for Mac, his dependence on her, his violence toward her, her isolation, her visa situation, and her financial dependency all played into her considerations about separation. Ultimately she succeeded in attaining permanent residency status via the IPV exception. The police were often called over the period of the interviews. By the time of interview 2, police had applied successfully for protection orders for both Shuang and Mac so they could be protected from each other. This was despite Mac's history of serious harm toward Shuang, including strangling her, and her explanation that the only time she is violent is in self-defense—pushing him away. In interview 3, Shuang disclosed she was charged with breach of the protection order on a couple of occasions. She described her relationship with Mac, and her situation, as a "dead circle"—something with no solution.

> ***Shuang, interview 1:*** *After that separation and later, he contact me and apologize and everything, yeah. Also his family talk to me about this and now he really changed a lot, yeah. I just don't understand, totally, he's—like, he's totally changed and not violent anymore. He always—like, after this, he always felt sorry and apologizing for everything and I kept forgiving him, but it's like a dead circle. . . . You never find a solution, you know.*

I meet Shuang, in her late 30s, at a coffee shop in a shopping mall near her home. She is a small, fine-boned woman and softly spoken. She discusses her experiences in a matter-of-fact way. She has a bachelor's degree from her home country and speaks several languages (English is her third language). Shuang came to Australia 3 years ago on a student visa, but this was canceled because she wasn't attending school. The visa cancellation coincided with meeting Mac online. Mac is Australian born and also in his 30s. Shuang initially moved in with Mac as a flatmate, but they fell in love and were married within a year. Mac agreed to sponsor her on a partner visa.[9]

Shuang says that at the beginning of the relationship Mac "showed her the city," cooked for her, and generally helped her out. She says, "We bought a dog together and we had a lot of fun going out." But he began to pick on her for small things, and she didn't know why. He hassled her about her previous sexual experiences and would easily become angry and break things like a chair or a cup or punch the refrigerator. He made threats to send her back home, kill her, and burn down the house. Sometimes the police attended. She told the police she didn't want anything to happen to Mac, but police said things like "You fight all the time, better just to finish the relationship, it's not a healthy relationship." Shuang's visa status relied on Mac's sponsorship, and she knows few other people in the city. Sometimes police told Mac to go away, but he always came back the next day and apologized. The police took out a protection order for Shuang. Mac had to be on good behavior, but they kept living together.

Shuang says that recently it got "worse and worse until he physically attacked me." He picked her up and pushed her against the wall; he strangled her and she briefly lost consciousness. Shuang ran to the neighbors, who called an ambulance, and she was taken to hospital. Her medical report states a diagnosis of postconcussive syndrome.[10] The hospital arranged for her to stay in a shelter for 3 weeks. The police also came to the hospital and told her Mac would be charged with an offense. She said: "I really want him to learn a lesson. You can't do this in a normal society, no matter what, there's a law here." In the end he was only charged with breaching the protection order. She thinks that Mac's father went to the police and talked them out of more serious charges.

Mac later apologized for his behavior, and Shuang moved back in. She says, "Basically I want to work on it, our marriage. I really put a lot of hope in this. . . . I'm very traditional . . . normally, like if you choose to marry, you're supposed to live with this guy the rest of your life." Little by little she found out more about Mac. He has PTSD after spending many years of his youth in prison, where he served a long sentence for serious theft and violence-related offenses. She says things have been tolerable with Mac over the past couple of months since she came back. She likes having the protection order in place and thinks it keeps her safe because Mac doesn't want to go back to prison.

Shuang's visa status is complicated. When she was in the shelter, she planned to go back to Mac, but shelter workers told her about the option of applying for permanent residency under the IPV exception. They assisted her with the process, and she is currently on a "bridging visa" waiting for the result of her application. She says the bridging visa makes things very hard because she can't work or study or leave the country to visit her family. She still relies on Mac to support her. Shuang says the immigration department is "very suspicious" and believes she got married to Mac to get permanent residency.

> ***Shuang, interview 2:*** *I was very scared, actually, very scared because I have no experience with people using drugs, I have no idea what will happen and . . . his very bad temper. So, yeah, I just like, I'm very scared but I decide to go back to him and keep an eye on him. I really feel very . . . guilty because I left him and that trigger him to use the drugs.*

Shuang and I catch up in the same coffee shop a year after the first interview, this time on a Saturday morning. We joke that it is our local. Shuang is in a celebratory mood because she now has permanent residency. She's working in a restaurant and lives by herself with her own lease, although she stays with Mac sometimes. Since the first interview, Shuang spent another period in a shelter for 3 months. She says there was more violence, and she was being "run down" by Mac all the time. She couldn't take it and rang the police, who were able to find her a place in a shelter.

Shuang was staying at Mac's just the week before our second interview and while there she called the police because Mac "pushed [her] in the neck." The police attended and encouraged her to leave Mac, telling her, "Look, your relationship doesn't work anymore . . . it's a waste of our time coming here. You have to make the right decisions, otherwise it will never end." Shuang says she will still see Mac for now but in 6 months she will reconsider. He is continuing to break their things and insult her, and she is scared of him. She says, "He doesn't have a bottom line, something you shouldn't do, and . . . after . . . he regrets it and it's too late."

Since the time of the first interview, police have taken out new protection orders against both Shuang and Mac so they must both be on good behavior toward each other.[11] The protection orders end this month, and the police have suggested Shuang should renew hers. She says the only time she is violent toward Mac is when she pushes him away. She thinks police "didn't like really trust in me and also listen to Mac's story . . . I reckon maybe because he's local." Shuang says, "At the moment I just follow my heart, I couldn't leave him alone, he is not well." She describes her situation as "complicated" and "stressful."

> ***Shuang interview 3:*** *Yeah. I do [love him]. I do actually. He's not a bad person. That's why I didn't give him up. He's not bad at all. He's just always hang around with the wrong people. Got in trouble all the time. His nature is not that.*

I meet Shuang again 10 months after the second interview. The police renewed the protection orders against both Shuang and Mac. It turned out that one of the conditions on Mac's order was that Shuang was not allowed to contact him. Twice she was charged with breaching the order because she went to Mac's house to check on him, and she was ordered to pay fines of $200 (USD131). She got a payment plan and paid them off. She says the police were watching her and alleged that she went to his place to disturb him and cause trouble. Police took her to the watch-house the first time and told her she wasn't allowed to visit Mac. The next two times they charged her. She thinks the police "got sick of us—they just want to do something to give us a lesson."

Although Shuang and Mac now live separately, Shuang sometimes stays overnight at Mac's house if he is all right. She still loves him. They have the protection orders, and they must be on good behavior toward each other, but the police changed the order so they can be in contact. She hasn't divorced Mac yet because she is waiting to see if he can remain stable. She says: "I'm already 40 years old, [but] if he can't settle down and have a normal life, I better just leave him."

THE FAMILY LAW SYSTEM AND SEPARATION

One of the underlying expectations of the family law system is that parents share the care of their children after separation.[12] Family court orders almost always allow the father to have contact with the children in the relationship (Australian Institute of Family Studies, 2019), with shared parenting increasingly associated with the best interests of the child (DeKeseredy, Dragiewicz, & Schwartz, 2018, p. 127). Postseparation contact orders provide opportunities for abuse (Khaw, Bermea, Hardesty, Saunders, & Whittaker, 2018, p. 18; Stubbs & Wangmann, 2015, p. 121), and many women who engage with the family law system report experiencing fear and coercion or control from their partner around parenting issues after separation (Hooker, Kaspiew, & Taft, 2016, p. 26; Kaspiew et al., 2015; Laing, 2017, p. 1321). Abusive men often use threats about ongoing care of the children as part of their strategy of coercive control (Hooker et al., 2016, p. 28).

Many women in the study understood that on separation their abusive partner would likely be ordered unsupervised contact with the children if they try to sort out parenting arrangements through the family courts, but they also feared worse might happen, which would be that the family courts would order the children to live with their abusive partner. The continued safety of children, something many women feel will be easier to monitor if they are present, also underpinned decisions about separating (S. Miller, 2018, p. 106; Saunders, Faller, & Tolman, 2011). Hilary shared in her first interview: "I don't want some magistrate deciding what is best—in their best interests. . . . That's why I stayed with Bruce [ex-partner] for as long as I did because he used to say things to me like that. 'You'll have to give me the children if we separate, you realize that, don't you?' . . . So the absolute terror of having to give them to him and him not keeping them safe."

As is clear from some of the women's experiences explored in Chapter 8, women often make complex arrangements to avoid the family law system. Others, in their efforts to sidestep the family court, put off separating in order to wait for their children to be old enough to make their own decisions. For example, Fiona said in her first interview: "I'd always been planning when the kids were old enough, I would go. I knew that."

Faith's Experience

Faith separated from her partner, Ryan, several times before "completely" separating. Key obstacles for her leaving included his constant threats that he would take the children if she left and the reality of the poverty she and the children would experience after separation. On previous occasions when she left, she had gone as far as applying for a protection order only to find that Ryan had applied for one against her. Faith finally decided to proceed with separation when Ryan slept with another woman in Faith's bed. Since separating, she has struggled to get a protection order as Ryan has adjourned proceedings many times, and once she had the order, she struggled to get police to charge any breaches of the order. Contact and property arrangements through the family court took 4 years to resolve. By the time of interview 3, she remained separated from Ryan, although she did not discount the idea of reuniting.

> ***Faith, interview 1:*** *I'd refer to him as my heroin. I'd say it's—I know he's going to kill me and I can't stop wanting him. I'd say that's the only thing that I can see it as. I know it's bad, I know he's going to kill me, and I actually had a conversation with my . . . sister and I said, you realize if I ever go missing he's done it, because I will never ever leave these kids.*

Faith meets me on the weekend while her children are on a contact visit with their father. We meet at the home of Pearl, a retired social worker who has been helping Faith navigate the legal system. Pearl leaves us on the porch and heads inside, telling us, "Call me if you need me."

Faith and Ryan are in their 40s. They were in a relationship for more than 15 years and have several school-aged children together. She has a bachelor's degree and works full-time. Ryan has a trade and was fully employed when they were together, but currently he receives social security. She says, "I think it has a lot to do with child support."

When I ask Faith when she separated from Ryan, she asks: "Cut it completely, really cut it?" "Yes," I say. "Last year," Faith answers, "but it's been breaking up, breaking up, and breaking up a lot of times." She separated 4 years ago and applied for a protection order but then "backed out." Two years ago they separated again, and she applied for another protection order. That time Ryan also applied for a protection order against her, so the lawyer suggested they sign an undertaking.[13] The legal aid lawyer was worried that Faith would lose her job if a protection order was made against her—so then Faith and Ryan signed an undertaking. They were back living together shortly after this. She says her most recent separation from Ryan was just over 6 months ago, after she discovered he had sex with someone else in her bed: "I just went, OK, thank you for telling me that because you've just solidified that I will never ever get back with him again. . . . It was like he will stop at nothing."

Faith says there were a couple of early incidents in which Ryan's temper flared, and this surprised her, but the abuse really started when she was pregnant with their first child. Then Ryan started calling her abusive names, telling her she was fat and ugly. They had a joint account, and she would rush to pay the bills before the money disappeared; sometimes he would blow his entire paycheck on the way home from work on slot machines and alcohol. There were also degrading forms of physical abuse: He spat at her, threw drinks at her, and pulled her hair. She sometimes had bruises after he smashed her head into a wall, and he often kicked her. Sometimes he walked past her when she was on the couch and kicked her casually. She had many bruises on her legs. On one occasion "he choked" her, but she kicked him off. He told her he had a five-step plan to destroy her: "Take my job from me. . . . Take my kids from me. Take my house from me, I think take my freedom. I think it's to report me to the police for doing all this stuff and destroy my name." On one occasion he described exactly how he was going to kill her: "He'd rung me up and he said, I'm going to smash your head through the back door, it's glass, until you're all cut up, drag you by your hair down the stairs, put you in the [car], drive up to the . . . bridge and push you into oncoming traffic and then I'm going to jump off the bridge." She says she stayed because she "always wanted to keep my family together. . . . I didn't want the kids having to grow up with two different parents." Ryan also always said that he would take the kids; she says that "he had me convinced."

Faith explains that "by the end, when I was going back and forward, I was actually lying to my friends and saying 'yep, we're still separated, yep,' but we'd be back together." She says, "He'd really manipulated my brain, big time, and that's a big thing. When I . . . saw my therapist I knew, I said to him, I need you to retrain how I think. I realize that my brain has been manipulated."

Faith has a protection order, and Ryan must stay away from her. The protection order application was adjourned by Ryan many times before it was set down for a hearing. Eventually Ryan consented to it being made on the basis that he made no admissions.[14] She is currently navigating the family law system and has been refused legal aid. She and Ryan have been to a conciliation conference.[15] Initially the conciliator had not read the documents and so ushered them in to a room together. Faith resisted, explaining the history of IPV, and then they were separated. Faith says that initially the conciliator didn't believe her, but eventually, after Faith's disclosures, the conciliator discouraged going to trial and said, "You do realize at the end of the day, it's whoever is the better actor." Faith has submitted all the documents required of her, but Ryan has submitted none. She comments: "Well he's been acting his whole life, that's what an abuser is, they're a very good actor."

There is now an interim family court order about child contact. For now the children live with Faith but see their father under the supervision of his parents one day each weekend. Faith wanted the contact to happen at a contact center, but the judge did not make that order. She says she has told the police that Ryan makes constant suicide threats.[16] A police officer has helped her install a recording app on her phone to record Ryan's threats.[17]

> ***Faith, interview 2:*** *Staying away was really hard. But it was so worth it in the end. I literally had to rebuild myself. I didn't know my*

favorite color. I was a robot. There are huge parts of my life I honestly cannot remember. Now, though, what I have now is just—I'm still single and I'm fine with that—but I just have happiness. I still get angry or whatever. I still—just normal emotions—but I come home to peace. That is so different. When I used to come home and not know what I was coming home to. The anxiety would already start at the thought of going home. But now just to come home and go, "Oh, I'm just going to sit down and have a coffee or have a wine."

Ten months after our first interview, I meet Faith in a coffee shop. Faith is not eligible for legal aid and so has been managing the continuing requirements of the family court on her own. The court ordered that the children have an independent children's lawyer.[18] Faith received a bill for $3,000 (USD2,000) for the independent children's lawyer costs and had to "make a hardship case" because she couldn't afford to pay it. Meanwhile, Ryan is receiving social security and thus does not have to pay.

Faith's main aim in the property settlement was to keep the house, but she needs 10 years to refinance it. She sought advice from several lawyers who advised this would not be possible. Recently, however, after representing herself, she received the order that she sought and has 10 years to refinance the house. Because she is a single wage earner with several dependent children, banks would not lend the amount she needs now, but in 10 years, when house prices go up, she will be in a better position to refinance. She still has significant debt, including for a car that she has never driven (Ryan drove it). It's been repossessed, but the debt is in her name. She says she will have paid that off in a few years.

She has also had to change contact handovers. A friend was dropping the children off with Ryan and then picking them up, but Faith didn't want to rely on a third party. Faith wanted handovers to happen at a contact center; this idea was rejected. The judge suggested a police station, but Faith did not think that was appropriate. She says she might have been a bit emotional about this. She said to the judge, "Would you do that with your own children?" She says the judge yelled at her and said: "How dare you? I can hold you in contempt of court right now." Both Faith and the judge apologized to each other. For a while handovers happened at a police station. There have been at least four appearances before the family court since Faith and I first met less than a year ago; both Ryan and Faith have been ordered to do parenting courses, and Ryan has been ordered to take some behavior management courses.

Faith still has a protection order, which she thinks is helpful. Ryan is not supposed to contact her, but he emails all the time. She took the emails to police, but because Ryan mentions the children in them, the police refused to charge him: "He's worked out how far he can go. He goes to that line."

She says she had a full year in which she saw Ryan only at court; her friend was doing all the child handovers. This break from seeing Ryan was important. She says: "I felt that anger. For a long time, I had a lot of anger. I've still got that in the back of my mind, that fear. I don't know if that will ever go away. It's getting more to the nothing. It's not quite there because he still manipulates me with the kids."

> ***Faith, interview 3:*** *I'm a completely different person now who was abused. He's a different person as well . . . that doesn't mean we'll reconnect or anything like that, but it means at the moment we can communicate and we can get on. . . . I started . . . letting Ryan come over . . . it's early days. Like it's been less than 5, 6 months. You know, I mean yes, we have . . . kids together. Yes we've known each other for 16 years. Yes, we've been through a lot . . . we sat and talked about quite a lot of things. . . . I'm not going to put everything in it. I'm just—let's just wait and see.*

Faith and I meet 7 months after the second interview, again in a coffee shop. Faith says that she and Ryan both did their court-ordered courses. She completed a parenting after separation course and found it really helpful because it "allowed me to really separate myself from the situation." She says that being a single parent is very hard. The kids are a couple of years older now, so when they went back to court to set a date for trial, she offered Ryan a week on and week off with the children. He accepted that arrangement, and court orders were ultimately made by consent a few months ago. Ryan has never sought to look after the children for a week since the order was made. Faith says:

> But it meant that that whole court business could stop . . . and we sort of started communicating. He's seen the kids a lot more and that took all that out of it . . . he had done those courses and he had those major changes in the way he was treating me and talking to me . . . he owned what he did. That was a massive one. . . . It's only new, it's only fresh. But it seems to be working at the moment.

Ryan has done a "perpetrator course," and he told Faith that "quite often, he'd be the only one who turned up at it. So he'd just have this one-on-one with this guy and it was just life-changing for him." Faith says that in order for them to get on for the kids, she "had to let a lot of stuff go as well. A lot of anger and a lot of hurt." Despite this, she still has a protection order in place. Faith tells me, "There was no line before. . . . He could just do whatever and I would just—you know, I was a shell." She says she wants to make sure the changes are "real" before she changes "anything." Faith says:

> The domestic violence had such a hold. It's like this octopus that holds my brain. . . . In order to break away from that, I had to have no contact. Because I couldn't see or think of anything apart from him. Not him entirely. It just had that much hold on me. . . . It was just covered in that black ink that they spurt. That's what I was like. That's why there's huge parts I can't remember. I honestly can't remember. Huge gaps in my life.

CONCLUSION

Consistent with what has been found in other research, the study women's reasons for staying, leaving and returning are complex and multilayered. For some women, improved employment options, financial support, child care, public housing, and other material support may help. These material things are worth continuing to fight for because they not only are likely to make it safer for some women to leave violent relationships but also are likely to improve women's equality and may reduce violence, making it safer for some women to stay (Stark, 2007, p. 381). Had Faith, Melissa, and Shuang been able to secure improved material support, they might have separated earlier, or at least found life easier when they did leave, and they may have been able to live free of the abuse for longer. But this is only part of the story. For Melissa, Shuang, and Faith, emotional connections, feelings of love and commitment, and a need for intimacy were also part of the pull to stay and return (Hamby, 2014, pp. 89–90).

It is clear that an abusive partner's violence, abuse, and efforts to exert control often continue or even increase after separation. Long after her separation, Melissa experienced serious assaults and nighttime trespass into her home, and Anna received death threats. When women separate from an abuser, they no longer know where he is, which sometimes places them in a constant state of fear and/or danger. This was Anna and Melissa's experience throughout the period of the interviews.

For many women, the legal system did not keep them safe; sometimes, as many of the chapters show, engagement with law after separation complicated their lives and exacerbated their danger. Anna, Melissa, Shuang, and Faith did not find that protection orders improved their safety. Protection orders were not taken seriously by Anna and Melissa's ex-partners, who constantly breached them, filing away their fines or simply failing to turn up at court for judgment. For Shuang, the protection order process resulted in her being punished. Police took out protection orders against both Shuang and her partner—charging Shuang for breaches of no-contact orders on several occasions. For many women, like Shuang, with insecure visa status or no visa, separation meant poverty, hunger, and, for some, deportation.

When a woman has children with her abusive partner, separation may result in lengthy litigation in the family courts and enmeshment with her abusive partner for years, managing financial and contact arrangements about the children (Fleury, Sullivan, & Bybee, 2000, p. 1381; Goodmark,

2012, p. 83). The response of the family law system was a significant consideration for Anna and Faith in their decisions to leave. Both were concerned that their children would be taken from their care or ordered to have unsafe contact with their abusive partners. For both women their fears they would be ordered to agree to unsafe contact were realized. Throughout the interviews, child contact arrangements were in a constant state of flux for Anna and Faith. After separation they were drawn in to their ex-partner's adversarial engagement with legal processes, adding to the stress they experienced.

The disconnectedness of legal systems and the inconsistent expectations related to separation—from police, child protection services, protection orders, family law, and victims assistance—added to the practical and emotional burdens faced by women at separation. The women's stories clearly demonstrate that legal definitions of separation fail to reflect women's experiences (Smart, 1989, p. 4). Separation is not a moment in time but a process or a journey; it is not linear, and it may be, as in Shuang's words, a "dead circle." If safety is an aspiration of the legal response to IPV (Goodmark, 2012, pp. 104–105), then separation should not be part of the assessment of the worthiness of a woman's claim for legal and other support.

NOTES

1. There is no requirement under Australian protection order statutes for the applicant to be separated (either physically or legally) from the respondent to the application (Australasian Institute of Judicial Administration [AIJA], 2020, [3.3]).
2. An administrative system exists for victims of crime to claim payments for various costs including, for example, counseling, changes to locks, and so forth (Daly, Holder, & Meyer, 2019).
3. Reviews of IPV-related deaths have identified that gang affiliation increased the risk of future harm after separation (Domestic and Family Violence Death Review and Advisory Board, 2018, p. 69).
4. Pregnancy has been shown to increase and escalate a woman's risk and experience of domestic and family violence by her intimate partner (D. Walsh, 2008).
5. When parents can agree on parenting arrangements after separation, they can make a parenting plan. Although these are not legally enforceable, they can be used

as evidence of agreement between the parties at a particular point in time (Harland et al., 2015, pp. 133–155).

6. Family law disputes can engage a variety of approaches, including mediation (termed *family dispute resolution*) (Harland et al., 2015, pp. 90–94).
7. Child support is dealt with administratively in Australia, and it is possible to claim an exemption from collecting it on the basis that collection would increase the risk of future IPV (Douglas & Nagesh, 2019).
8. See Chapter 4.
9. See Chapter 4.
10. Postconcussive syndrome is associated with nonfatal strangulation (J. C. Campbell et al., 2018).
11. Mutual orders, sometimes called cross orders, are reasonably common in Australia, and there has been significant criticism about their use (Douglas & Fitzgerald, 2013; Wangmann, 2012).
12. In Australia, family law legislation includes a presumption of shared care defined as being at least 35% of nights with each parent (Harland et al., 2015, pp. 24–25; see also Dragiewicz, 2015, pp. 134–136).
13. An undertaking is an informal promise made by a person to the court. A breach of such an undertaking has no formal implications (AIJA, 2020, [7.11]).
14. Where a protection order is made by consent without admission, there may be no admission of fact capable of being relied upon in later family law proceedings (AIJA, 2020, [7.7]).
15. A conciliation conference is conducted by a family court registrar and aims to help parties settle their dispute to avoid trial (Cooper & Brandon, 2007).
16. The abuser's threat to commit suicide may increase the risk of future harm and death (J. Campbell et al., 2003, p. 1091).
17. Despite the police assisting Faith to install a recording app on her phone, it is not clear any recordings can be admitted in evidence, although they can be helpful for women in convincing lawyers, police, and child protection workers (Douglas & Burdon, 2018).
18. Independent children's lawyers (ICLs) are appointed to represent the interests of children who are the subject of a dispute between their parents or guardians (Kaye, 2019a, p. 101).

10

Conclusion

THE IMPORTANCE OF EXPERIENCE

This book has placed women's experiences of the interaction between law and intimate partner violence (IPV) at its center (Ahmed, 2017, p. 203; R. Campbell & Wasco, 2000, p. 778). Talking with women over time provided an opportunity to better understand women's journeys through law (Kelly, Sharp, & Klein, 2014; Slote et al., 2005). Women's decisions about, and experiences of, law varied widely, depending on their resources, context, backgrounds, and needs. Some women used law selectively and in creative ways. Although some women chose to turn away from law (Smart, 1989), most had little choice but to engage with it, fearing the loss of safety, children, citizenship, and even liberty if they did not. The women's narratives demonstrate the level of resourcefulness, endurance, tenacity, time, and money; the "hardiness" that engaging with law requires (Goodmark, 2012, p. 5; S. Miller, 2018, pp. 176–177; Silbey, 2005, p. 353).[1]

Although women experienced positive moments in law, overall, their interactions with law reflect an accumulation of negative experiences over time, in different parts of the legal system, not just one negative interaction with an "out-of-touch" police officer, lawyer, or judge or an adverse court experience. Many women found their ex-partners used legal processes to continue to try to control, intimidate, and abuse them, and that justice actors, including child protection workers, police, lawyers, and judges, often failed, or took too long, to recognize it and respond. In this way

Women, Intimate Partner Violence, and the Law. Heather Douglas, Oxford University Press (2021). © Oxford University Press.
DOI: 10.1093/oso/9780190071783.003.0010

justice actors sometimes facilitated secondary abuse and contributed to women's trauma. The risk of double victimization, at home through IPV and then through law, is well recognized (Bumiller, 2008, p. 97; Herman, 2003, 2005). For most women in this study, their legal engagements did not deliver the safety and closure they sought, or if they did, the response was slow and stressful (Goodmark, 2012, p. 8). For some women, the time law took was too long and the losses were too great. At best, women's experiences of law can be described as ambivalent and uneven (Ewick & Silbey, 1992, p. 749).

Women's engagements with law did change, in different ways, over time. For some women the passage of time meant their children grew older, leading them to feel a little more comfortable to consent to orders for their child to have contact with an ex-partner they still perceived to be unsafe. Most women from culturally and linguistically diverse backgrounds had achieved permanent residency status by the time of the second or third interview and were financially independent, and some were able to finally consider returning to their birth countries along with their children to visit extended family. Some women developed connections and relationships over time with police officers, lawyers, and judges, believing by the time of later interviews that these justice actors finally understood their experience of IPV and their ex-partner's role in perpetrating it, but sometimes this recognition took years. Many women pointed to the financial costs of law that they struggled with for years. Some thought they had closure and that their legal interactions in response to IPV were finished, only to have their abusive partner restart litigation. By the time of the third interview, many of the women were starting to experience less law, and their contact with their ex-partner had ended, lessened, and sometimes improved.

Although, overall, this is a story of legal system failure and a broken legal system, throughout their interviews women often suggested, or pointed to, ways that their journeys through law could have been improved, both in the sense of increasing their safety and in reducing the secondary trauma they experienced through interacting with law. Many recommendations based on their interviews are suggested in earlier chapters. In this chapter I explore some possibilities for a more safety-focused legal system.

A SAFE LEGAL SYSTEM

In her consideration of battered women's protective strategies, Hamby concludes that those who work with people who have experienced IPV must be more respectful, properly trained, and educated, and services must be integrated, sufficiently and consistently funded, and work from a strengths-based holistic paradigm (Hamby, 2014, pp. 184–187). Many of the women interviewed in this study had similar ideas to those of Hamby (2018) about the kinds of changes needed in the legal context: respectful justice actors who understand IPV, an integrated legal system, well-funded services (such as legal aid and police and judges who have time), and for the legal system to mitigate their risk and harm rather than increase it.[2]

Respectful Justice Actors Who Understand IPV

Some of the women's stories showed that how legal system actors respond can make an important and positive difference to their legal trajectory toward safety and to reducing the potential for them to experience secondary trauma through the legal process. Their stories showed that the opposite is also true: When legal actors fail to understand IPV, they can contribute to law being experienced as a form of secondary victimization (see Chapters 5–8) (Ptacek, 1999, pp. 174–176).

Reviews of the legal response to IPV routinely highlight the importance of training justice actors about IPV (DeKeseredy, Dragiewicz, & Schwartz, 2017, p. 157; Hamby, 2014, p. 182; State of Victoria, 2016a, p. 15). In its wide-ranging review of the response to family violence, the Victorian Royal Commission Into Family Violence observed that changing laws has only a symbolic effect, and that to gain changes in practice, training and education are essential (State of Victoria, 2016a, p. 27). Given the extent to which law and legal systems are relied on to respond to IPV (Barlow & Walklate, 2020; State of Victoria, 2016a), it is insufficient to depend on a small group of specially trained individuals as resource points, although this is a start. A solid education base about IPV needs to be provided to all those whose work intersects with IPV, and that education needs to be consistent between professions, as well as updated and refreshed regularly. University courses such as those in social work,[3] criminology, and law should incorporate introductory modules about IPV within their degree structures, as many of those who graduate from these courses are likely to confront IPV in their working lives. Refresher training for those working in child protection,[4] criminal law, and family law, where IPV is a common feature of everyday practice, should be provided regularly. As women in this study frequently identified, there are still too many professionals working in the legal system who fail to understand the dynamics of IPV, including coercive control and the key role of nonphysical abuse in women's experience of IPV, and who focus on separation as a goal (Goodmark, 2012, p. 5) (see Chapters 3 and 9). Training should address these issues but also consider ways that legal practices can avoid secondary traumatization. Herman has identified some of the ways in which engaging with law is retraumatizing for victims of abuse:

> Victims need social acknowledgment and support; the court requires them to endure a public challenge to their credibility. Victims need to establish a sense of power and control over their lives; the court requires them to submit to a complex set of rules and procedures that they may not understand, and over which they have no control. Victims need an opportunity to tell their stories in their own way, in a setting of their choice; the court requires them to respond to a set of yes-or-no questions that break down any personal attempt to construct a coherent and meaningful narrative. Victims often need to control or limit their exposure to specific reminders of the trauma; the court requires them to relive the experience by directly confronting the perpetrator. (2003, p 163)

In light of Herman's comments, the legal process may be less traumatizing when justice actors are respectful to the parties and when judges avoid any appearance of being aligned with either party. It might be less traumatizing when justice actors show they understand the dynamics of IPV and when they are attuned to the possibility that the legal process may be being used to extend abuse. In the context of legal systems abuses, judges might make better use of their powers to stop irrelevant questions and minimize delays and the need for court attendances. Justice actors more generally would minimize trauma by preparing in advance, including reading files and ensuring clear information is included in files in the event that there is a change in personnel (AIJA, 2020, [5.3]; Ptacek, 1999, p. 176; Ward, 2016). In particular, this careful recording would help to avoid the need for a victim to tell her story over and over again. If justice actors clearly explained procedures and court orders and their consequences to the parties, and gave them time to ask questions, this might help to reduce the secondary trauma of going to law. If justice actors used the resources available to make the court experience as safe as possible (e.g., provide and use safe rooms, exclude unnecessary people from the court, ensure safe or staggered departure of parties from the court, and use witness protection options), this would also help to avoid trauma (Kelly et al., 2014, p. 43). In taking these measures, justice actors may not only reduce trauma but also help to make going to law an empowering experience (Ptacek, 1999, pp. 172–178; Stark, 2007, p. 403).

Online Courts

Separation from an abusive partner is a dangerous time for women, and abuse often continues after separation (J. Campbell et al., 2003; Fleury, Cris, Sullivan, & Bybee, 2000; Mahoney, 1991). However, once the parties have separated, many of the methods of abuse previously employed by the abuser may no longer be an option. The abuser may no longer have physical access to the victim and might look for new ways to perpetuate abuse (Slote et al., 2005, p. 1387; DeKeseredy et al., 2017; Dobash & Dobash, 2015, p. 39). At the point of separation, many women who have been abused go to law to seek protection from further violence, to get assistance in breaking ties with the abuser, and to determine issues that cannot be resolved without legal system intervention (Lewis, Dobash, Dobash, & Cavanagh, 2001, p. 109). Indeed after separation, for any relationship, regardless of whether there is IPV, there are many legitimate reasons to go to law. However, as many of the women's stories in this book show, for many abusive partners, who may be court-ordered not to contact their previous partner, litigation may be the only way they can have contact. In circumstances where women must come to court to defend their rights, abusers are incentivized to increase opportunities to see them at court by adjourning proceedings, trying to split their cases into different parts, and making multiple applications in multiple courts. Furthermore, as Herman (2003, p. 160) points out, recovery from the trauma of IPV is facilitated by limiting exposure to reminders of the trauma. For many women each court date is a new exposure to the reminders of the trauma; this is experienced not just on the actual court date but also in the days leading up to it (Ptacek, 1999, p. 149; Roberts, Chamberlain, & Delfabbro, 2015, p. 609).

As more of the work of the courts is shifted online, this might reduce the incentive for abusers to extend litigation. Increasingly, courts accept online applications, the filing of documents, applications involving those in custody, and the conduct of applications and hearings in the context of bail and adjournments (Ellison, 2002; Treadway Johnson & Wiggins, 2006; T. Walsh, 2018). As technology becomes increasingly sophisticated, it already allows for separate virtual "rooms" to be created—for example, for lawyers and their clients, lawyers together, or with the judge or the entire court—there will be more opportunities for online justice. Potentially one could imagine a scenario in which a woman could "attend" court online from the safety of her lawyer's office or that of her support worker.[5] Training in the use of technology may be needed, and discrepancies in the availability of internet service, approved software, and necessary hardware between organizations would need to be managed and accounted for. However, these developments offer some promise in helping to reduce legal systems abuse and the secondary trauma of court attendance.

An Integrated Legal System

Ensuring the definitions of IPV are the same across systems (see Appendix 2) and that, where possible, the same screening and risk assessment tools are utilized have yet to occur but are important steps toward an integrated system. Given the ubiquity of IPV in contested matters in the family courts, IPV should be accounted for and the safety of children should truly be at the center of decision-making around child contact (DeKeseredy et al., 2017, pp. 157–159).

Criminal responses are part of an integrated system, and women (and the wider community) should be able to expect a strong criminal response (Hill, 2019, p. 253). As presented in Chapters 4 and 6, women in this study expressed frustration and disappointment about the use of the criminal law, especially the failure of police and judges to take seriously nonphysical breaches of civil protection orders. Women highlighted the failure of justice actors to take seriously breaches of no-contact conditions in protection orders, especially when women had children with their abuser. They expressed frustration when police "dropped" serious charges and proceeded with less serious charges (such as a breach of protection order charge) or preferred non-IPV charges (such as drunk driving or drug possession) or when numerous reported breach incidents were "rolled up" into one charge (Kelly et al., 2014, p. 42). Several women also reported they were misrecognized by police as abusers. Women in this study also expressed frustration that when they attended a police station or called the police, the police officer often knew nothing about them. Improved and regular training and careful shift handovers may address some of these concerns.

A number of recent reviews call for more criminalization (DeKeseredy et al., 2017, pp. 153–154; McMahon & McGorrery, 2020), in particular, the introduction of an offense of coercive control based on research by Stark (2007).[6] It is possible the existence of an offense of coercive control would have made a small difference to some of the women in this study. If such an offense had existed, some abusers may have been charged with it rather than escaping punishment altogether; then again, some women in this study may have been charged with it too. It is possible that the introduction of such an offense might lead, more generally, to greater awareness of the seriousness of nonphysical forms of abuse and coercive control (Hill, 2019), although there may be more nuanced ways to raise community awareness (Our Watch, 2020). Certainly, one of the simplest things to do would be to introduce a new offense. However, it is clear that, in the Australian context, greater focus on criminalization leads to ever-higher levels of incarceration, particularly of Aboriginal and Torres Strait Islander people. Notably, in Australia, Aboriginal and Torres Strait Islander women are the fastest-growing group to be incarcerated because of family violence (Douglas & Fitzgerald, 2018; Nancarrow, 2019). The situation is similar in the United States for African American women (D. Coker & Macquoid, 2015, p. 588). Tolmie (2018; also Goodmark, 2018, p. 221) raises further concerns about focusing on criminalization of coercive control. In particular, Tolmie argues that the risks of introducing this offense include "that it could be used in a manner that minimizes IPV, invalidates the victim's experiences or, worst of all, recasts their resistance to abuse as abuse" (2018, p. 62).

For most of the women in this study, the issue related to police and criminal justice was not a lack of powers, options, or offenses being available to police but a failure to properly exercise available powers and to follow through on appropriate charges that were available. One suggestion was that women should have one or two key points of contact with police and that police should know about their history and the risks of their particular circumstances. Having a couple of key contacts within the police could reduce women's trauma of having to explain the abuse all over again and would also enable those officers to acquire a more comprehensive picture of the pattern of abuse experienced, perhaps leading to more appropriate outcomes more quickly. This worked well for some women in this study, but it was ad hoc and driven by individual women rather than by police policy

Resourcing Services and Responses

The women in this study also pointed to the need for a well-resourced system that ensures sufficient time is allocated to their case across all systems. Many women highlighted the inadequacy of the legal aid system (Chapter 7). Their experiences demonstrate that in the absence of a well-resourced legal aid system, women may bargain away their rights and agree to legal orders that undercut their safety and the safety of their children. In the absence of sufficient legal aid, they may turn to private lawyers, resulting in high levels of personal debt. These debts often had implications for the rest of their lives and the lives of their children, including impacting on their health, contributing to a cycle of poverty and housing stress, and reducing their superannuation.

Although there is a need for IPV training for all justice actors who interact with IPV, there is also a deep need for well-resourced specialist support services in this context (Hill, 2019, p. 243). Kelly and colleagues have referred to the "triple defensiveness" of women from marginalized groups who seek support after experiencing IPV, noting that women "are defensive with professionals about their victimisation; how their mothering will be judged; and about being a minority woman. This is why many appreciate being able to access specialist services run by women from minorities, it creates a different basis for interaction" (2016, pp. 4–5; see also Crenshaw, 1991; Slote et al., 2005, p. 1377). Many of the services that supported and recruited women to this study were independent specialist support services; some worked with minority groups, and some were legal. These services effectively provide supportive case management for women, connecting them with the range of services and supports they need, of which law is one. There was a high level of engagement throughout the period of the study between these services and many of the women they supported. For many of the women, this support was pivotal to their survival and helped them on their journey toward safety, independence, and freedom from violence.

CONCLUSION

For some women in this study, their engagement with law often challenged, reduced, or delayed their safety. For most women, their safety is a work in progress, and the law's role is only a small part of that progression. Since the 1970s and 1980s, law has been identified as an important tool in responding to women who have experienced IPV (E. Schneider, 2000, p. 440). This belief has become entrenched (Goodmark, 2012, p. 4), resulting, perhaps, in communities expecting too much from law. In different ways over many years, scholars have pointed at the limitations of law as a response and the need to decenter it as a solution (Scales, 2006, p. 118; Smart, 1989, p. 5). Although it should be decentered, law cannot be ignored; too many women who have experienced IPV are enmeshed in its web and have hopes for what it can deliver, and it should deliver greater safety more safely than it does. It is important to continue to work toward making law a safe place for victims of violence, and this book has attempted to make a contribution to that work.

NOTES

1. In her consideration of paths to survivorship, Miller highlights the "hardiness" of most of the women she interviewed. She describes hardiness as having three dimensions: being committed to finding meaning or purpose in life, a belief that one can influence one's surroundings and the outcome of events, and the belief that one can learn and grow from positive and negative experiences (S. Miller, 2018, p. 176).
2. Similar aspirations for law have appeared over and over again in numerous law reform projects (e.g., Special Taskforce on Domestic and Family Violence in Queensland, 2015; State of Victoria, 2016).
3. Notably, in 2019 the Australian Association of Social Workers required that university degrees in social work must include "power, oppression and exploitation" in relations as part of their required curriculum (Australian Association of Social Workers, 2019, p. 8).
4. In Australia and the United States, the "Safe and Together" model is an increasingly important framework in working with parents in child protection cases where there is IPV (Humphreys, Healey, & Mandel, 2018).
5. Notably, one of the techniques identified to deal with trauma is to diffuse it; one technique is to imagine it an image on television (Scent & Boes, 2014).
6. Coercive control–type offenses have been introduced in England, Wales, and Scotland in the United Kingdom, and there continues to be discussion about their implementation (Scott, 2020; Wiener, 2020).

APPENDIX 1

Women's Experiences

Woman's Name	Chapter
Anna	9
Bianca	5
Cassie (Aboriginal and Torres Strait Islander [ATSI])	5
Doya (culturally and linguistically diverse [CALD])	6
Faith	9
Felicity	8
Fiona	3
Hilary	7
Ingrid (CALD)	4
Julia	6
Lisa	8
Melissa (ATSI)	9
Rosa (CALD)	3
Sandra	4
Shelley	5
Shuang (CALD)	9
Susan	6
Trisha (CALD)	7

APPENDIX 2

Definitions of Intimate Partner Violence Across Systems

DOMESTIC AND FAMILY VIOLENCE PROTECTION ACT 2012 (QLD)

Section 8: Meaning of Domestic Violence

(1) **"Domestic violence"** means behaviour by a person (the **"first person"**) towards another person (the **"second person"**) with whom the first person is in a relevant relationship that—
   a) is physically or sexually abusive; or
   b) is emotionally or psychologically abusive; or
   c) is economically abusive; or
   d) is threatening; or
   e) is coercive; or
   f) in any other way controls or dominates the second person and causes the second person to fear for the second person's safety or wellbeing or that of someone else.

(2) Without limiting *subsection (1)*, domestic violence includes the following behaviour—
   a) causing personal injury to a person or threatening to do so;
   b) coercing a person to engage in sexual activity or attempting to do so;
   c) damaging a person's property or threatening to do so;
   d) depriving a person of the person's liberty or threatening to do so;

e) threatening a person with the death or injury of the person, a child of the person, or someone else;
f) threatening to commit suicide or self-harm so as to torment, intimidate or frighten the person to whom the behaviour is directed;
g) causing or threatening to cause the death of, or injury to, an animal, whether or not the animal belongs to the person to whom the behaviour is directed, so as to control, dominate or coerce the person;
h) unauthorised surveillance of a person;
i) unlawfully stalking a person.

(3) A person who counsels or procures someone else to engage in behaviour that, if engaged in by the person, would be domestic violence is taken to have committed domestic violence.

(4) To remove any doubt, it is declared that, for behaviour mentioned in *subsection (2)* that may constitute a criminal offence, a court may make an order under this Act on the basis that the behaviour is domestic violence even if the behaviour is not proved beyond a reasonable doubt.

(5) In this section—

"coerce," a person, means compel or force a person to do, or refrain from doing, something.

"unauthorised surveillance," of a person, means the unreasonable monitoring or tracking of the person's movements, activities or interpersonal associations without the person's consent, including, for example, by using technology.

FAMILY LAW ACT 1975 (CTH)

Section 4AB Definition of family violence etc.

(1) For the purposes of this Act, *family violence* means violent, threatening or other behaviour by a person that coerces or

controls a member of the person's family (the *family member*), or causes the family member to be fearful.

(2) Examples of behaviour that may constitute family violence include (but are not limited to):
   a) an assault; or
   b) a sexual assault or other sexually abusive behaviour; or
   c) stalking; or
   d) repeated derogatory taunts; or
   e) intentionally damaging or destroying property; or
   f) intentionally causing death or injury to an animal; or
   g) unreasonably denying the family member the financial autonomy that he or she would otherwise have had; or
   h) unreasonably withholding financial support needed to meet the reasonable living expenses of the family member, or his or her child, at a time when the family member is entirely or predominantly dependent on the person for financial support; or
   i) preventing the family member from making or keeping connections with his or her family, friends or culture; or
   j) unlawfully depriving the family member, or any member of the family member's family, of his or her liberty.

(3) For the purposes of this Act, a child is *exposed* to family violence if the child sees or hears family violence or otherwise experiences the effects of family violence.

(4) Examples of situations that may constitute a child being exposed to family violence include (but are not limited to) the child:
   a) overhearing threats of death or personal injury by a member of the child's family towards another member of the child's family; or
   b) seeing or hearing an assault of a member of the child's family by another member of the child's family; or
   c) comforting or providing assistance to a member of the child's family who has been assaulted by another member of the child's family; or

(d) cleaning up a site after a member of the child's family has intentionally damaged property of another member of the child's family; or

(e) being present when police or ambulance officers attend an incident involving the assault of a member of the child's family by another member of the child's family.

MIGRATION REGULATIONS 1994 (CTH)

Regulation 1.21

"*relevant family violence*" means conduct, whether actual or threatened, towards:

a) the alleged victim; or
b) a member of the family unit of the alleged victim; or
c) a member of the family unit of the alleged perpetrator; or
d) the property of the alleged victim; or
e) the property of a member of the family unit of the alleged victim; or
f) the property of a member of the family unit of the alleged perpetrator;

that causes the alleged victim to reasonably fear for, or to be reasonably apprehensive about, his or her own wellbeing or safety. . . .

"*violence*" includes a threat of violence.

APPENDIX 3

Visa Status

Name	Woman's Visa Before Interview	Interview 1	Interview 2	Interview 3	Partner's or Ex-partner's Visa Status
Angelina	1 Student 2 Sponsored spouse	Bridging (intimate partner violence [IPV] exception)	Not interviewed (but advised PR [IPV])	Not interviewed	Australian-born Permanent resident (PR)
Bisera	Sponsored parent	PR	PR	PR	Australian-born: daughter's partner
Celina	1 Tourist 2 Sponsored spouse	Bridging (IPV)	PR (IPV)	PR	Overseas-born PR
Chi	Work	PR	PR	PR	Australian-born citizen
Dalila	Refugee	Refugee	Refugee	Refugee	Overseas-born refugee
Dara	Sponsored spouse	PR (IPV)	PR	PR	Overseas-born PR
Doya	Tourist (lapsed)	Bridging (IPV)	Bridging (IPV)	PR (IPV)—department discretion)	Australian-born citizen
Euni	Student	Student	Bridging - Student	Bridging—student	Overseas-born Student
Ingrid	Sponsored spouse	PR (IPV)	PR	PR	Australian-born citizen
Jamila	Refugee	Refugee	Refugee	Refugee	Overseas-born refugee
Lahleh	Sponsored spouse	Bridging (applied for refugee status)	Bridging (applied for refugee status)	Not interviewed	Overseas-born PR
Leah	1 Tourist 2 Sponsored spouse	Bridging (IPV)	PR (IPV)	PR	Overseas-born PR
Luciana	1 Tourist 2 Student 3 Sponsored spouse	PR (IPV)	PR	PR	Overseas-born—skilled work

Name	Woman's Visa Before Interview	Interview 1	Interview 2	Interview 3	Partner's or Ex-partner's Visa Status
Mira	1 Tourist 2 Sponsored spouse	Bridging (IPV)	PR (IPV)	PR	Overseas-born PR
Pari	1 Tourist 2 Skilled work	PR	PR	PR	1 Tourist 2 Sponsored (wife's work visa) PR
Perlah	1 Tourist 2 Sponsored spouse	Bridging (IPV)	PR (IPV)	PR	Australian-born citizen
Radha	Sponsored spouse	Bridging (IPV)	PR (IPV)	PR	Overseas-born PR
Rosa	Sponsored spouse	Sponsored spouse (but separated)	Sponsored spouse (but separated)	Bridging visa	Overseas-born—skilled work
Sara	Refugee	Refugee	Refugee	Refugee	Overseas-born Refugee
Shuang	Student—canceled Sponsored spouse	Bridging (IPV)	PR (IPV)	PR	Australian-born citizen
Tabora	Sponsored spouse	Sponsored spouse (but separated)	Sponsored spouse (but separated)	Not interviewed	Overseas-born—skilled work
Trisha	Sponsored spouse	PR	PR	PR	Australian-born citizen
Valeria	Sponsored spouse	Bridging (IPV)	PR (IPV)	PR	Australian-born citizen
Vera	Sponsored spouse	PR	PR	PR	Australian-born citizen

REFERENCES

Ackerman, J., & Love, T. P. (2014). Ethnic group differences in police notification about intimate partner violence. *Violence Against Women, 20*(2), 162–185. doi:10.1177/1077801214521327

Adams, W. (2015). Conducting semi-structured interviews. In K. Newcomer, P. Hatry, & J. Wholey (Eds.), *Handbook of practical program evaluation* (pp. 492–505). Hoboken, NY: Jossey-Bass.

Agnew-Brune, C., Moracco, K. E., Person, C. J., & Bowling, J. M. (2017). Domestic violence protective orders: A qualitative examination of judges' decision-making processes. *Journal of Interpersonal Violence, 32*(13), 1921–1942. doi:10.1177/0886260515590126

Ahmed, S. (2017). *Living a feminist life*. Durham, NC: Duke University Press.

Alexander, M. (2010). *The new Jim Crow: Mass incarceration in the age of colorblindedness.* New York, NY: The New Press.

Alexander, R. (2018). *Family violence in Australia: The legal response*. Leichardt, New South Wales: Federation Press.

Allen, M. (2011). Violence and voice: Using a feminist constructivist grounded theory to explore women's resistance to abuse. *Qualitative Research, 11*(1), 23–45. doi:10.1177/1468794110384452

Allimant, A., & Ostapiej-Piatkowski, B. (2011). *Supporting women from CALD backgrounds who are victim/survivors of sexual violence: Challenges and opportunities for practitioners* (Wrap No. 9). Melbourne, Victoria: Australian Centre for the Study of Sexual Assault. Retrieved from https://aifs.gov.au/publications/supporting-women-cald-backgrounds-who-are-victimsurvivors-sexual-violen

Amanor-Boadu, Y., Messing, T., Stith, S., Anderson, J., O'Sullivan, C., & Campbell, J. (2012). Immigrant and nonimmigrant women: Factors that predict leaving an abusive relationship. *Violence Against Women, 18*(5), 611–633. doi:10.1177/1077801212453139

Anderson, C., & Kirkpatrick, S. (2016). Narrative interviewing. *International Journal of Clinical Pharmacy, 38*(3), 631–634. doi:10.1007/s11096-015-0222-0

Anderson, D., & Saunders, D. (2003). Leaving an abusive partner: An empirical review of predictors, the process of leaving, and psychological well-being. *Trauma, Violence & Abuse, 4*(2), 163–191. doi:10.1177/1524838002250769

Anitha, S. (2019). Understanding economic abuse through an intersectional lens: Financial abuse, control, and exploitation of women's productive and reproductive labor. *Violence Against Women, 25*(15), 1854–1877. doi:10.1177/1077801218824050

Anitha, S., Roy, A., & Yalamarty, H. (2016). *Disposable women: Abuse, violence and abandonment in transnational marriages: Issues for policy and practice in the UK and India.* Retrieved from http://eprints.lincoln.ac.uk/20091/

Australasian Institute of Judicial Administration. (2020). *National domestic and family violence bench book.* Sydney, New South Wales: Australasian Institute of Judicial Administration. Retrieved from http://www.dfvbenchbook.aija.org.au

Australian Association of Social Workers. (2019). *Australian social work education and accreditation standards.* North Melbourne, Victoria: Australian Association of Social Work. Retrieved from https://www.aasw.asn.au/careers-study/careers-in-social-work-2/careers-in-social-work.

Australian Bureau of Statistics. (2016a). 2071.0 Census of population and housing: Reflecting Australia—Stories from the census, Australia. Retrieved from http://www.abs.gov.au/ausstats/abs@.nsf/Lookup/by%20Subject/2071.0~2016~Main%20Features~Aboriginal%20and%20Torres%20Strait%20Islander%20Population%20Data%20Summary~10

Australian Bureau of Statistics. (2016b). 3412.0 Migration, Australia, 2015–16, Australia. Retrieved from http://www.abs.gov.au/ausstats/abs@.nsf/Latestproducts/3412.0Main%20Features42015-16?opendocument&tabname=Summary&prodno=3412.0&issue=2015-16&num=&view=

Australian Bureau of Statistics. (2017). 6227.0 Education and work, Australia. Retrieved from http://www.abs.gov.au/ausstats/abs@.nsf/mf/6227.0

Australian Institute of Family Studies. (2019). *Parenting arrangements after separation.* Melbourne, Victoria: Australian Institute of Family Studies.

Australian Institute of Health and Welfare. (2019). *Child protection in Australia 2017–18.* Canberra, Australian Capital Territory: Australian Government. Retrieved from https://www.aihw.gov.au/reports/child-protection/child-protection-australia-2017-18/contents/table-of-contents

Australian Institute of Health and Welfare. (2020). *Australia's children in brief.* Canberra, Australian Capital Territory: Australian Government.

Australian Law Reform Commission. (2019). *Family law for the future—an inquiry into the family law system* (Report No. 135). Brisbane, Queensland: Australian Law Reform Commission.

Australian Law Reform Commission and New South Wales Law Reform Commission. (2010). *Family violence—A national legal response.* Sydney, New South Wales: Australian Law Reform Commission.

Bagaric, M., Alexander, T., & Bagaric, B. (2019). Offenders risking deportation deserve a sentencing discount—but the reduction should be provisional. *Melbourne University Law Review 43*(1). Advance copy. https://law.unimelb.edu.au/__data/assets/pdf_file/0008/3288761/Bagaric-Alexander-and-Bagaric-432-Advance.pdf

Bagshaw, D., Chung, D., Couch, M., Lilburn, S., & Wadham, B. (2000). *Reshaping responses to domestic violence* (Final report, University of South Australia and Partnerships Against Domestic Violence). Adelaide, South Australia: Pirie.

Baker, P. (1997). And I went back: Battered women's negotiation of choice. *Journal of Contemporary Ethnography 26*(1), 55–74. doi:10.1177/089124197026001003

Ball, J. (2009). Fathering in the shadows: Indigenous fathers and Canada's colonial legacies. *Annals of the American Academy of Political and Social Science, 624*(1), 29–48. doi:10.1177/0002716209334181

Bancroft, L., Silverman, J. G., & Ritchie, D. (2012). *The batterer as parent: Addressing the impact of domestic violence on family dynamics* (2nd ed.). Thousand Oaks, CA: Sage.

Barata, P. (2007). Abused women's perspectives on the criminal justice system's response to domestic violence. *Psychology of Women Quarterly, 31*(2), 202–215. doi:10.1111/j.1471-6402.2007.00353.x

Barlow, C., & Walklate, S. (2020). Policing intimate partner violence: The "golden thread" of discretion. *Policing: A Journal of Policy and Practice.14*(2), 404–413. doi:10.1093/police/pay001

Barrett, B. J., Peirone, A., Cheung, C. H., & Habibov, N. (2017). Pathways to police contact for spousal violence survivors: The role of individual and neighborhood factors in survivors' reporting behaviors. *Journal of Interpersonal Violence*. Advance online publication. doi:10.1177/0886260517729400

Barrett, B. J., & St. Pierre, M. (2011). Variations in women's help seeking in response to intimate partner violence: Findings from a Canadian population-based study. *Violence Against Women, 17*(1), 47–70.

Belknap, J., & Sullivan, C. (2003). *Longitudinal study of battered women in the system: The victim's and decision makers' perceptions: Final report*. Washington, DC: US Department of Justice.

Bell, M. E., Perez, S., Goodman, L. A., & Dutton, M. A. (2011). Battered women's perceptions of civil and criminal court helpfulness: The role of court outcome and process. *Violence Against Women, 17*(1), 71–88. doi:10.1177/1077801210393924

Bennett, L., Goodman, L., & Dutton, M. A. (2000). Risk assessment among batterers arrested for domestic assault: The salience of psychological abuse. *Violence Against Women, 6*(11), 1190–1203. doi:10.1177/10778010022183596

Bent-Goodley, T. B., & Fowler, D. N. (2006). Spiritual and religious abuse: Expanding what is known about domestic violence. *Journal of Women in Social Work, 21*(3), 282–295. doi:10.1177/0886109906288901

Beuthin, R. E. (2014). Breathing in the mud: Tensions in narrative interviewing. *International Journal of Qualitative Methods, 13*(1), 122–134. doi:10.1177/160940691401300103

Birdsey, E., & Snowball, L. (2013). *Reporting violence to police: A survey of victims attending domestic violence services* (Issue Paper No. 91). Sydney, New South Wales: New South Wales Bureau of Crime Statistics. Retrieved from https://www.women.nsw.gov.au/__data/assets/pdf_file/0004/280912/Reporting_Violence_to_the_Police_-_BOCSAR_survey.pdf

Blagg, H., Bluett-Boyd, N., & Williams, E. (2015). *Innovative models in addressing violence against indigenous women: State of knowledge paper*. Sydney, New South Wales: Australia's National Research Organisation for Women's Safety.

Blagg, H., Williams, E., Cummings, E., Hovane, V., Torres, M., & Woodley, J. (2018). *Innovative models in addressing violence against Indigenous women: Final report.*

Sydney, New South Wales: Australia's National Research Organisation for Women's Safety.

Bluett-Boyd, N. (2005). *In search of justice in family violence: Exploring alternative responses in the Victorian Indigenous Australian community*. Melbourne, Victoria: Victorian Aboriginal Legal Service.

Blumstein, A., & Cohen, J. (1987). Characterizing criminal careers. *Science, 238*(4818), 985–991.

Bond, C., Holder, R., Jeffries, J., & Fleming, C. (2017). *Evaluation of the specialist domestic and family violence court trial in Southport: Summary and final report*. Mount Gravatt, Queensland: Griffith Criminology Institute, Griffith University. Retrieved from https://www.courts.qld.gov.au/__data/assets/pdf_file/0007/515428/dfv-rpt-evaluation-dfv-court-southport-summary-and-final.pdf

Borges Jelenic, A. (2019). I loved him and he scared me: Migrant women, partner visas and domestic violence. *Emotion, Space and Society, 32*. doi:10.1016/j.emospa.2019.100582

Borges Jelenic, A. (2020). Australia's family violence provisions in migration law: A comparative study. *Flinders Law Journal, 21*(2), 259–294.

Bowstead, J. (2016). Women on the move: Theorizing the geographies of domestic violence journeys in England. *Gender, Place and Culture, 24*(1), 108–121. doi:10.1080/0966369X.2016.1251396

Braun, V., & Clarke, V. (2006). Using thematic analysis in psychology. *Qualitative Research in Psychology, 3*(2), 77–101. doi:10.1191/1478088706qp063oa

Breger, M. L. (2017). Reforming by re-norming: How the legal system has the potential to change a toxic culture of domestic violence. *Journal of Legislation, 44*(2), 170–200.

Broady, T., & Gray, R. (2018). The intersection of domestic violence and child protection in Australia: Program participant accounts. *Australian Social Work, 71*(2), 189–201. doi:10.1080/0312407X.2017.1422774

Brooks, A., & Hesse-Biber, S. N. (2012). An invitation to feminist research. In S. N. Hesse-Biber (Ed.), *Handbook of feminist research: Theory and praxis* (pp. 1–24). London, England: Sage. doi:10.4135/9781483384740

Bruton, C., & Tyson, D. (2018). Leaving violent men: A study of women's experiences of separation in Victoria, Australia. *Australian & New Zealand Journal of Criminology, 51*(3), 339–354. doi:10.1177/0004865817746711

Buckley, H., Whelan, S., & Carr, N. (2011). "Like waking up in a Franz Kafka novel": Service users' experiences of the child protection system when domestic violence and acrimonious separations are involved. *Children and Youth Services Review, 33*, 126–133. doi:10.1016/j.childyouth.2010.08.022

Bumiller, K. (2008). *In an abusive state: How neo-liberalism appropriated the feminist movement against sexual violence*. Durham, NC: Duke University Press.

Burgess-Proctor, A. (2012). Backfire: Lessons learned when the criminal justice system fails help-seeking battered women. *Journal of Crime and Justice, 35*(1), 68–92. doi:10.1080/0735648X.2011.631393

Burman, J. (2003). Lawyers and domestic violence: Raising the standard of practice. *Michigan Journal of Gender & Law, 9*(2), 208–259.

Burton, L., Purvin, D., & Garrett-Peters, R. (2009). Longitudinal ethnography: Uncovering domestic abuse in low-income women's lives. In G. Elder & J. Giele (Eds.), *The craft of lifecourse research* (pp. 70–92). New York, NY: Guilford Press.

Campbell, J., Webster, D., Koziol-McLain, J., Block, C., Campbell, D. Curry, M. A., . . . Laughon, K. (2003). Risk factors for femicide in abusive relationships: Results from a multisite case control study. *American Journal of Public Health, 93*(7), 1089–1097. doi:10.2105/ajph.93.7.1089

Campbell, J. C., Anderson, J. C., McFadgion, A., Gill, J., Zink, E., Patch, M., . . . Campbell, D. (2018). The effects of intimate partner violence and probable traumatic brain injury on central nervous system symptoms. *Journal of Women's Health, 27*(6), 761–767. doi:10.1089/jwh.2016.6311

Campbell, R., & Wasco, S. (2000). Feminist approaches to social science: Epistemological and methodological tenets. *American Journal of Community Psychology, 28*(6), 773–791. doi:10.1023/A:1005159716099

Capezza, N. M., & Arriaga, X. B. (2008). Factors associated with acceptance of psychological aggression against women. *Violence Against Women, 14*(6), 612–633. doi:10.1177/1077801208319004

Carrington, K., Guala, N., Puyol, M., & Sozzo, M. (2020). How women's police stations empower women, widen access to justice and prevent gender violence. *International Journal for Crime, Justice and Social Democracy, 8*(1), 42–67. doi:10.5204/ijcjsd.v9i1.1494

Castles, M. (2016). Barriers to unbundled legal services in Australia: Canvassing reforms to better manage self-represented litigants in courts and in practice. *Journal of Judicial Administration, 25*, 237–256.

Cattaneo, L. B., Grossman, J., & Chapman, A. R. (2016). The goals of IPV survivors receiving orders of protection: An application of the empowerment process model. *Journal of Interpersonal Violence, 31*(17), 2889–2911. doi:10.1177/0886260515581905

Child Protection Act 1999 (Qld).

Choice, P., & Lamke, L. (1997). A conceptual approach to understanding abused women's stay/leave decisions. *Journal of Family Issues, 18*, 290–314. doi:10.1177/019251397018003004

Coker, A. L., Davis, K. E., Arias, I., Desai, S., Sanderson, M., Brandt, H. M., & Smith, P. H. (2002). Physical and mental health effects of intimate partner violence for men and women. *American Journal of Preventive Medicine, 23*(4), 260–268. doi:10.1016/S0749-3797(02)00514-7

Coker, D., & Macquoid, A. (2015). Why opposing hyper-incarceration should be central to the work of the anti–domestic violence movement. *University of Miami Race and Social Justice Law Review, 5*, 585–618. Retrieved from https://repository.law.miami.edu/cgi/viewcontent.cgi?article=1061&context=umrsjlr

Collins, P. H., & Bilge, S. (2016). *Intersectionality.* Cambridge, England: Polity.

Cooper, D., & Brandon, M. (2007). How can family lawyers effectively represent their clients in mediation and conciliation processes? *Australian Journal of Family Law, 21*(3), 288–308.

Corbett, N., & Summerfield, A. (2017). *Alleged perpetrators of abuse as litigants in person in private family law: The cross-examination of vulnerable and intimidated witnesses.* London, England: Ministry of Justice. Retrieved from https://www.gov.uk/government/publications/alleged-perpetrators-of-abuse-as-litigants-in-person-in-private-family-law

Council of Australian Governments. (2019). *Fourth action plan: National plan to reduce violence against women and their children 2010–2022*. Canberra, Australian Capital Territory: Commonwealth of Australia.

Crenshaw, K. (1989). Demarginalizing the intersection of race and sex: A black feminist critique of antidiscrimination doctrine, feminist theory and antiracist politics. *University of Chicago Legal Forum*, *8*(1), 139–167.

Crenshaw, K. (1991). Mapping the margins: Intersectionality, identity politics and violence against women of color. *Stanford Law Review*, *43*(6), 1241–1299.

Crock, M., & Berg, L. (2011). *Immigration, refugees and forced migration: Law policy and practice in Australia*. Leichardt, New South Wales: Federation Press.

Crossman, K., & Hardesty, J. (2018). Placing coercive control at the center: What are the processes of coercive control and what makes control coercive? *Psychology of Violence*, *8*(2), 196–206. doi:10.1037/vio0000094

Crossman, K., Hardesty, J., & Raffaelii, M. (2016). "He could scare me without laying a hand on me": Mothers' experiences of nonviolent coercive control during marriage and after separation. *Violence Against Women*, *22*(4), 454–473. doi:/10.1177/1077801215604744

Daly, K., Holder, R., & Meyer, V. (2019). *The FAVE project, financial assistance and victims' experiences. Technical Report No. 7: Victims' experiences seeking financial assistance for sexual offences*. Brisbane, Queensland: School of Criminology and Criminal Justice and Griffith Criminology Institute, Griffith University.

Day, A., Jones, R., Nakata, M., & McDermott, D. (2013). Indigenous family violence: An attempt to understand the problems and inform appropriate and effective responses to criminal justice system intervention. *Psychiatry, Psychology and Law*, *19*(1), 104–117. doi:10.1080/13218719.2010.543754

DeKeseredy, W. S., & Dragiewicz, M. (2014). Woman abuse in Canada: Sociological reflections on the past, suggestions for the future. *Violence Against Women*, *20*(2), 228–244. doi:10.1177/1077801214521325

DeKeseredy, W. S., Dragiewicz, M., & Schwartz, M. (2017). *Abusive endings: Separation and divorce violence against women*. Oakland, CA: University of California Press.

Dobash, R. E., & Dobash, R. P. (1979). *Violence against wives: A case against the patriarchy*. New York, NY: Free Press.

Dobash, R. E., & Dobash, R. P. (2015). *When men murder women*. Oxford, England: Oxford University Press.

Domestic and Family Violence Death Review and Advisory Board. (2018). *2017–2018 Annual report*. Brisbane, Queensland: Queensland Government.

Domestic and Family Violence Protection Act 2012 (Qld).

Dosanjh, S., Lewis, G., Mathews, D., & Bhandari, M. (2008). Child protection involvement and victims of domestic violence: Is there a bias? *Violence Against Women*, *14*(7), 833–843. doi:10.1177/1077801208320247

Douglas, H. (2008). The criminal law's response to domestic violence: What's going on? *Sydney Law Review*, *30*(3), 439–469.

Douglas, H. (2012). Battered women's experiences of the criminal justice system: Decentering the law. *Feminist Legal Studies, 20*, 121–134. doi:10.1007/s10691-012-9201-1

Douglas, H. (2018). Legal systems abuse and coercive control. *Criminology and Criminal Justice, 18*(1), 84–91.

Douglas, H., & Bartlett, B. (2016). Practice and persuasion: Women, feminism and judicial diversity. In R. Ananian-Welsh, & J. Crowe (Eds.), *Judicial independence: Contemporary challenges, future directions* (pp. 76–88). Annandale, New South Wales: Federation Press.

Douglas, H., & Burdon, M. (2018). Legal responses to non-consensual smartphone recordings in the context of domestic and family violence. *University of New South Wales Law Journal, 41*(1), 157–184.

Douglas, H., & Fell, E. (2020). Mothers, domestic and family violence: Malicious reports of child maltreatment as coercive control. *Journal of Family Violence*, published 3 January 2020. doi:10.1007/s10896-019-00128

Douglas, H., & Fitzgerald, R. (2013). Legal processes and gendered violence: Cross-applications for domestic violence protection orders. *University of New South Wales Law Journal, 36*(1), 56–87.

Douglas, H., & Fitzgerald, R. (2018). The domestic violence protection order system as entry to the criminal justice system for Aboriginal and Torres Strait Islander people. *International Journal for Crime, Justice and Social Democracy, 7*(3), 41–57. doi:10.5204/ijcjsd.v7i3.499

Douglas, H., & Harpur, P. (2016). Intellectual disabilities, domestic violence and legal engagement. *Disability & Society, 31*(3), 305–321. doi:10.1080/09687599.2016.1167673

Douglas, H., Harris, B., & Dragiewicz, M. (2019). Technology-facilitated domestic and family violence: Women's experiences. *British Journal of Criminology, 59*(3), 551–570. doi:10.1093/bjc/azy068

Douglas, H., & Nagesh, R. (2019). Domestic and family violence, child support and "the exemption." *Journal of Family Studies*. Advance online publication. doi:10.1080/13229400.2019.1653952

Douglas, H., & Walsh, T. (2010). Mothers, domestic violence and child protection. *Violence Against Women, 16*(5), 489–508. doi:10.1177/1077801210365887

Dowling, C., Morgan, A., Boyd, C., & Voce, I. (2018). *Policing domestic violence: A review of the evidence* (Research report No. 13). Canberra, Australian Capital Territory: Australian Institute of Criminology. Retrieved from https://aic.gov.au/publications/rr/rr13

Dragiewicz, M. (2015). Family law reform and domestic violence. In R. Goel & L. Goodmark (Eds.), *Comparative perspectives on gender violence: Lessons from efforts worldwide* (pp. 127–140). New York, NY: Oxford University Press. doi:10.1093/acprof:oso/9780199346578.001.0001

Durfee, A. (2015). "Usually it's something in the writing": Reconsidering the narrative requirement for protection order petitions. *University of Miami Race & Social Justice Law Review, 5*, 469–484.

Durfee, A., & Goodmark, L. (2019). Is there a protection order to prison pipeline? Gendered dimensions of cross-petitions. *Journal of Aggression, Maltreatment and Trauma*. Advance online publication. doi:10.1080/10926771.2019.1685044

Dutton, M., Goodman, L., Lennig, D., Murphy, J., & Kaltman, K. (2006). *Ecological model of battered women's experience over time*. Washington, DC: National Institute of Justice.

Elizabeth, V. (2019). "It's an invisible wound": The disenfranchised grief or post-separation mothers who lose care time. *Journal of Social Welfare and Family Law, 41*(1), 34–52. doi:10.1080/09649069.2019.1554788

Ellis, D. (2017). Marital separation and lethal male partner violence. *Violence Against Women, 23*(4), 503–519. doi:10.1177/1077801216644985

Ellison, L. (2002). *The adversarial process and the vulnerable witness.* Oxford, England: Oxford University Press.

Epstein, D. A., & Goodman, L. A. (2019). Discounting women: Doubting domestic violence survivors' credibility and dismissing their experiences. *University of Pennsylvania Law Review, 167*(2), 399–461.

Estefan, L. F., Coulter, M. L., & VandeWeerd, C. (2016). Depression in women who have left violent relationships: The unique impact of frequent emotional abuse. *Violence Against Women, 22*(11), 1397–1413. doi:10.1177/1077801215624792

Ewick, P., & Silbey, S. (1992). Conformity, contestation and resistance: An account of legal consciousness. *New England Law Review 26*, 731–749.

Ewick, P., & Silbey, S. (1998). *The common place of law: Stories from everyday life.* Chicago: University of Chicago Press.

Exum, M. L., Hartman, J. L., Friday, P. C., & Lord, V. B. (2014). Policing domestic violence in the post-SARP era: The impact of a domestic violence police unit. *Crime & Delinquency, 60*(7), 999–1032. doi:10.1177/0011128710382345

Family Law Act 1975 (Cth).

Farrington, D., Piquero, A., & Jennings, W. (2013). *Offending from childhood to late middle age: Recent results from the Cambridge Study in Delinquent Development.* New York, NY: Springer.

Fawole, O. I. (2008). Economic violence to women and girls: Is it receiving the necessary attention? *Trauma, Violence & Abuse, 9*(3), 167–177. doi:10.1177/1524838008319255

Fehlberg, B., & Millward, C. (2014). Family violence and financial outcomes after parental separation. In A. Hayes & D. Higgins,(Eds.), *Families, policies and the law: Selected essays on contemporary issues for Australia* (pp. 235–244). Melbourne, Victoria: Australian Institute of Family Studies.

Felson, R. B., Ackerman, J. M., & Gallagher, C. A. (2005). Police intervention and the repeat of domestic assault. *Criminology, 43*(3), 563–588. doi:10.1111/j.0011-1348.2005.00017.x

Feresin, M., Folla, N., Lapierre, S., & Romito, P. (2018). Family mediation in child custody cases and the concealment of domestic violence. *Journal of Women and Social Work, 33*(4), 509–525. doi:10.1177/0886109918766659

Fernandez, M. (2010). *Restorative justice for domestic violence victims: An integrated approach to their hunger for healing.* Plymouth, MA: Lexington Books.

Ferraro, K. (2006). *Neither angels nor demons: Women, crime, and victimization.* Lebanon, NH: North Eastern University Press.

Field, R., Jeffries, S., Rathus, Z., & Lynch, A. (2016). Family reports and family violence in Australian family law proceedings: What do we know? *Journal of Judicial Administration, 25*(4), 212–236.

Fine, M. (1989). The politics of research and activism: Violence against women. *Gender and Society, 3*, 549–558. doi:10.1177/089124389003004012

Fitzgerald, R., & Douglas, H. (2019). The whole story: The dilemma of the domestic violence protection order narrative. *British Journal of Criminology, 60*(1), 180–197. doi:10.1093/bjc/azz043

Fleury, R. (2002). Missing voices: Patterns of battered women's satisfaction with the criminal legal system. *Violence Against Women, 8*(2), 181–205. doi:10.1177/10778010222183008

Fleury, R., Sullivan, C., & Bybee, D. (2000). When ending the relationship does not end the violence: Women's experiences of violence by former partners. *Violence Against Women 6*(1): 1363–1383. doi:10.1177/10778010022183695

Flynn, A., & Freiberg, A. (2018). *Plea negotiation: Pragmatic justice in an imperfect world.* Cham, Switzerland: Palgrave.

Follingstad, D., Rutledge, R., Berg, L., Hause, L., & Polek, B. (1990). The role of emotional abuse in physically abusive relationships. *Journal of Family Violence, 5*(2), 107–120. doi:10.1007/BF00978514

Fusco, R. A. (2013). "It's hard enough to deal with all the abuse issues": Child welfare workers' experiences with intimate partner violence on their caseloads. *Children and Youth Services Review, 35*, 1946–1953. doi:10.1016/j.childyouth.2013.09.020

Genn, H. (1997). Understanding civil justice. *Current Legal Problems, 50*(1), 155–187. doi:10.1093/clp/50.1.155

Genn, H. (1999). *Paths to justice: What people do and think about going to law.* Oxford, England: Hart Publishing.

George, A., & Harris, B. (2014). *Landscapes of violence: Women surviving family violence in regional and rural Victoria.* Retrieved from https://www.deakin.edu.au/__data/assets/pdf_file/0003/287040/Landscapes-of-Violence-online-pdf-version.pdf

Ghafournia, N. (2011). Battered at home, played down in policy: Migrant women and domestic violence in Australia. *Aggression and Violent Behavior, 16*(3), 207–213. doi:10.1016/j.avb.2011.02.009

Ghafournia, N., & Easteal, P. (2018). Are immigrant women visible in Australian domestic violence reports that potentially influence policy? *Laws, 7*(32), 1–16. doi:10.3390/laws7040032

Gondolf, E., & White, R. (2001). Batterer program participants who repeatedly reassault: Psychopathic tendencies and other disorders. *Journal of Interpersonal Violence, 16*(4), 361–380. doi:10.1177/088626001016004006

Goodman-Delahunty, J., & Corbo Crehan, A. (2015). Enhancing police responses to domestic violence incidents: Reports from client advocates in New South Wales. *Violence Against Women, 22*(8), 1007–1026. doi:10.1177/1077801215613854

Goodmark, L. (2005). Telling stories, saving lives: The Battered Mothers' Testimony Project, women's narratives, and court reform. *Arizona State Law Journal, 37*(3), 710–757.

Goodmark, L. (2009). Reframing domestic violence law and policy: An anti-essentialist proposal. *Journal of Law and Policy, 31*, 39–56.

Goodmark, L. (2012). *A troubled marriage: Domestic violence and the legal system*. New York, NY: New York University Press.

Goodmark, L. (2018). *Decriminalizing domestic violence: A balanced policy approach to intimate partner violence*. Oakland, CA: University of California Press.

Gordon, S. (2006). Cultural conceptualisation of child abuse and responses to it: An Aboriginal perspective. *Social Policy Journal of New Zealand, 28*, 1–18.

Gover, A. R., Paul D. P., & Dodge M. (2011). Law enforcement officers' attitudes about domestic violence. *Violence Against Women, 17*(5), 619–636. doi:10.1177/1077801211407477

Gray, L., Easteal, P., & Bartels, L. (2014). Immigrant women and family violence: Will the new exceptions help or hinder victims? *Alternative Law Journal, 39*(3), 167–171.

Greiner, D., J., Pattanayak, C. W., & Hennessy, J. (2013). The limits of unbundled legal assistance: A randomized study in a Massachusetts district court and prospects for the future. *Harvard Law Review, 126*, 901–989.

Gutowski, E., & Goodman, L. (2020). "Like I'm invisible": IPV survivor-mothers' perceptions of seeking child custody through the family court system. *Journal of Family Violence, 35*, 441–457. doi:10.1007/s10896-019-00063-1

Hague Convention of 25 October 1980 on the Civil Aspects of International Child Abduction. Opened for signature October 25, 1980, 1343 UNTS 89 (entered into force December 1, 1993).

Halliday, S., & Schmidt, P. (2009). Patricia Ewick and Susan Silbey and the *Common place of law*. In S. Halliday & P. Schmidt (Eds.), *Conducting law and society research* (pp. 214–226). Cambridge, England: Cambridge University Press.

Halsey, M. (2007). Assembling recidivism: The promise and contingencies of post-release life. *Journal of Criminal Law and Criminology, 97*(4), 1209–1260.

Hamby, S. (2014). *Battered women's protective strategies: Stronger than you know*. Oxford, England: Oxford University Press.

Hanna, C. (2009). The paradox of progress: Translating Evan Stark's coercive control into legal doctrine for abused women. *Violence Against Women, 15*(12), 1458–1476. doi:10.1177/1077801209347091

Harland, A., Cooper, D., Rathus, Z., & Alexander, R. (2015). *Family law principles* (2nd ed.). Pyrmont, New South Wales: Thomson Reuters Australia.

Head, E. (2009). The ethics and implications of paying participants in qualitative research. *International Journal of Social Research Methodology, 12*(4), 335–344. doi:10.1080/13645570802246724

Henderson, A., Bartholomew, K., & Dutton, D. (1997). He loves me; he loves me not: Attachment and separation resolution of abused women. *Journal of Family Violence, 12*(2), 169–191. doi:10.1023/A:1022836711637

Herman, J. (2003). The mental health of crime victims: Impact of legal intervention. *Journal of Traumatic Stress, 16*, 159–166. doi:10.1023/A:1022847223135

Herman, J. (2005). Justice from the victim's perspective. *Violence Against Women, 11*(5), 571–602. doi:10.1177/1077801205274450

Hess, C., & Del Rosario, A. (2018). *Dreams deferred: A survey on the impact of intimate partner violence on survivor's education, careers and economic security*. Washington, DC: Institute for Women's Policy.

Hesse-Biber, S. (2015). Feminist approaches to mixed methods research: Linking theory and praxis. In A. Tashakkori & C. Teddlie (Eds.). *Sage Handbook of Mixed Methods in Social and Behavioral Research* (pp. 169–192). Thousand Oaks, CA: Sage.

Hester, M. (2012). The "three planet model": Towards an understanding of contradictions in approaches to women and children's safety in contexts of domestic violence. In L. McMillan & N. Lombard (Eds.), *Violence against women: Current theory and practice in domestic abuse, sexual violence and exploitation* (pp. 35–52). London, England: Jessica Kingsley.

Heward-Belle, S. (2017). Exploiting the "good mother" as a tactic of coercive control: Domestically violent men's assaults on women as mothers. *Affilia*, *32*(3), 374–389. doi:10.1177/0886109917706935

Heward-Belle, S., Laing, L., Humphreys, C., & Toivonen, C. (2018). Intervening with children living with domestic violence: Is the system safe? *Australian Social Work*, *71*(2), 135–147. doi:10.1080/0312407X.2017.1422772

Hill, J. (2019). *See what you made me do: Power, control and domestic abuse*. Sydney: Black Inc. Books.

Hirschel, D., & Hutchison, I. (2003). The voices of domestic violence victims: Predictors of victim preference for arrest and the relationship between preference for arrest and re-victimization. *Crime & Delinquency*, *49*(2), 313–336. doi:10.1177/00111287 02251067

Holder, R. (2018). *Just Interests: Victims, Citizens and the Potential for Justice.* Northampton, MA: Edward Elgar.

Holder, R., & Daly, K. (2017). Sequencing justice: A longitudinal study of justice goals of domestic violence victims. *British Journal of Criminology*, *58*(4), 787–804. doi:10.1093/bjc/azx046

Hooker, L., Kaspiew, R., & Taft, A. (2016). *Domestic and family violence and parenting: Mixed methods insights into impact and support needs: State of knowledge paper* Sydney, New South Wales: Australia's National Research Organisation for Women's Safety.

Hoyle, C., & Sanders, A. (2000). Police response to domestic violence: From victim choice to victim empowerment. *British Journal of Criminology*, *40*(1), 14–36. doi:10.1093/bjc/40.1.14

Huggins, J. (1998). *Sister girl: The writings of Aboriginal activist and historian Jackie Huggins.* Brisbane, Queensland: University of Queensland Press.

Hughes, J., & Chau, S. (2012). Children's best interests and intimate partner violence in the Canadian family law and child protection systems. *Critical Social Policy*, *32*(4), 677–695. doi:10.1177/0261018311435025

Human Rights and Equal Opportunity Commission. (1997). *Bringing them home: Report of the national inquiry into the separation of Aboriginal and Torres Strait Islander children from their families.* Sydney, New South Wales: Human Rights and Equal Opportunity Commission. Retrieved from https://www.humanrights.gov.au/our-work/bringing-them-home-report-1997

Humphreys, C., Healey, L., Kirkwood, D., & Nicholson, D. (2018). Children living with domestic violence: A differential response through multi-agency collaboration. *Australian Social Work*, *71*(2), 162–174. doi:10.1080/0312407X.2017.1415366

Humphreys, C., Healey, L., & Mandel, D. (2018). Case reading as a practice and training intervention in domestic violence and child protection. *Australian Social Work, 71*(3), 277–291. doi:10.1080/0312407X.2017.1413666

Humphreys, C., Thiara, R. K., Sharp, C., & Jones, J. (2015). Supporting the relationship between mothers and children in the aftermath of domestic violence. In N. Stanley & C. Humphreys (Eds.), *Domestic violence and protecting children: New thinking and approaches* (pp. 130–147). London, England: Jessica Kingsley.

Hunter, R. (2008). *Domestic violence law reform and women's experiences in court.* New York, NY: Cambria Press.

Hunter, R. (2019). Contemporary issues in family law in England and Wales. In S. Choudhry & J. Herring (Eds.), *The Cambridge companion to comparative family law* (pp. 19–47). Cambridge, England: Cambridge University Press.

Hunter, R., Burton, M., & Trinder, L. (2020). *Assessing risk of harm to children and parents in private law and children cases: Final Report.* London, England: Ministry of Justice.

InTouch. (2010). *Barriers to the justice system faced by CALD women experiencing family.* Melbourne, Victoria: InTouch.

Jaffe, P. G., Johnston, J. R., Crooks, C. V., & Bala, N. (2008). Custody disputes involving allegations of domestic violence: Toward a differentiated approach to parenting plans. *Family Court Review, 46*(3), 500–522. doi:10.1111/j.1744-1617.2008.00216.x

James, C., & Ross, N. (2016). Did he ever hit you? Exploring the attitudes of lawyers in the assessment of the seriousness of threats and violent histories in domestic violence cases. *Australian Journal of Family Law, 30*(3), 205–239.

Jarnkvist, K., & Brannstrom, L. (2019). Stories of victimization: Self-positioning and construction of gender in narratives of abused women. *Journal of Interpersonal Violence, 34*(21–22), 4687–4712. doi:10.1177/0886260516676474

Jeffries, S., Bond, C. E. W., & Field, R. (2013). Australian domestic violence protection order legislation: A comparative quantitative content analysis of victim safety provisions. *Current Issues in Criminal Justice, 25*(2), 627–643.

Jeffries, S., Field, R., & Bond, C. E. W. (2015). Protecting Australia's children: A cross-jurisdictional review of domestic violence protection order legislation. *Psychiatry, Psychology and Law, 22*(6), 800–813. doi:10.1080/13218719.2015.1015204

Jeffries, S., Field, R., Menih, H., & Rathus, Z. (2016). Good evidence, safe outcomes in parenting matters involving family report writing practice from the perspective of professionals working in the family violence system. *University of New South Wales Law Journal, 39*(4), 1355–1388.

Jeffs, N., Kelly, L., & Klein, R. (2018). Long journeys toward freedom: The relationship between coercive control and space for action—measurement and emerging evidence. *Violence Against Women, 24*(2), 163–185. doi:10.1177/1077801216686199

Johnson, H., & Hotton, T. (2003). Losing control: Homicide risk in estranged and intact intimate relationships. *Homicide Studies, 7*(1), 58–84. doi:0.1177/1088767902239243

Johnson, S. P., & Sullivan, C. M. (2008). How child protection workers support or further victimize battered mothers. *Affilia, 23*(3), 242–258. doi:10.1177/0886109908319113

Jordan, L., & Phillips, L. (2013). *Women's experiences of surviving family violence and accessing the magistrates' court in Geelong, Victoria: Phase 1 of the family violence and the Victorian regional magistrates' courts research project*. Geelong, Victoria: Centre for Rural and Regional Law and Justice, Deakin University. Retrieved from https://www.deakin.edu.au/__data/assets/pdf_file/0004/258133/pubs-4.pdf

Kaspiew, R., Carson, R., Coulson, M., Dunstan, J., & Moore, S. (2015). *Responding to family violence: A survey of family law practices and experiences*. Melbourne, Victoria: Australian Institute of Family Studies. Retrieved from https://aifs.gov.au/sites/default/files/efva-rfv.pdf

Kaspiew, R., Carson, R., Dunstan, J., De Maio, J., Moore, S., Moloney, L., . . . Tayton, S. (2015). *Experience of separated parents study*. Melbourne, Victoria: Australian Institute of Family Studies. Retrieved from https://aifs.gov.au/sites/default/files/efva-esps.pdf

Kaye, M. (2019a). Accommodating violence in the family courts. *Australian Family Law Journal, 33*, 100–118.

Kaye, M. (2019b). The increasing demands on the role of children's lawyers in family law proceedings in Australia. *Child and Family Law Quarterly, 2*, 143–163.

Kaye, M., Wangmann, J., & Booth, T. (2017). Preventing personal cross-examination of parties in family law proceedings involving family violence. *Australian Journal of Family Law, 31*(2), 94–117.

Kelly, L., Meyersen, T., Hagemann-White, C., Jalusic, M., & Magalhaes, M. (2016). *Transnational foundations for ethical practice in interventions against violence against women and child abuse*. London, England: London Metropolitan University.

Kelly, L., Sharp, N., & Klein, R. (2014). *Finding the costs of freedom: How Women and children rebuild their lives after domestic violence*. London, England: Solace Women's Aid. Retrieved from https://www.endviolenceagainstwomen.org.uk/wp-content/uploads/Costs_of_Freedom_Report_-_SWA.pdf

Khaw, L., Bermea, A., Hardesty, J., Saunders, D., & Whittaker, M. (2018). "The system had me choked too": Abused mothers' perceptions of the custody determination process that resulted in negative custody outcomes. *Journal of Interpersonal Violence*. Published July 30, 2018. doi:10.1177/0886260518791226

Kim, J., & Gray, K. A. (2008). Leave or stay? Battered women's decision after intimate partner violence. *Journal of Interpersonal Violence, 23*(10), 1465–1482. doi:10.1177/0886260508314307

Klein, A. R. (2009). *Practical implications of current domestic violence research: For law enforcement, prosecutors and judges*. Washington, DC: National Institute of Justice. Retrieved from https://www.ncjrs.gov/pdffiles1/nij/225722.pdf

Kothari, C. L., Rhodes, K. V., Wiley, J. A., Fink, J., Overholt, S., Dichter, M. E., . . . Cerulli, C. (2012). Protection orders protect against assault and injury: A longitudinal study of police-involved women victims of intimate partner violence. *Journal of Interpersonal Violence, 27*(14), 2845–2868. doi:10.1177/0886260512438284

Kurz, D. (1996). Separation, divorce and woman abuse. *Violence Against Women, 2*(1), 63–81. doi:10.1177/1077801296002001004

Laing, L. (2008). A perilous journey: Seeking protection in the aftermath of domestic violence. *Communities Children and Families Australia, 3*(2), 19–28.

Laing, L. (2013). *"It's like this maze that you have to make your way through": Women's experiences of seeking a domestic violence protection order in NSW*. Sydney, New South

Wales: University of Sydney. Retrieved from https://ses.library.usyd.edu.au/handle/2123/9267

Laing, L. (2017). Secondary victimization: Domestic violence survivors navigating the family law system. *Violence Against Women*, *23*(11), 1314–1335. doi:10.1177/1077801216659942

Laing, L., Heward-Belle, S., & Toivonen, C. (2018). Practitioner perspectives on collaboration across domestic violence, child protection, and family law: Who's minding the gap? *Australian Social Work*, *71*(2), 215–227. doi:10.1080/0312407X.2017.1422528

Laird, L. (2018, September 1). The job is killing them: Family lawyers experience threats, violence. *ABA Journal*. Retrieved from http://www.abajournal.com/magazine/article/the_job_is_killing_them_family_ lawyers_experience_threats_violence

Langenderfer-Magruder, L., Alven, L., Wilke, D., & Spinelli, J. (2019). "Getting everyone on the same page": Child welfare workers' collaboration challenges on cases involving intimate partner violence. *Journal of Family Violence*, *34*(1), 21–31. doi:10.1007/s10896-018-0002-4

Laub, J., & Sampson, S. (2001). Understanding desistance from crime. *Crime and Justice: A Review of Research*, *28*, 1–69.

Lea, S. J., & Callaghan, L. (2016). "It gave me my life back": An evaluation of a specialist legal domestic abuse service. *Violence Against Women*, *22*(6), 704–721. doi:10.1177/1077801215610013

Legal Aid Queensland. (2018). *Annual report 2017–2018*. Brisbane, Queensland: Legal Aid Queensland. Retrieved from http://www.legalaid.qld.gov.au/ About-us/Corporate-publications/Annual-reports/2017%E2%80%9318-annual-report

Legal Aid Queensland. (2019a). *Grants policy manual*. Brisbane, Queensland: Legal Aid Queensland. Retrieved from https://www.legalaid.qld.gov.au/About-us/Policies-and-procedures/Grants-Policy-Manual

Legal Aid Queensland. (2019b). Scale of fees. Brisbane, Queensland: Legal Aid Queensland. Retrieved from http://www.legalaid.qld.gov.au/About-us/Policies-and-procedures/Grants-Handbook/Fees-and-payments/Scale-of-fees

Leisenring, A. (2012). Victims' perceptions of police response to intimate partner violence. *Journal of Police Crisis Negotiations*, *12*(2), 146–164. doi:10.1080/15332586.2012.728926

Lemon, N. K. D. (2018). *Domestic violence law* (5th ed.). St. Paul, MN: West Academic.

Lewis, R., Dobash, R. P., Dobash R. E., & Cavanagh, K. (2000). Protection, prevention, rehabilitation or justice? Women's use of the law to challenge domestic violence. *International Review of Victimology*, *7*(1–3), 179–205. doi:10.1177/026975800000700310

Lewis, R., Dobash, R. P., Dobash R. E., & Cavanagh, K. (2001). Law's progressive potential: The value of engagement with the law for domestic violence. *Social Legal Studies*, *10*(1), 105–130. doi:10.1177/a017834

Li, S., Levick, A., Eichman, A., & Chang, J. C. (2015). Women's perspectives on the context of violence and role of police in their intimate partner violence arrest experiences. *Journal of Interpersonal Violence*, *30*(3), 400–419. doi:10.1177/0886260514535100

Littrich, J., & Murray, K. (2019). *Lawyers in Australia*. Leichardt, New South Wales: Federation Press.

Littwin, A. (2012). Coerced debt: The role of consumer credit in domestic violence. *California Law Review*, *100*(4), 951–1026. doi:10.15779/Z38VR6G

Logan, T. K., Walker, R., Shannon, L., & Cole, J. (2008). Combining ethical considerations with recruitment and follow-up strategies for partner violence victimisation research. *Violence Against Women, 14*(11), 1226–1251. doi:10.1177/1077801208323976

Loxton, D., Schofield, M., & Hussain, R. (2006). Psychological health in midlife among women who have ever lived with a violent partner or spouse. *Journal of Interpersonal Violence, 21*(8), 1092–1107. doi:10.1177/0886260506290290

Lynch, D., & Laing, L. (2013). *"Women get lost in the gaps": Service providers' perspectives on women's access to legal protection from domestic violence*. Sydney, New South Wales: University of Sydney. Retrieved from https://ses.library.usyd.edu.au/handle/2123/9195

Macdonald, G. S. (2016). Domestic violence and private family court proceedings: Promoting child welfare or promoting contact? *Violence Against Women, 22*(7), 832–852. doi:10.1177/1077801215612600

MacDonald, H. (1998). *What's in a name? Definitions and domestic violence*. Brunswick, Victoria: Domestic Violence and Incest Resource Centre.

MacQueen, S., & Norris, P. A. (2016). Police awareness and involvement in cases of domestic and partner abuse. *Policing and Society, 26*(1), 55–76. doi:10.1080/10439463.2014.922084

Magistrates' Court of Victoria. (2019). *Annual report 2018–2019*. Melbourne, Victoria: Magistrates' Court of Victoria.

Maher, J., & Segrave, M. (2018). Family violence risk, migration status and "vulnerability": Hearing the voices of immigrant women. *Journal of Gender-Based Violence, 2*(3), 503–518. doi:10.1332/239868018X15375304047178

Mahoney, M. (1991). Legal images of battered women: Redefining the issue of separation. *Michigan Law Review, 90*, 1–94. Retrieved from https://repository.law.miami.edu/fac_articles/386/

Malhotra, A. (2014). To return or not to return: Hague Convention vs. non-convention countries. *Family Law Quarterly, 48*(2), 297–318.

Mandel, D. (2010). Child welfare and domestic violence: Tackling thorny questions that stand in the way of collaboration and improvement of child welfare practice. *Violence Against Women, 16*(5), 530–536. doi:10.1177/1077801210366455

Manjoo, R. (2015). Gaps and challenges in states' responses in the quest to eliminate violence against women. In R. Goel & L. Goodmark (Eds.), *Comparative perspectives on gender violence: Lessons from efforts worldwide* (pp. 15–30). New York, NY: Oxford University Press. doi:10.1093/acprof:oso/9780199346578.001.0001

Markovits, D. (2010). *A modern legal ethics*. Princeton, NJ: Princeton University Press.

Maruna, S. (2001). *Making good: How ex-convicts reform and rebuild their lives*. Washington, DC: American Psychological Association.

Matsuda, M. (1987). Looking to the bottom: Critical legal studies and reparations. *Harvard Civil Rights–Civil Liberties Law Review, 22*(2), 323–400.

McGorrery, P., & McMahon, M. (2019). Criminalising "the worst" part: Operationalising the offence of coercive control in England and Wales. *Criminal Law Review, 11*, 957–965.

McMahon, M., & McGorrery, P. (2020). Criminalizing coercive control: An introduction. In M. McMahon & P. McGorrery (Eds.), *Criminalizing coercive control: Family violence and the criminal law* (pp. 3–32). New York, NY: Springer.

McMahon, M., McGorrery, P., & Burton, K. (2019). Prosecuting non-physical abuse between current intimate partners: Are stalking laws an under-utilised resource? *Melbourne University Law Review, 42*(2), 551–592.

Mechanic, M. B., Weaver, T. L., & Resick, P. A. (2000). Intimate partner violence and stalking behaviors: Exploration of patterns and correlates in a sample of acutely battered women. *Violence and Victims, 15*(1), 55–72. doi:10.1891/0886-6708.15.1.55

Menard, S. (1991). *Longitudinal research.* Newbury Park, CA: Sage.

Merry, S. (2003). Rights talk and the experience of law: Implementing women's human rights to protection from violence. *Human Rights Quarterly, 25*(2), 343–381. Retrieved from https://muse.jhu.edu/article/41999

Meyer, S. (2011). Seeking help for intimate partner violence: Victims' experiences when approaching the criminal justice system for IPV-related support and protection in an Australian jurisdiction. *Feminist Criminology, 6*(4), 268–290. doi:10.1177/1557085111414860

Meyersfeld, B. (2010). *Domestic violence and international law.* Oxford, England: Bloomsbury Publishing.

Migration Regulations 1994 (Cth).

Miller, S. (2018). *Journeys: Resilience and growth for survivors of intimate partner violence.* Oakland, CA: University of California Press.

Miller, S. L., & Smolter, N. L. (2011). "Paper abuse": When all else fails, batterers use procedural stalking. *Violence Against Women, 17*(5), 637–650. doi:10.1177/1077801211407290

Mitra-Kahn, T., Newbigin, C., & Hardefeldt, S. (2016). *Invisible women, invisible violence: Understanding and improving data on the experiences of domestic and family violence and sexual assault for diverse groups of women: State of knowledge* (ANROWS Landscapes No. DD01/2016). Sydney, New South Wales: Australia's National Research Organisation for Women's Safety.

Moloney, L., Smyth, B., Weston, R., Richardson, N., Qu, L., & Gray, M. (2007). Allegations of family violence and child abuse in family law children's proceedings: Key findings of Australian Institute of Family Studies (Research report No. 15). *Family Matters, 77*, 8–15.

Montesanti, S. R., & Thurston, W. E. (2015). Mapping the role of structural and interpersonal violence in the lives of women: Implications for public health interventions and policy. *BMC Women's Health, 15*(100), 1–13. doi:10.1186/s12905-015-0256-4

Morgan, A. (2011). Police and crime prevention: Partnering with the community. In J. Putt (Ed.), *Community policing in Australia.* Research and public policy series no. 111. Canberra, Australian Capital Territory: Australian Institute of Criminology. Retrieved from https://aic.gov.au/publications/rpp/rpp111

Mullender, A., Hague, G., Imam, U., Kelly, L., Malos, E., & Regan, L. (2002). *Childrens's perspectives on domestic violence.* Thousand Oaks, CA: Sage.

Myhill, A. (2019). Renegotiating domestic violence: Police attitudes and decisions concerning arrest. *Policing and Society, 29*(1), 52–68. doi:10.1080/10439463.2017.1356299

Nagin, D. S., Farrington, D., & Moffitt, T. (1995). Life-course trajectories of different types of offenders. *Criminology, 33*(1), 111–140. doi:10.1111/j.1745-9125.1995.tb01173.x

Nancarrow, H. (2019). *Unintended consequences of domestic violence law: Gendered aspirations and racialised realities*. London, England: Palgrave Macmillan.

Naughton, C. M., O'Donnell, A. T., Greenwood, R. M., & Muldoon, O. T. (2015). "Ordinary decent domestic violence": A discursive analysis of family law judges' interviews. *Discourse & Society, 26*(3), 349–365. doi:10.1177/0957926514564738

Neilson, C., & Renou, B. (2015). *Will somebody listen to me? Insight, actions and hope for women experiencing family violence in regional Victoria*. Bendigo, Victoria: Loddon Campaspe Community Legal Centre. Retrieved from http://lcclc.org.au/wp-content/uploads/2015/05/FV_FULL_online_v2.pdf

Nichols, A. (2014). No-drop prosecution in domestic violence cases: Survivor-defined and social change approaches to victim advocacy. *Journal of Interpersonal Violence, 29*(11), 2114–2142. doi:10.1177/0886260513516385

Oakley, A. (1981). Interviewing women: A contradiction in terms. In H. Roberts (Ed.), *Doing feminist research* (pp. 30–61). London, England: Routledge.

Oakley, A. (2016). Interviewing women again: Power, time and the gift. *Sociology, 50*(1), 195–213. doi:10.1177/0038038515580253

Office of the Administrative Rules Coordinator Division of Financial Management. (2020). Pending rules, committee rules review book, 65th Idaho Legislature. Retrieved from https://adminrules.idaho.gov/legislative_books/2020/pending/20H_HealthWelfare.pdf#nameddest=G71.999750

Ornstein, P., & Rickne, J. (2013). When does intimate partner violence continue after separation? *Violence Against Women, 19*(5), 617–633. doi:10.1177/1077801213490560

Our Watch. (2020). Melbourne: OurWatch. https://www.ourwatch.org.au/

Parkinson, P., & Cashmore, J. (2009). *The voice of a child in family law disputes*. Oxford, England: Oxford University Press. doi:10.1093/acprof:oso/9780199237791.001.0001

Pence, E., & Paymar, M. (1993). *Education groups for men who batter: The Duluth model*. New York, NY: Springer.

Person, C. J., Moracco, K. E., Agnew-Brune, C., & Bowling, J. M. (2018). "I don't know that I've ever felt like I got the full story": A qualitative study of courtroom interactions between judges and litigants in domestic violence protective order cases. *Violence Against Women, 24*(12), 1474–1496. doi:10.1177/1077801217738582

Petrie, E. (2018). *Small claims large battles: Achieving economic equality in the family law system*. Melbourne, Victoria: Women's Legal Service. Retrieved from https://womenslegal.org.au/files/file/WLSV%20Small%20Claims,%20Large%20Battles%20Research%20Report%202018.pdf

Pittaway, E., Muli, C., & Shteir, S. (2009). "I have a voice-hear me!": Findings of an Australian study examining the resettlement and integration experience of refugees and migrants from the Horn of Africa in Australia. *Refuge, 26*(2), 133–146.

Productivity Commission Steering Committee for the Review of Government Service Provision. (2016). *Overcoming Indigenous disadvantage: Key indicators 2016—report*. Canberra: Commonwealth of Australia. Retrieved from https://www.pc.gov.au/research/ongoing/overcoming-indigenous-disadvantage/2016/report-documents/oid-2016-overcoming-indigenous-disadvantage-key-indicators-2016-report.pdf

Ptacek, J. (1999). *Battered women in the courtroom: The power of judicial responses*. Boston, MA: Northeastern University Press.

Purske, M. (Producer), & Behrendt, L. (Director). (2019). *After the apology* [Motion picture] Screen Australia, Australia.

Queensland Courts. (2019). *Magistrates courts of Queensland: Annual report 2018–2019*. Brisbane, Queensland: Queensland Courts.

R v. Conde [2015] QCA 63 (April 21, 2015).

Radford, L., & Hester, M. (2001). Overcoming mother blaming? Future directions for research on mothering and domestic violence. In S. A. Graham-Bermann & J. L. Edleson (Eds.), *Domestic violence in the lives of children: The future of research, intervention, and social policy* (pp. 135–155). Washington, DC: APA Books. doi:10.1037/10408-007

Radford, L., & Hester, M. (2006). *Mothering through violence*. London, England: Jessica Kingsley.

Ragusa, A. T. (2012). Rural Australian women's legal help seeking for intimate partner violence: Women intimate partner violence victim survivors' perceptions of criminal justice support services. *Journal of Interpersonal Violence, 28*(4), 685–717. doi:10.1177/0886260512455864

Rathus, Z. (2013). Shifting language and meanings between social science and the law: Defining family violence. *University of New South Wales Law Journal, 36*(2), 359–389.

Rathus, Z., Jeffries, S., Menih, H., & Field, R. (2019). "It's like standing on a beach, holding your children's hands, and having a tsunami coming towards you": Intimate partner violence and "expert" assessments in Australian family law. *Victims & Offenders, 14*(4), 408–440. doi:10.1080/15564886.2019.1580646

Reissman, C. K. (2008). *Narrative methods for human sciences*. Los Angeles, CA: Sage.

Renner, L. M., & Hartley, C. C. (2018). Psychological well-being among women who experienced intimate partner violence and received civil legal services. *Journal of Interpersonal Violence*. Advance online publication. doi:10.1177/0886260518777552

Rezey, M. (2020). Separated women's risk for intimate partner violence: A multiyear analysis using the National Crime Victimization Survey. *Journal of Interpersonal Violence, 35*(5), 1055–1080. doi:10.1177/0886260517692334

Riger, S. (1992). Epistemological debates, feminist voices: Science, social values and the study of women. *American Psychologist, 47*(6), 730–740. doi:10.1037/0003-066X.47.6.730

Roberts, D., Chamberlain, P., & Delfabbro, P. (2015). Women's experiences of the processes associated with the family court of Australia in the context of domestic violence: A thematic analysis. *Psychiatry, Psychology and Law, 22*(4), 599–615. doi:10.1080/13218719.2014.960132

Robinson, A. L., Myhill, A., & Wire, J. (2018). Practitioner (mis)understandings of coercive control in England and Wales. *Criminology & Criminal Justice, 18*(1), 29–49. doi:10.1177/1748895817728381

Rumney, P. N., & McCartan, K. F. (2017). Purported false allegations of rape, child abuse and non-sexual violence: Nature, characteristics and implications. *Journal of Criminal Law, 81*(6), 497–520. doi:10.1177/0022018317746789

Ryan, G., & Bernard, H. R. (2003). Techniques to identify themes. *Field Methods, 165*(1), 85–109. doi:10.1177/1525822X02239569

Saini, M., Black, T., Fallon, B., & Marshall, A. (2013). Child custody disputes within the context of child protection investigations: Secondary analysis of the Canadian incident study of reported child abuse and neglect. *Child Welfare, 92*(1), 115–137.

Saini, M., Black, T., Godbout, E., & Deljavan, S. (2019). Feeling the pressure to take sides: A survey of child protection workers' experiences about responding to allegations of child maltreatment within the context of child custody disputes. *Children and Youth Services Review, 96*, 127–133. doi:10.1016/j.childyouth.2018.11.044

Saldo & Tindall [2013] FamCA 951 (December 5, 2013).

Sandefur, R. (2015). Elements of professional expertise: Understanding relational and substantive expertise through lawyers' impact. *American Sociological Review, 80*(5), 909–933. doi:10.1177/0003122415601157

Sanders, C. (2007). *Domestic violence, economic abuse and implications of a program for building economic resources for low-income women: Findings from interviews with participants in a women's economic action program*. St Louis, MO: Washington University in St Louis. Retrieved from https://csd.wustl.edu/07-12/

Sarat, A. (1990). "The law is all over": Power, resistance and the legal consciousness of the welfare poor. *Yale Journal of Law & the Humanities, 2*, 343–379. Retrieved from https://digitalcommons.law.yale.edu/cgi/viewcontent.cgi?article=1039&context=yjlh

Saunders, D., Faller, K., & Tolman, R. (2011). *Custody evaluators' beliefs about domestic abuse in relation to custody outcomes*. Washington, DC: National Institute of Justice.

Saunders, D. G., Faller, K. C., & Tolman, R. M. (2016). Beliefs and recommendations regarding child custody and visitation in cases involving domestic violence: A comparison of professionals in different roles. *Violence Against Women, 22*(6), 722–744. doi:10.1177/1077801215608845

Saxton, M. D., Olszowy, L., MacGregor, J. C. D., MacQuarrie, B. J., & Wathen, C. N. (2018). Experiences of intimate partner violence victims with police and the justice system in Canada. *Journal of Interpersonal Violence*. Advance online publication. doi:10.1177/0886260518758330

Scales, A. (2006). *Legal feminism: Activism, lawyering and legal theory*. New York, NY: New York University Press.

Scent, C., & Boes, S. (2014). Acceptance and commitment training: A brief intervention to reduce procrastination among college students. *Journal of College Student Psychotherapy, 28*(2), 144–156. doi:10.1080/87568225.2014.883887

Schindeler, E. (2019). Family law court orders for supervised contact in custodial disputes—unanswered questions. *Children Australia, 44*(4), 194–201.

Schneider, A., & Mills, N. (2006). What family lawyers are really doing when they negotiate. *Family Court Review, 44*, 612–622. doi:10.1111/j.1744-1617.2006.00114.x

Schneider, E. (2000). *Battered women and feminist lawmaking*. New Haven, CT: Yale University Press.

Schwartz, M., & Cunneen, C. (2009). From crisis to crime: The escalation of civil and family law issues to criminal matters in Aboriginal communities in NSW. *Indigenous Law Bulletin*, 7(15), 18–25.

Scott, M. (2020). The making of the new "gold standard": The Domestic Abuse (Scotland) Act 2018. In M. McMahon & P. McGorrery (Eds.), *Criminalizing coercive control: Family violence and the criminal law* (pp. 177–194). New York, NY: Springer.

Segrave, M. (2017). *Temporary migration and family violence: An analysis of victimisation, vulnerability and support.* Clayton, Victoria: Monash University. Retrieved from https://www.monash.edu/arts/gender-and-family-violence/research-projects/completed-projects/temporary-migration-and-family-violence.

Segrave, M. (2018). Temporary migration and family violence: The borders of coercive control. In K. Fitz-Gibbon, S. Walklate, J. McCulloch, & J. Maher (Eds.), *Intimate partner violence, risk and security: Securing women's lives in a global world* (pp. 126–149). New York, NY: Routledge.

Segrave, M., Wilson, D., & Fitz-Gibbon, K. (2018). Policing intimate partner violence in Victoria (Australia): Examining police attitudes and the potential of specialisation. *Australian and New Zealand Journal of Criminology, 51*(1), 99–116. doi:10.1177/0004865816679686

Semaan, I., Jasinski, J., & Bubriski-McKenzie, A. (2013). Subjection, subjectivity, and agency: The power, meaning, and practice of mothering among women experiencing intimate partner abuse. *Violence Against Women, 19*(1) 69–88. doi:10.1177/1077801212475335

Sentencing Advisory Council. (2019). *Sentencing practices for breach of family violence protection orders: Final report.* Melbourne, Victoria: Sentencing Advisory Council. Retrieved from https://www.sentencingcouncil.vic.gov.au/sites/default/files/2019-08/Sentencing_Practices_for_Breach_of_Family_Violence_Intervention_Orders_Final_Report.pdf

Seuffert, N. (1999). Domestic violence, discourses of romantic love and complex personhood and the law. *Melbourne University Law Review, 23*, 212–240.

Seuffert, N., Mundy, T., & McLaine, M. (2018). *Evaluation of the YWCA NSW Domestic Violence Intervention Service: Report.* Woolongong, New South Wales: University of Wollongong.

Shabbar, F. (2012). Protecting our non-citizens: Iraqi women on Australian temporary spouse visas. *Sociological Review, 60*(1), 149–168. doi:10.1111/j.1467-954X.2011.02046.x

Shanahan, M. J., Carter, R. F., Ryan, S., Costanzo, J. J., Hoare, A., & Rafter, A. J. (2018). *Carter's criminal law of Queensland* (22nd ed.). Chatswood, NSW: LexisNexis Butterworths.

Sharpe, G. (2017). Sociological stalking? Methods, ethics and power in longitudinal criminological research. *Criminology & Criminal Justice, 17*(3), 233–247. doi:10.1177/1748895816669214

Sharp-Jeffs, N., Kelly, L., & Klein, R. (2018). Long journeys toward freedom: The relationship between coercive control and space for action—measurement and emerging evidence. *Violence Against Women, 24*(2), 163–185. doi:10.1177/1077801216686199

Shepard, M. F., & Hagemeister, A. K. (2013). Perspectives of rural women: Custody and visitation with abusive ex-partners. *Journal of Women and Social Work, 28*(2), 165–176. doi:10.1177/0886109913490469

Sherman, L., & Harris, H. (2013). Increased homicide victimization of suspects arrested for domestic assault: A 23 year follow-up of the Milwaukee Domestic Violence Experiment. *Journal of Experimental Criminology, 9*(4), 491–514. doi:10.1007/s11292-013-9193-0

Silbey, S. (2005). After legal consciousness. *Annual Review of Law and Social Science, 1*, 323–368. doi:10.1146/annurev.lawsocsci.1.041604.115938

Slote, K. Y., Cuthbert, C., Mesh, C. J., Driggers, M. G., Bancroft, L., & Silverman, J. G. (2005). Battered mothers speak out: Participatory human rights documentation as a model for research and activism in the United States. *Violence Against Women, 11*(11), 1367–1395. doi:10.1177/1077801205280270

Smart, C. (1989). *Feminism and the power of law*. London, England: Routledge.

Sommerlad, H. (2013). Let history judge? Gender, race, class and performative identity: A study of women judges in England and Wales. In U. Schultz & G. Shaw (Eds.), *Gender and judging* (pp. 355–376). London, England: Hart Publishing. doi:10.5040/9781474200127

Special Taskforce on Domestic and Family Violence in Queensland. (2015). *Not now, not ever: Putting an end to domestic and family violence in Queensland*. Brisbane, Queensland: Queensland Government. Retrieved from https://www.csyw.qld.gov.au/campaign/end-domestic-family-violence/about/not-now-not-ever-report

Spencer, P. (2016). Strengthening the web of accountability: Criminal courts and family violence offenders. *Alternative Law Journal, 41*(4), 225–229. doi:10.1177/1037969X1604100402

Stark, E. (2007). *Coercive control: How men entrap women in personal life*. Oxford, England: Oxford University Press.

Stark, E. (2012a). Coercive control. In L. McMillan & N. Lombard (Eds.), *Violence against women: Current theory and practice in domestic abuse, sexual violence and exploitation* (pp. 17–34). London, England: Jessica Kingsley.

Stark, E. (2012b). Looking beyond domestic violence: Policing coercive control. *Journal of Police Crisis Negotiations, 12*(2), 199–217. doi:10.1080/15332586.2012.725016

Stark, E., & Hester, M. (2019). Coercive control: Update and review. *Violence Against Women, 25*(1), 81–104. doi:10.1177/1077801218816191

State of Victoria. (2016a). *Royal Commission Into Family Violence: Report and recommendations*. Melbourne, Victoria: State of Victoria.

State of Victoria. (2016b). *Royal Commission Into Family Violence: Summary and recommendations*. Melbourne, Victoria: Victorian Government.

Steinberg, J. (2011). In pursuit of justice: Case outcomes and the delivery of unbundled legal services. *Georgetown Journal of Poverty Law and Policy, 18*(3), 453–505.

Stewart, C. C., Langan, D., & Hannem, S. (2013). Victim experiences and perspectives on police responses to verbal violence in domestic settings. *Feminist Criminology, 8*(4), 269–294. doi:10.1177/1557085113490782

Stubbs, J., & Wangmann, J. (2015). Competing conceptions of victims of domestic violence with legal processes. In D. Wilson & S. Ross (Eds.), *Crime, victims and policy* (pp. 107–132). New York, NY: Springer.

Sullivan, C., Rumptz, M., Campbell, R., Eby, K., & Davidson, W. (1996). Retaining participants in longitudinal community research: A comprehensive protocol. *Journal of Applied Behavioral Science, 32*(3), 262–276. doi:10.1177/0021886396323002

Swain, S. (2014). *History of Australian inquiries reviewing institutions providing care for children*. Report for the Royal Commission Into Institutional Responses to Child Sexual Abuse. Retrieved from https://safeguardingchildren.acu.edu.au/research_

and_resources/history_of_australian_inquiries_reviewing_institutions_providing_care_for_children

Sweet, P. L. (2019). The sociology of gaslighting. *American Sociological Review, 84*(5), 851–875. doi:10.1177/0003122419874843

Tilbury, C. (2009). The over-representation of Indigenous children in the Australian child welfare system. *International Journal of Social Welfare, 18*(1), 57–64. doi:10.1111/j.1468-2397.2008.00577.x

Titterton, A. (2017). Indigenous access to family law in Australia and caring for Indigenous children. *University of New South Wales Law Journal, 40*(1), 146–185.

Toews, M., & Bermea, A. (2017). I was naive in thinking, "I divorced this man, he is out of my life": A qualitative exploration of post-separation power and control tactics experienced by women. *Journal of Interpersonal Violence, 32*(14), 2166–2189. doi:10.1177/0886260515591278

Tolmie, J. (2018). Coercive control: To criminalize or not to criminalize? *Criminology & Criminal Justice, 18*(1), 50–66. doi:10.1177/1748895817746712

Tolmie, J., Smith, R., Short, J., Wilson, D., & Sach, J. (2018). Social entrapment: A realistic understanding of the criminal offending of primary victims of intimate partner violence. *New Zealand Law Review, 2*, 181–213.

Treadway Johnson, M., & Wiggins, E. (2006). Videoconferencing in criminal proceedings: Legal and empirical issues and directions for research. *Law and Policy, 28*(2), 211–227. doi:10.1111/j.1467-9930.2006.00224.x

Trinder, L., Hunter, R., Hitchings, E., Miles, J., Smith, L., Moorhead, R., . . . Pearce, J. (2014). *Litigants in person in private family law cases*. London, England: Ministry of Justice. Retrieved from https://www.gov.uk/government/publications/litigants-in-person-in-private-family-law-cases

Trocmé, N., & Bala, N. (2005). False allegations of abuse and neglect when parents separate. *Child Abuse & Neglect, 29*, 1333–1345. doi:10.1016/j.chiabu.2004.06.016

Trocmé, N., Knoke, D., & Blackstock, C. (2004). Pathways to the overrepresentation of Aboriginal children in Canada's child welfare system. *Social Service Review, 78*(4), 577–600. doi:10.1086/424545

Tuerkheimer, D. (2017). Incredible women: Sexual violence and the credibility discount. *University of Pennsylvania Law Review, 166*(1), 1–58.

Ullman, S. E. (2011). Longitudinal tracking methods in a study of adult women sexual assault survivors. *Violence Against Women, 17*(2), 189–200. doi:10.1177/1077801210397702

Ursel, J. (2013). *An examination of the Manitoba front-end project*. Winnipeg, MB: RESOLVE, University of Manitoba, Canada. Retrieved from https://umanitoba.ca/centres/resolve/media/FINAL_REPORT_June_for_the_Maxbell_Foundation.pdf

Ursel, J., & Hagyard, C. (2008). The Winnipeg family violence court. In J. Ursel, L. Tutty, & J. leMaistre (Eds.), *What's law got to do with it? The law, specialized courts and domestic violence in Canada* (pp. 95–119). Toronto, ON: Cormorant Books.

Ursel, J., Tutty, L. M., & leMaistre, J. (2008). The justice system response to domestic violence: Debates, discussions and dialogues. In J. Ursel, L. M. Tutty, & J. leMaistre (Eds.), *What's law got to do with it? The law, specialized courts and domestic violence in Canada* (pp. 1–21). Toronto, ON: Cormorant Books.

Van Camp, T., & Wemmers, J. (2013). Victim satisfaction with restorative justice more than simply procedural justice. *International Review of Victimology, 19*(2), 117–143. doi:10.1177/0269758012472764

Vaughan, C., Davis, E., Murdolo, A., Chen, J., Murray, L., Block, K., . . . Warr, D. (2015). *Promoting community-led responses to violence against immigrant and refugee women in metropolitan and regional Australia: The ASPIRE project* (ANROWS Landscapes No. 12/2015). Sydney, New South Wales: Australia's National Research Organisation for Women's Safety.

Walby, S., Towers, J., & Francis, B. (2016). Is violent crime increasing or decreasing? A new methodology to measure repeat attacks making visible the significance of gender and domestic violence. *British Journal of Criminology, 56*(6), 1203–1234. doi:10.1093/bjc/azv131

Walklate, S., McCulloch, J., Fitz-Gibbon, K., & Maher, J. M. (2019). Criminology, gender and security in the Australian context: Making women's lives matter. *Theoretical Criminology, 23*(1), 60–77. doi:10.1177/1362480617719449

Walsh, C., McIntyre, S-J., Brodie, L., Bugeja, L., & Hauge, S. (2012). *Victorian systemic review of family violence deaths: First report.* Melbourne, Victoria: Coroners Court of Victoria. Retrieved from https://www.coronerscourt.vic.gov.au/sites/default/files/2018-11/vsrfvd%2Bfirst%2Breport%2B-%2Bfinal%2Bversion.pdf

Walsh, D. (2008). The hidden experience of violence during pregnancy: A study of 400 pregnant Australian women. *Australian Journal of Primary Health, 14*(1), 97–105. doi:10.1071/PY08013

Walsh, T. (2018). Video links in youth justice proceedings: When rights and convenience collide. *Journal of Judicial Administration, 27*, 161–181.

Wangmann, J. (2012). Incidents v context: How does the NSW protection order system understand intimate partner violence? *Sydney Law Review, 34*, 695–719.

Ward, D. (2016). In her words: Recognising and preventing abusive litigation against domestic violence survivors. *Seattle Journal for Social Justice, 14*(2), 429–464. https://digitalcommons.law.seattleu.edu/sjsj/vol14/iss2/11/

Westmarland, L. (2001). *Gender and policing: Sex, power and police culture.* Cullompton, England: Willan.

Wiener, C. (2017). Seeing what is "invisible in plain sight": Policing coercive control. *Howard Journal of Crime and Justice, 56*(4), 500–515. doi:10.1111/hojo.12227

Wiener, C. (2020). From social construct to legal innovation: The offence of controlling or coercive behaviour in England and Wales. In M. McMahon & P. McGorrery (Eds.), *Criminalizing coercive control: Family violence and the criminal law* (pp. 159–175). New York, NY: Springer.

Willis, M. (2011). Non-disclosure of violence in Australian Indigenous communities. Trends & issues in crime and criminal justice no. 405. Canberra, Australian Capital Territory: Australian Institute of Criminology.

Wilson, M., & Daly, K. (1992). Till death do us part. In J. Radford & D. Russell (Eds.), *Femicide: The politics of women killing,* 83–98. New York, NY: Twayne.

Young, A., Powers, J., & Bell, S. (2006). Attrition in longitudinal studies: Who do you lose? *Australian and New Zealand Journal of Public Health, 30*(4), 353–361. doi:10.1111/j.1467-842X.2006.tb00849.x

INDEX

For the benefit of digital users, indexed terms that span two pages (e.g., 52–53) may, on occasion, appear on only one of those pages.

Tables and figures are indicated by *t* and *f* following the page number